Vocabulary Workshop

Complete Course

Norbert Elliot

HOLT, RINEHART AND WINSTON

Austin • *New York* • *Orlando* • *Chicago* • *Atlanta*
San Francisco • *Boston* • *Dallas* • *Toronto* • *London*

Printed in the United States of America

ISBN 0-03-043023-2

4 5 6   164   00 99 98 97

Author

Norbert Elliot, the author and general editor of this new edition of *Vocabulary Workshop,* has a Ph.D. in English from The University of Tennessee. He is an associate professor of English at New Jersey Institute of Technology. A former site director for the National Writing Project, he has directed summer language arts institutes for kindergarten through twelfth-grade teachers in the public schools. A specialist in test development and evaluation of writing, Norbert Elliot has written books and articles on writing assessment, communication, and critical thinking. Dr. Elliot is the father of five children and is married to Lorna Jean Elliot, under whose care, he says, "everything thrives."

Contributing Writers

Raymond and Sylvia Teague collaborated on the writing of *Making New Words Your Own* and *Reading New Words in Context* for this edition of *Vocabulary Workshop.* The Teagues have been writing educational materials for eight years. After graduating from Texas Christian University, Raymond worked for the *Fort Worth Star-Telegram* as a writer and editor of news and features. He is now the newspaper's children's book editor. Sylvia earned her bachelor's and master's degrees from the University of Texas at Arlington, where she taught economics. Raymond and Sylvia have a daughter, Alexandra, who now attends college. The Teagues live on a mountaintop outside Eureka Springs, Arkansas, where they share a wonderful view, a crowded office, two cats, and an aging goldfish.

Lorna Jean Elliot wrote the *Connecting New Words and Patterns* sections for this edition of *Vocabulary Workshop.* She is a graduate of Susquehanna University, where she taught composition for several years. She earned her Master of Arts degree in English Literature from the Bread Loaf School of English in Middlebury, Vermont. The author of an award-winning novella, Mrs. Elliot currently has her hands full as a freelance writer and as the mother of five thriving children.

CONTENTS

British Literature and Culture

MAKING NEW WORDS YOUR OWN

How We Make New Words Our Own

How do you learn new vocabulary? You probably already have some strategies for guessing the meanings of new words. When you first meet a new word, for example, you may try to figure out what it means by studying the context in which it appears. Or maybe you take a guess at the word and try substituting your guess in the sentence.

Below are three kinds of exercises that can help you develop your strategies for learning new words on your own.

EXERCISE 1 *Mapping* 👈

In these exercises, you will see a new word used in a sentence, and you will be asked to guess its meaning. You will check that guess against the dictionary definition of the word. Then you will be asked to list other forms of that word.

Here's an example of a mapping exercise:

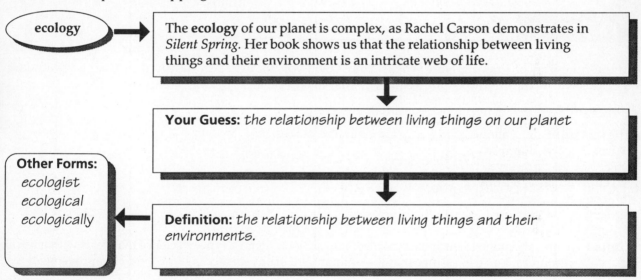

ecology

The **ecology** of our planet is complex, as Rachel Carson demonstrates in *Silent Spring*. Her book shows us that the relationship between living things and their environment is an intricate web of life.

Your Guess: *the relationship between living things on our planet*

Other Forms:
ecologist
ecological
ecologically

Definition: *the relationship between living things and their environments.*

Hint #1 Think about the word ecology. Have you heard the word before? If so, what other words do you associate it with?

Hint #2 Look for clues in the sentence. Ecology seems to be associated with the word planet and the idea that the relationship between living things is similar to a web.

Hint #3 Base your guess on an informed hunch. The example shows that the writer guesses ecology means the relationship between living things on our planet.

Hint #4 When you go to the dictionary to check your guess, be sure to read through all the definitions in order to select the one that best fits the given sentence. In the example, the writer chose the definition of ecology that seemed to make the most sense in the passage.

Hint #5 Take a moment to think about the ways that other forms of the word could be used. The writer of the example found ecologist and ecological in the dictionary and guessed that the adverb form of the word would be ecologically.

EXERCISE 2 *Context Clues* ✍

Again, you will see the new word used in a sentence. This time, however, you're actually given a set of definitions, and you must match the new word with its meaning.

Here's an example of a context-clue exercise:

COLUMN A	**COLUMN B**

_G_ word: _____ecology_____

n. the relationship between living things and their environments; the science of such relationships

(G) Aldo Leopold (1866–1948) learned to think like a mountain so that he could understand and preserve the **ecology** of nature. Nature's rights, he felt, must be respected.

Hint #1 Read Column B first, and look for clues to the meaning of the word. You might imagine that thinking like a mountain would give you strong opinions about how nature should be treated. For example, as part of the earth, you would make sure that the rights of the earth were respected.

Hint #2 You should scan Column A for a likely definition of the word. In this case, the idea of relationships suggests that the sample definition is the correct one.

Hint #3 As you write the word in the blank, say it to yourself to get a sense of the sound of the word.

EXERCISE 3 *Sentence Completion* ✍

In the final part of **Making New Words Your Own**, you are asked to supply the missing vocabulary word or words in order to create a sentence that makes sense.

Here's an example of a sentence-completion exercise:

The science of _____ allows us to _____ our natural resources.
(A) zoology . . . diminish
(B) ecology . . . preserve
(C) cultivation . . . destroy
(D) zoology . . . ignore
(E) ecology . . . exhaust

Hint #1 Think about the logic of the sentence. You are looking for a type of science that deals with natural resources. You can assume that the ultimate aim of any science is some kind of improvement.

Hint #2 Substitute the words in choices (A) through (E) in the sentence to see which pair of words completes the logic of the sentence.
  • The pairs containing the word zoology can probably be ruled out, since zoology deals with animals in particular, not all natural resources.
  • Cultivation has something to do with natural resources, but it is unlikely that the aim of any science is to destroy.
  • Similarly, you can rule out answer (E) because the aim of ecology is not to exhaust but to preserve our natural resources. This conclusion leads to the correct answer, (B).

As you complete these three types of exercises, you will develop the ability to make an educated guess about the meaning of a word by thinking about its context.

Name _____ Date _____ Class _____

MAKING NEW WORDS YOUR OWN

Lesson 1 | **CONTEXT: Literary Figures**
British Poets

For more than a thousand years, writers from England, Wales, Scotland, and Ireland have interpreted the world through poetry. During this long history, the style and subject of British poetry have varied dramatically. Yet all great British poets hold this in common: They have contributed immeasurably to the beauty of the English language and to the richness of the world's literature.

In the following exercises, you will have the opportunity to expand your vocabulary by reading about some of Britain's great poets. Below are ten vocabulary words that will be used in these exercises.

banal	finesse	lampoon	nefarious	pseudonym
bellicose	glib	lugubrious	nemesis	purloin

EXERCISE 1 | *Mapping*

Directions. In the item below, a vocabulary word is provided and used in a sentence. Take a guess at the word's meaning and write it in the box labeled **Your Guess**. Then look the word up in your dictionary and write the definition in the box labeled **Definition**. In the **Other Forms** box, write as many other forms of the word, such as adjective and noun forms, as you can think of or find in your dictionary.

Then, following the same procedure, draw your own map for each of the nine remaining vocabulary words. Use a separate sheet of paper.

1.

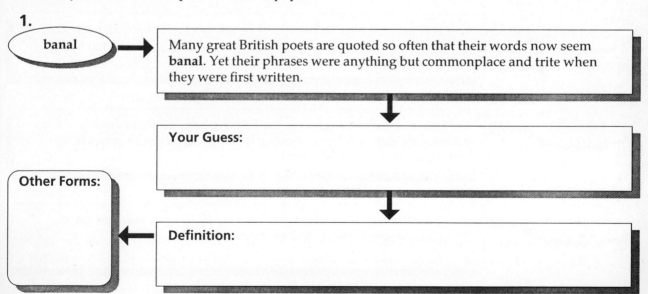

banal → Many great British poets are quoted so often that their words now seem **banal**. Yet their phrases were anything but commonplace and trite when they were first written.

Your Guess:

Other Forms:

Definition:

2.

bellicose →

A variety of colorful individuals have contributed to Britain's poetic heritage. Alexander Pope (1688–1744), for example, was small and physically weak, yet he was often aggressive and **bellicose** in his writing, using words almost as weapons.

3.

finesse →

The poet Sir Thomas Wyatt (1503–1542) handled relationships with **finesse**. He demonstrated such delicate skill in dealing with people that he served as a diplomat for King Henry VIII.

4.

glib →

No one would accuse Sir Francis Bacon (1561–1626) of being **glib**. He was a smooth talker, to be sure, but his statements had substance.

5.

lampoon →

British poets who were somewhat cynical liked to **lampoon** the institutions of their day. They had to be careful, though: Satirists could be punished severely for making fun of those in power.

6.

lugubrious →

British poets have written verse in every conceivable tone. Some poems are so joyful that they are almost ecstatic; others are so sad that they could be considered **lugubrious**.

7.

nefarious →

This is in keeping with the variety of people who have become poets. Some great British poets had sweet, calm dispositions, while others had wicked, **nefarious** temperaments.

8.

nemesis →

Unfortunately, many students view British poetry as their **nemesis**. With patience, though, most stop viewing this verse as an unconquerable foe and come to see it as a valued friend.

9.

pseudonym →

It was not unusual for a British poet of the past to use a **pseudonym**, although most wrote under their own names.

10.

purloin →

If you were to **purloin** a book of British poetry, you would be stealing something worthwhile. Still, you should buy or borrow the volume instead and read your poetry with a clear conscience.

EXERCISE 2 *Context Clues* ✍

Directions. Scan the definitions in Column A. Then think about how the boldface words are used in the sentences in Column B. To complete the exercise, match each definition in Column A with the correct vocabulary word from Column B. Write the letter of your choice on the line provided; then write the vocabulary word on the line before the definition.

| COLUMN A | COLUMN B |

COLUMN A

_____ **11.** word: _____
adv. easily spoken; speaking too smoothly to be sincere

_____ **12.** word: _____
adj. sad or mournful, often to an exaggerated degree; doleful

_____ **13.** word: _____
n. delicate skill; subtlety; *v.* to bring about with skill; to evade

_____ **14.** word: _____
n. an avenger; an unbeatable rival; a person who punishes another for evil deeds

_____ **15.** word: _____
v. to steal

_____ **16.** word: _____
adj. commonplace; trite; stale from overuse

_____ **17.** word: _____
n. a fictitious name assumed by an author; a pen name

_____ **18.** word: _____
n. strongly satirical writing; *v.* to ridicule or satirize

_____ **19.** word: _____
adj. very wicked; infamous; having a bad reputation

_____ **20.** word: _____
adj. warlike; inclined to fighting

COLUMN B

(A) One of the greatest British poets was Alexander Pope, whose **finesse** with the English language is legendary. Few others have used words with such skill.

(B) One of Pope's most famous poems is *The Rape of the Lock,* a **lampoon** intended to ridicule the petty daily lives of eighteenth-century England's aristocracy.

(C) The title of the poem refers to the theft of a lock of hair, which an adventurous baron **purloins** from the fair Belinda.

(D) The action in the poem is based on an actual event. Pope wrote the poem, in part, to ridicule the people involved, who treat the **banal,** insignificant event as a major crisis.

(E) Pope himself was a fascinating individual. He was a literary success, yet he often felt **lugubrious;** his sadness and depression led him to refer to his life as a "long disease."

(F) Pope was also **bellicose.** He frequently attacked his contemporaries in his writings, often with great vigor and always with great skill.

(G) Those who suffered from his attacks considered Pope to be vicious, even **nefarious.** They called him the "Wicked Wasp of Twickenham," after the villa in which he lived.

(H) To lesser literary figures of the day, Pope was sometimes seen as a **nemesis,** a rival who could not be beaten.

(I) Pope's pride in his work is revealed by the fact that he never used a **pseudonym** but always published under his own name.

(J) Today we **glibly** use the expressions "To err is human, to forgive, divine," "Hope springs eternal in the human breast," and "For fools rush in where angels fear to tread." We should take these phrases more seriously—after all, they are quotations from the great British poet Alexander Pope.

EXERCISE 3 *Sentence Completion* 👆

Directions. For each of the following items, circle the letter of the choice that best completes the meaning of the sentence or sentences.

21. A British poet who wished to remain anonymous could use a _____.
- (A) banality
- (B) pseudonym
- (C) finesse
- (D) nemesis
- (E) mesmerism

22. Although some modern readers find his writing heavy-handed and lacking subtlety, others think poet and essayist John Milton (1608–1674) wrote with great _____.
- (A) finesse
- (B) banality
- (C) bellicosity
- (D) glibness
- (E) nemesis

23. Satirist Jonathan Swift (1667–1745) was a master of the _____. His satires, which ridicule conventions of his day, are still considered to be among the best ever written.
- (A) lampoon
- (B) finesse
- (C) nemesis
- (D) propriety
- (E) euphemism

24. All of us _____ phrases from British poets. However, our theft of their words may be considered a tribute to their genius.
- (A) feign
- (B) allay
- (C) finesse
- (D) revile
- (E) purloin

25. A failed love affair left a young William Wordsworth (1770–1850) _____. With both care and _____, his friend and fellow poet Samuel Taylor Coleridge (1772–1834) helped Wordsworth move beyond his sadness and depression.
- (A) glib . . . lampoon
- (B) lugubrious . . . finesse
- (C) banal . . . nemesis
- (D) nefarious . . . glibness
- (E) bellicose . . . finesse

26. Much of Robert Burns's (1759–1796) poetry is about the commonplace, even _____, events experienced by ordinary people.
- (A) glib
- (B) nefarious
- (C) banal
- (D) lugubrious
- (E) bellicose

27. The shy Alfred, Lord Tennyson (1809–1892) and the aggressive, almost _____, Arthur Henry Hallam (1811–1833) were friends. Hallam's early death left Tennyson feeling _____ and heartbroken for years.
- (A) bellicose . . . lugubrious
- (B) glib . . . nefarious
- (C) nefarious . . . banal
- (D) banal . . . lugubrious
- (E) banal . . . bellicose

28. Percy Bysshe Shelley (1792–1822) believed that the good could triumph over the _____. He himself worked as the _____ of evil in order to avenge oppressed people.
- (A) glib . . . finesse
- (B) lampoon . . . pseudonym
- (C) banal . . . lampoon
- (D) bellicose . . . finesse
- (E) nefarious . . . nemesis

29. Among the memorable characters created by William Shakespeare are the angry, _____ Tybalt and Falstaff, whose humor and ability to _____ people and situations make him a merry, witty figure.
- (A) bellicose . . . lampoon
- (B) nefarious . . . finesse
- (C) glib . . . purloin
- (D) lugubrious . . . lampoon
- (E) bellicose . . . purloin

30. Tuberculosis was John Keats's (1795–1821) _____. Knowing at age twenty-five that the disease would cause his death, he wrote poetry that was sincere and deepfelt, not _____.
- (A) nemesis . . . glib
- (B) pseudonym . . . bellicose
- (C) lampoon . . . lugubrious
- (D) finesse . . . banal
- (E) nemesis . . . nefarious

MAKING NEW WORDS YOUR OWN

Lesson 2 | CONTEXT: Literary Figures
The Revolution of Mary Wollstonecraft

The late 1700s was a time of revolution, with freedom fighters struggling to overcome oppression in the British colonies and in France. In England, writer Mary Wollstonecraft (1759–1797) fought a revolution of her own—a revolution fought on behalf of women's rights. An early feminist, Wollstonecraft's most famous book is *A Vindication of the Rights of Woman* (1792). In this brief but forceful book, she argued that women should be men's equals in politics, economics, and law.

In the following exercises, you will have the opportunity to expand your vocabulary by reading about Mary Wollstonecraft. Below are ten vocabulary words that will be used in these exercises.

abject	commensurate	euphemism	phlegmatic	prosaic
admonish	distraught	nebulous	propriety	revile

EXERCISE 1   *Mapping* ✍

Directions. In the item below, a vocabulary word is provided and used in a sentence. Take a guess at the word's meaning and write it in the box labeled **Your Guess**. Then look the word up in your dictionary and write the definition in the box labeled **Definition**. In the **Other Forms** box, write as many other forms of the word, such as adjective and noun forms, as you can think of or find in your dictionary.

Then, following the same procedure, draw your own map for each of the nine remaining vocabulary words. Use a separate sheet of paper.

1.

(abject) ➡ Wollstonecraft believed that many women lived **abject** lives because they were made miserable by men, many of whom treated women as members of an inferior class.

⬇

Your Guess:

Other Forms:

Definition:

2.

admonish →

In her writings, Wollstonecraft **admonished** men for not giving women the respect they deserve. Men were not used to such polite but serious scoldings from an educated woman.

3.

commensurate →

Wollstonecraft believed that women should be treated in a way that was **commensurate** with their abilities. If she were alive today, she would support the idea that men and women who do the same work should be given the same wages.

4.

distraught →

Although Wollstonecraft was a bold champion of women's rights in her writings, she suffered a series of difficult personal relationships. **Distraught** over these failures, she used the mental conflicts that arose from these relationships as material for her novels.

5.

euphemism →

In the introduction to *A Vindication of the Rights of Woman*, Wollstonecraft states that she wants to avoid "flowery diction." Based on this information, one would not expect her writing to include **euphemisms**, mild expressions used in place of expressions considered harsh or distasteful.

6.

nebulous →

Whether or not they agree with her views, readers cannot accuse Wollstonecraft of being **nebulous**, for she clearly defines her ideas about society's tendency to glorify "feminine inferiority."

7.

phlegmatic →

Wollstonecraft had witnessed and experienced many injustices, and it was not her nature to remain **phlegmatic**. Far from remaining indifferent, she tried to persuade women to stand up for their rights.

8.

propriety →

Conventional standards made women "weak and wretched," Wollstonecraft wrote. She criticized such forms of **propriety** and urged women to "acquire strength, both of mind and body."

9.

prosaic →

Wollstonecraft said that society and men's attitudes toward women often kept women in **prosaic** or ordinary situations, when, in fact, women were capable of exceptional achievements.

10.

revile →

Although she attacked men for treating women as inferior beings, Wollstonecraft did not **revile** men. Rather than resorting to name-calling, she attempted to explain what she thought men were doing wrong.

EXERCISE 2   *Context Clues* ✍

Directions. Scan the definitions in Column A. Then think about how the boldface words are used in the sentences in Column B. To complete the exercise, match each definition in Column A with the correct vocabulary word from Column B. Write the letter of your choice on the line provided; then write the vocabulary word on the line preceding the definition.

COLUMN A

_____ **11.** word: _____
n. a mild expression used in place of a harsh, crude, or distasteful expression

_____ **12.** word: _____
adj. hazy; vague; not clearly defined

_____ **13.** word: _____
adj. hopelessly low; wretched; miserable; without self-respect

_____ **14.** word: _____
n. acceptable behavior; conformity with conventional standards

_____ **15.** word: _____
v. to attack with abusive language; to call insulting names

_____ **16.** word: _____
adj. in a state of mental conflict; agitated; crazed

_____ **17.** word: _____
v. to reprove mildly and kindly, but seriously; to caution or warn; to urge

_____ **18.** word: _____
adj. matter-of-fact; ordinary; commonplace

_____ **19.** word: _____
adj. sluggish; indifferent; calm

_____ **20.** word: _____
adj. in proper proportion; having the same scale, measure, or size; proportionate

COLUMN B

(A) Wollstonecraft's early home life, which greatly influenced her views about men and women, was not a model of **propriety,** or acceptable behavior.

(B) As a child, Wollstonecraft was often **distraught.** She was especially agitated by her father's cruelty to her mother.

(C) Wollstonecraft's father not only physically abused her mother but also probably **reviled,** or verbally abused, her.

(D) You might say that Wollstonecraft's father was often "under the influence," which is a **euphemism** for "drunk."

(E) Wollstonecraft's passive, submissive mother was **phlegmatic** in her reaction to the abuse. Wollstonecraft, on the other hand, reacted quickly and tried to help her mother.

(F) Wollstonecraft's father made the family's **abject** home life even more wretched by wasting an inherited fortune.

(G) Surely, no one would **admonish,** or reprove, Wollstonecraft for leaving home at the age of nineteen.

(H) Wollstonecraft needed a job that matched her abilities. Becoming a companion to a widow was **commensurate** with her limited experience at the time.

(I) Her physical circumstances may have been **prosaic,** but Wollstonecraft's independence was out of the ordinary for women of her time.

(J) Even if her overall plans for her life were **nebulous,** Wollstonecraft had one definite goal: to educate herself.

EXERCISE 3 Sentence Completion ✍

Directions. For each of the following items, circle the letter of the choice that best completes the meaning of the sentence or sentences.

21. Mrs. Epstein's plan for the seminar in our English literature class was _____ until she made a definite decision to focus on Mary Wollstonecraft's feminist views.
    - (A) nebulous
    - (B) phlegmatic
    - (C) distraught
    - (D) abject
    - (E) commensurate

22. When they heard what the topic was, students were at first _____, but they became actively interested when they learned more about Wollstonecraft's ideas.
    - (A) commensurate
    - (B) prosaic
    - (C) omniscient
    - (D) phlegmatic
    - (E) abject

23. Each day our discussions grew more lively, becoming _____ with our increased knowledge of Wollstonecraft's writings.
    - (A) abject
    - (B) prosaic
    - (C) commensurate
    - (D) distraught
    - (E) nebulous

24. Wollstonecraft flew in the face of _____, Mrs. Epstein said, for she openly criticized conventional standards.
    - (A) nebulousness
    - (B) abjection
    - (C) euphemism
    - (D) commensuration
    - (E) propriety

25. One boy in our class, Ruben Paré, is idealistic and sensitive, which is really just _____ for "hopelessly romantic."
    - (A) an admonishment
    - (B) a euphemism
    - (C) a commensuration
    - (D) a propriety
    - (E) an abjection

26. Ruben was upset when Bruce, a real chauvinist, _____ Wollstonecraft for her feminist ideals. Ruben _____ Bruce for his narrow-minded views, politely reproving him.
    - (A) reviled . . . absolved
    - (B) admonished . . . inveigled
    - (C) reviled . . . admonished
    - (D) feigned . . . reviled
    - (E) admonished . . . purloined

27. Bruce doesn't like to be reproved, but he accepted Ruben's _____ without becoming angry. However, I could tell that Ruben was _____, upset that such attitudes still exist.
    - (A) propriety . . . nebulous
    - (B) abjection . . . phlegmatic
    - (C) euphemism . . . commensurate
    - (D) revilement . . . prosaic
    - (E) admonishment . . . distraught

28. "Look around," Mrs. Epstein continued. "There are miserable people living in _____ poverty, and there are women whose jobs are not _____ with, or equal to, their abilities."
    - (A) commensurate . . . nebulous
    - (B) distraught . . . phlegmatic
    - (C) phlegmatic . . . abject
    - (D) abject . . . commensurate
    - (E) euphemistic . . . distraught

29. "Wollstonecraft was agitated, or _____, over injustices suffered by women she knew. Her pain was _____ with, or proportionate to, her awareness of inequalities."
    - (A) distraught . . . commensurate
    - (B) prosaic . . . abject
    - (C) nebulous . . . phlegmatic
    - (D) commensurate . . . distraught
    - (E) nebulous . . . abject

30. "Whether women lead ordinary, _____ lives or extraordinary ones, they should be treated with respect. We should all care about women's rights, and not be sluggish, or _____, in rising to their defense."
    - (A) phlegmatic . . . commensurate
    - (B) nebulous . . . prosaic
    - (C) prosaic . . . phlegmatic
    - (D) distraught . . . euphemistic
    - (E) prosaic . . . commensurate

Name _____ Date _____ Class _____

MAKING NEW WORDS YOUR OWN

Lesson 3 | **CONTEXT:** Literary Figures

A Gothic Story

Have you ever been part of a collaborative creative writing project, working with a group of students? One person starts a story, and then each group member in turn adds to it. Our class created a Gothic story in this way after studying the Romantic Movement in literature in the late 1700s and early 1800s. Gothic stories involve mysterious, gloomy, remote settings, sometimes suggesting medieval times. Elements of the setting may include haunted castles, ruins, eerie landscapes, and ghostly visitors. Would you like to hear a portion of the story we wrote?

In the following exercises, you will have the opportunity to expand your vocabulary by reading excerpts from a Gothic story written by a group of students. Below are ten vocabulary words that will be used in these exercises.

assimilate	discursive	farcical	hyperbole	mesmerism
cognizant	ennui	fortuitous	incognito	omniscient

EXERCISE 1 *Mapping* 👉

Directions. In the item below, a vocabulary word is provided and used in a sentence. Take a guess at the word's meaning and write it in the box labeled **Your Guess**. Then look the word up in your dictionary and write the definition in the box labeled **Definition**. In the **Other Forms** box, write as many other forms of the word, such as adjective and noun forms, as you can think of or find in your dictionary.

Then, following the same procedure, draw your own map for each of the nine remaining vocabulary words. Use a separate sheet of paper.

1.

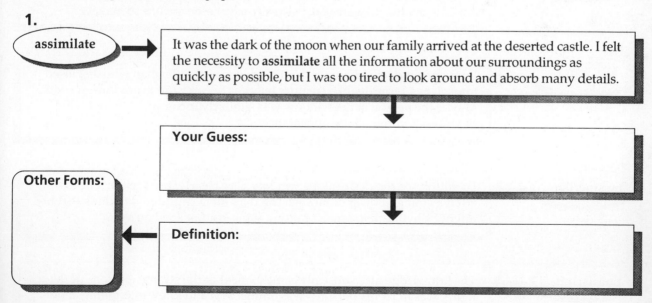

assimilate → It was the dark of the moon when our family arrived at the deserted castle. I felt the necessity to **assimilate** all the information about our surroundings as quickly as possible, but I was too tired to look around and absorb many details.

Your Guess:

Other Forms:

Definition:

2.

cognizant →

Suddenly, I was keenly aware of someone or something watching us. I do not know what made me **cognizant** of this; perhaps it was merely instinct. Nevertheless, all I could see were huge trees, their branches swaying in the fierce wind.

3.

discursive →

Eric, my brother, started talking excitedly, rambling on about various subjects that nobody else cared about. I think he was trying to hide his fear with his **discursive** speech.

4.

ennui →

Clearly, no one wanted to get out of the car. **Ennui** usually is a problem if we're stuck in the car too long on trips, but I think this time everyone stayed put not because they were bored and listless, but because they were frightened.

5.

farcical →

I started laughing, and my laughter startled all of us. "This is so **farcical**," I said. "We must look ridiculous sitting out here in the middle of the night, lost and tired but afraid to get out of the car."

6.

fortuitous →

"Well," my father said, "you have to admit it's **fortuitous** that we've found this house . . . or castle, or whatever it is. And it's also fortunate that someone inside appears to be awake. Look—there's a light on upstairs."

7.

hyperbole →

I peered up through the darkness and saw a large figure at an upstairs window. Whoever it was seemed as big as a gorilla, and that's no **hyperbole**. I'm not exaggerating to scare you; I've really never seen anyone so massive.

8.

incognito →

I remembered an old horror movie I once saw about a man who disguised himself as a large apelike creature in order to carry out gruesome murders. Maybe the person at the window was similarly **incognito**, I thought, hiding himself under a false appearance.

9.

mesmerism →

I couldn't see the figure at the window very clearly, but I felt that he exerted a strange power of **mesmerism** over me. I shuddered to think that he might be hypnotizing me or putting some kind of spell on me.

10.

omniscient →

The knowledge also suddenly came to me that the strange person—if the figure was indeed a person—was **omniscient** and knew everything about me and my family.

EXERCISE 2 *Context Clues* ✍

Directions. Scan the definitions in Column A. Then think about how the boldface words are used in the sentences in Column B. To complete the exercise, match each definition in Column A with the correct vocabulary word from Column B. Write the letter of your choice on the line provided; then write the vocabulary word on the line preceding the definition.

<table>
<tr><td>COLUMN A</td><td>COLUMN B</td></tr>
</table>

COLUMN A

_____ **11.** word: _____
n. one who is in disguise or using an assumed name; *adj.* disguised; using a false name; *adv.* in disguise; under a fictitious name

_____ **12.** word: _____
adj. aware of or informed about something

_____ **13.** word: _____
adj. ridiculous; like a farce; exaggeratedly comical

_____ **14.** word: _____
adj. wandering or shifting from one subject to another; rambling; long winded

_____ **15.** word: _____
n. an obvious exaggeration, made for effect and not meant to be taken literally

_____ **16.** word: _____
adj. knowing everything; having complete or infinite knowledge

_____ **17.** word: _____
adj. occurring by chance; accidental; fortunate

_____ **18.** word: _____
v. to absorb and incorporate food or knowledge; to absorb one group into a larger culture

_____ **19.** word: _____
n. discontent and listlessness from lack of occupation or interest; boredom

_____ **20.** word: _____
n. hypnotism; hypnotic appeal; intense fascination

COLUMN B

(A) There must have been a million lion heads carved on the castle door. Well, that may be a **hyperbole**, but there certainly were many.

(B) The man who answered the doorbell seemed to exert a power of **mesmerism** over all of us, although I can't explain our intense, almost magnetic fascination.

(C) "Welcome, I am Rincent Brice," he said. I thought he was presenting himself **incognito** because that didn't sound like a real name.

(D) My father told our **farcical** story—the comedy of errors, wrong turns, and late starts that resulted in our arriving there.

(E) "I am already **cognizant** of all you are telling me," Mr. Brice said, but he did not explain how he knew about us.

(F) Obviously, unlike my brother Eric, Mr. Brice was not a **discursive** talker. He said as little as possible, and his speech was abrupt, but his eyes wandered over us all.

(G) Mr. Brice appeared to know everything about us, even our futures. "You will change your plans and stay here three weeks," our seemingly **omniscient** host announced, like a fortune teller making a prediction.

(H) "Your arrival here was not **fortuitous**. Chance had no part in it," Mr. Brice added, sending shivers down my spine. "It was meant to be."

(I) Well, I thought, we surely won't have any problem with **ennui** here. Who could be bored under circumstances like these?

(J) "You now want to **assimilate** some food," Mr. Brice said. "I know that your bodies, unlike my own, need to absorb food."

EXERCISE 3 Sentence Completion ✍

Directions. For each of the following items, circle the letter of the choice that best completes the meaning of the sentence or sentences.

21. The longer we stayed, the more convinced I was that Mr. Brice was _____, using a false name and, perhaps, a disguise.
- (A) cognizant
- (B) discursive
- (C) incognito
- (D) fortuitous
- (E) assimilated

22. We didn't see him for the next twenty-four hours, but I was _____ of his presence and equally aware that he was watching us.
- (A) discursive
- (B) cognizant
- (C) farcical
- (D) incognito
- (E) omniscient

23. You may think this merely _____, but I had goose bumps over every inch of my body.
- (A) an ennui
- (B) an incognito
- (C) a mesmerism
- (D) an assimilation
- (E) a hyperbole

24. The next day, I wandered around the gloomy ruins behind the castle and wondered how my family could avoid being _____ by this strange place. Its eerie atmosphere made me think that we were all in danger of being absorbed by the odd surroundings.
- (A) farcical
- (B) cognizant
- (C) omniscient
- (D) assimilated
- (E) discursive

25. Perhaps if I could have had _____ talks with Mr. Brice, I might have learned more about his plans for us, but he was not at all talkative.
- (A) discursive
- (B) omniscient
- (C) fortuitous
- (D) farcical
- (E) cognizant

26. Eric was bored and complained of _____, so I told him to go outside. To use _____, he ran out as swiftly as a cheetah.
- (A) mesmerism . . . an ennui
- (B) hyperbole . . . a mesmerism
- (C) ennui . . . a hyperbole
- (D) incognito . . . an omniscience
- (E) discursiveness . . . an incognito

27. It was lucky, or _____, that I happened to be outside just when Eric vanished into the woods. I ran in after him, but I soon realized I was involved in _____, or ridiculous, chase. Eric had vanished.
- (A) cognizant . . . a discursive
- (B) fortuitous . . . a farcical
- (C) farcical . . . an incognito
- (D) incognito . . . a cognizant
- (E) discursive . . . an omniscient

28. I wished I were _____, able to know not only what was happening to Eric but to everyone else as well. I would have realized that my father had fallen under the hypnotic spell, or _____, of Mr. Brice.
- (A) farcical . . . ennui
- (B) incognito . . . hyperbole
- (C) discursive . . . ennui
- (D) omniscient . . . mesmerism
- (E) fortuitous . . . hyperbole

29. I wanted to be completely aware, fully _____, so that perhaps I could figure out a way to get us out of this once _____, but now far from comic, situation.
- (A) discursive . . . fortuitous
- (B) farcical . . . incognito
- (C) fortuitous . . . cognizant
- (D) assimilative . . . discursive
- (E) cognizant . . . farcical

30. If I could only be _____! If I were all-knowing, I could not be fooled by anyone, whether undisguised or _____.
- (A) omniscient . . . incognito
- (B) discursive . . . cognizant
- (C) farcical . . . omniscient
- (D) fortuitous . . . discursive
- (E) mesmerized . . . incognito

MAKING NEW WORDS YOUR OWN

Lesson 4 | CONTEXT: Literary Figures
Macbeth: Truth and Legend

Macbeth ruled Scotland from A.D. 1040 to 1057, and, from historical accounts, he was a good king. His reputation suffered, however, when his story became a folk legend that changed through many retellings. By the early 1600s, when Shakespeare wrote his play about the ruler, Macbeth appeared in histories of Scotland as "a savage tyrant" who had met with witches and plotted King Duncan's murder. The histories themselves were as much legend as fact—and were all the more compelling for that reason. Shakespeare wove these tales and truths about Macbeth into one of his most powerful plays: *Macbeth*.

In the following exercises, you will have the opportunity to expand your vocabulary by reading about Shakespeare and Macbeth. Below are ten vocabulary words that will be used in these exercises.

adroit	blazon	choleric	confer	expatriate
allay	bravado	colloquy	dirge	feign

EXERCISE 1 | *Mapping*

Directions. In the item below, a vocabulary word is provided and used in a sentence. Take a guess at the word's meaning and write it in the box labeled **Your Guess**. Then look the word up in your dictionary and write the definition in the box labeled **Definition**. In the **Other Forms** box, write as many other forms of the word, such as adjective and noun forms, as you can think of or find in your dictionary.

Then, following the same procedure, draw your own map for each of the nine remaining vocabulary words. Use a separate sheet of paper.

1.

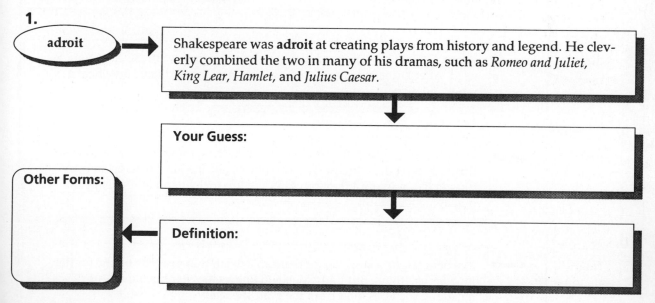

adroit → Shakespeare was **adroit** at creating plays from history and legend. He cleverly combined the two in many of his dramas, such as *Romeo and Juliet*, *King Lear*, *Hamlet*, and *Julius Caesar*.

Your Guess:

Other Forms:

Definition:

2.

allay →

The lack of historical accuracy in Shakespeare's plays does not **allay**, or lessen, people's interest in them. In fact, the plays have remained popular for nearly four hundred years.

3.

blazon →

Every year, Shakespeare's plays are performed all over the world. In towns and cities, audiences are attracted to theaters by posters that **blazon** information about performances.

4.

bravado →

Shakespeare's plays appeal to people because they dramatize universal human characteristics, such as pride, envy, love, ambition, cowardice, courage, and false bravery, or **bravado**.

5.

choleric →

Some of Shakespeare's characters are kind and good tempered, but some, like the **choleric** Macbeth, vent their bad tempers on all those around them. Macbeth's obsessive ambition drives him to react with quick anger.

6.

colloquy →

When Macbeth and Banquo, generals in King Duncan's army, are returning from a victorious battle, they meet and speak with three witches. In this **colloquy** the witches prophesy that Macbeth will be king of Scotland.

7.

confer →

When Duncan **confers**, or bestows, an honor on Macbeth by visiting his castle, Macbeth uses the occasion to fulfill the witches' prophecy. Macbeth murders Duncan in order to become king.

8.

dirge →

When *Macbeth* is performed, taped or live background music is sometimes used. After Duncan is murdered, for instance, the audience may hear a mournful **dirge**.

9.

expatriate →

Duncan's sons, Malcolm and Donalbain, fearing for their lives, **expatriate** themselves from Scotland. They do not plan to stay in a foreign country forever but only until they can safely return to Scotland and avenge the murder of their father.

10.

feign →

Macbeth **feigns** a story about Duncan's death that puts the blame for the murder on others. But Lady Macbeth knows that her husband's story is false, and she goes mad from the guilt she feels.

EXERCISE 2 *Context Clues*

Directions. Scan the definitions in Column A. Then think about how the boldface words are used in the sentences in Column B. To complete the exercise, match each definition in Column A with the correct vocabulary word from Column B. Write the letter of your choice on the line provided; then write the vocabulary word on the line preceding the definition.

COLUMN A

_____ **11.** word: _____

n. a funeral hymn; a poetic or musical expression of grief

_____ **12.** word: _____

v. to give, grant, or bestow; to have a conference or talk; to meet for discussion

_____ **13.** word: _____

v. to banish from one's native country; to withdraw from one's native land; *n.* one who is exiled or who has withdrawn from his or her native land

_____ **14.** word: _____

n. a conversation or conference, usually formal

_____ **15.** word: _____

v. to lessen; to relieve; to calm

_____ **16.** word: _____

v. to pretend; to make up

_____ **17.** word: _____

v. to proclaim; to display publicly; *n.* a coat of arms; a banner

_____ **18.** word: _____

adj. easily angered; bad tempered

_____ **19.** word: _____

adj. clever; skillful in a mental or physical way; expert

_____ **20.** word: _____

n. a show of false bravery or confidence

COLUMN B

(A) Macbeth is afraid that his actions after Duncan's death will **blazon** his guilt for all to see.

(B) Because he is obsessed with keeping the throne, Macbeth **confers** with underlings. When they meet, he orders them to kill Banquo and his son, Fleance, but Fleance escapes.

(C) Apparently Macbeth's friendship with Banquo was not genuine, but **feigned**. In reality, Macbeth is willing to kill Banquo to secure the throne.

(D) Banquo's ghost appears to Macbeth at a party. Macbeth's **bravado** is obvious; his false bravery when he faces the ghost makes the guests suspicious.

(E) In another **colloquy**, the witches warn Macbeth to "beware Macduff." After meeting with the witches, Macbeth orders Macduff's wife and children killed.

(F) Macduff leaves Scotland, **expatriating** himself to England. There he joins forces with Malcolm and Donalbain.

(G) Unlike her husband, Lady Macbeth is not **adroit**, or skillful, at intrigue and murder. Her guilt leads to madness.

(H) The **choleric** witches prophesy Macbeth's doom, but he does not understand what the bad-tempered women mean until it is too late.

(I) Macbeth's fears increase when he realizes that what he considered impossible is coming true. Nothing can **allay** Macbeth's fears; he cannot hope for relief.

(J) With all the deaths, including Macbeth's, there are many opportunities to play **dirges** during a performance of the play.

EXERCISE 3 *Sentence Completion* 🖎

Directions. For each of the following items, circle the letter of the choice that best completes the meaning of the sentence or sentences.

21. Scholars often hold _____ to discuss Shakespeare's writing. Some of these conferences are quite large.
(A) colloquies
(B) dirges
(C) expatriates
(D) blazons
(E) bravados

22. Shakespeare borrowed from other works and was _____, or skillful, at combining stories from different sources.
(A) choleric
(B) blazoned
(C) adroit
(D) conferrable
(E) gratuitous

23. Shakespeare took the idea of the murder of Duncan from a historical account of the murder of King Duff by Donwald, an ambitious, angry, and _____ king's subject.
(A) conferrable
(B) blazoned
(C) choleric
(D) expatriated
(E) prosaic

24. In the play, Macbeth takes on some of the dark traits associated with the historical Donwald. Like Donwald, Macbeth pretends to be braver than he actually is; he uses _____ to hide his fears.
(A) colloquy
(B) blazon
(C) conference
(D) bravado
(E) expatriation

25. Shakespeare may have based the witches, who bestow, or _____, prophecies on Macbeth and others, on the Norns of Scandinavian mythology.
(A) blazon
(B) expatriate
(C) allay
(D) feign
(E) confer

26. Shakespeare's _____, skillful descriptions make it easy to picture armies proudly displaying their _____, or coats of arms.
(A) choleric . . . bravado
(B) adroit . . . blazons
(C) conferrable . . . expatriates
(D) fortuitous . . . adroitness
(E) sanguine . . . bravado

27. Shakespeare may have _____ with people who had been _____ from England for political reasons, learning much from these talks.
(A) blazoned . . . allayed
(B) expatriated . . . feigned
(C) conferred . . . expatriated
(D) feigned . . . blazoned
(E) allayed . . . feigned

28. Shakespeare's witches _____ an interest in helping people, but actually they are skillful, or _____, at deceiving those to whom they reveal their prophecies.
(A) confer . . . choleric
(B) blazon . . . conferrable
(C) allay . . . choleric
(D) expatriate . . . adroit
(E) feign . . . adroit

29. If King James I attended a play, it was a major event that would have been _____ throughout England. The king disliked long plays, so to _____ any criticism, Shakespeare kept *Macbeth* short.
(A) feigned . . . expatriate
(B) allayed . . . blazon
(C) conferred . . . expatriate
(D) blazoned . . . allay
(E) feigned . . . confer

30. Apparently the king did not object to plays about _____ people whose rage leads them to commit murder. Nor, evidently, was he depressed by the somber chords of _____ played during death scenes.
(A) adroit . . . bravado
(B) choleric . . . dirges
(C) conferrable . . . blazons
(D) adroit . . . expatriates
(E) nebulous . . . colloquies

Name _____ Date _____ Class _____

| Lesson 5 | **CONTEXT:** Literary Figures |

The Pre-Raphaelites: Painters and Poets

In the mid-1800s, a small group of artists who called themselves Pre-Raphaelites formed in England. Since *pre-* means "before" and the artist Raphael lived from 1483–1520, the term doesn't make much sense until you learn that the group's aim was to return to an artistic style that predated Raphael. One of the group's artists, Dante Gabriel Rossetti (1828–1882), was also a poet, and before long he formed a group of Pre-Raphaelite poets. What was it that these artists admired in the art styles that were popular three hundred years before they were born?

In the following exercises, you will have the opportunity to expand your vocabulary by reading about the Pre-Raphaelite Brotherhood of painters and poets. Below are ten vocabulary words that will be used in these exercises.

| amorphous | decorum | facile | proffer | sanguine |
| ascetic | doggerel | guile | protégé | seraphic |

EXERCISE 1 *Mapping* 👈

Directions. In the item below, a vocabulary word is provided and used in a sentence. Take a guess at the word's meaning and write it in the box labeled **Your Guess.** Then look the word up in your dictionary and write the definition in the box labeled **Definition.** In the **Other Forms** box, write as many other forms of the word, such as adjective and noun forms, as you can think of or find in your dictionary.

Then, following the same procedure, draw your own map for each of the nine remaining vocabulary words. Use a separate sheet of paper.

1.

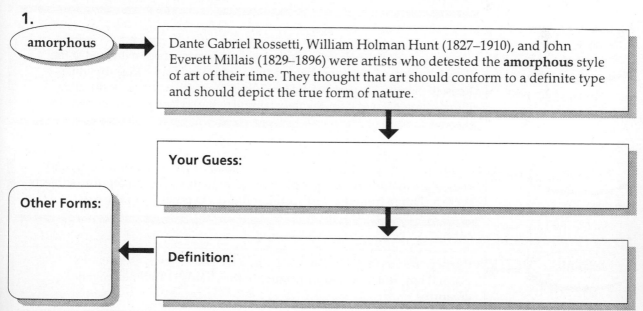

amorphous → Dante Gabriel Rossetti, William Holman Hunt (1827–1910), and John Everett Millais (1829–1896) were artists who detested the **amorphous** style of art of their time. They thought that art should conform to a definite type and should depict the true form of nature.

Your Guess:

Other Forms:

Definition:

2.

ascetic →

Dante Rossetti's sister, Christina Rossetti (1830–1894), was an **ascetic** who lived a life of simplicity and seclusion. She denied herself marriage for religious reasons. Her poetry is more devotional than that of the other Pre-Raphaelites.

3.

decorum →

Her good manners and behavior made Christina Rossetti an ideal model for her brother's paintings. He wanted someone with **decorum** to pose for his painting of the Virgin Mary.

4.

doggerel →

Christina Rossetti's poetry is simple but intense, and it is concerned with the relationship between worldly and spiritual matters. Because it is very well written, it could never be regarded as **doggerel**.

5.

facile →

Dante Rossetti was a **facile** artist and poet who moved easily and skillfully from one art form to another. He is highly respected in both fields.

6.

guile →

The Pre-Raphaelites wanted their works to be honest, totally lacking **guile**. They disliked the drab colors of the old masters' paintings and used bright, natural pigments and the simplicity of early Italian paintings in their works.

7.

proffer →

When the Pre-Raphaelites first **proffered** their works to the public in 1850, they were rejected. Two years later, when the artists offered their paintings to the Royal Academy, the public and critics alike praised their works.

8.

protégé →

The influential artist Holman Hunt, whose works had been exhibited at the Royal Academy in London, helped and encouraged Dante Rossetti while Rossetti painted *The Girlhood of Mary Virgin*. Rossetti, who was at this time Hunt's **protégé**, was painstakingly faithful to the style of the Pre-Raphaelites.

9.

sanguine →

Pre-Raphaelite paintings are filled with color and natural simplicity, and they often include robust people who seem happy. These **sanguine** subjects were a change from the dark, somber figures in other art of the day.

10.

seraphic →

Christ in the House of His Parents, by Millais, shows Jesus as a healthy, normal boy, not as a **seraphic** figure in the clouds with other angelic creatures.

EXERCISE 2 *Context Clues* ✍

Directions. Scan the definitions in Column A. Then think about how the boldface words are used in the sentences in Column B. To complete the exercise, match each definition in Column A with the correct vocabulary word from Column B. Write the letter of your choice on the line provided; then write the vocabulary word on the line preceding the definition.

COLUMN A

_____ **11.** word: _____
n. craftiness; deceit; cunning

_____ **12.** word: _____
v. to offer; *n.* an offer

_____ **13.** word: _____
adj. angelic; of the highest order of angels

_____ **14.** word: _____
adj. shapeless; of no particular form or type; not organized

_____ **15.** word: _____
n. proper action, speech, and dress; good manners and behavior; polite behavior

_____ **16.** word: _____
n. someone whose welfare or career is promoted by an influential person

_____ **17.** word: _____
adj. naturally cheerful and hopeful; confident; having a ruddy complexion; optimistic; hopeful

_____ **18.** word: _____
n. badly written or trivial verse, often with a singsong rhythm

_____ **19.** word: _____
n. a person who practices unusual self-denial or discipline, often for religious reasons; *adj.* self-denying

_____ **20.** word: _____
adj. easily done; performing or working with ease; adroit; not sincere or profound; superficial

COLUMN B

(A) Eventually, the openness and the lack of **guile** of Pre-Raphaelite art attracted more people to the movement.

(B) But other schools of art, such as Impressionism, were also attracting followers, so the Pre-Raphaelites had few **protégés**. Young artists did not seek out their influence.

(C) Many Pre-Raphaelites were criticized for their sensual subject matter. The public expected them to be **ascetics** as artists and felt that neither their art nor their lives reflected an attitude of discipline and self-denial.

(D) The painters were condemned for their informal lifestyles and what the public considered a lack of **decorum** in their actions, speech, and dress.

(E) They were certainly not **seraphic**, like angels, but they did not deserve to have their works condemned because of their personal lives.

(F) Because the Pre-Raphaelites believed strongly in portraying realistic detail, their works were never **amorphous**.

(G) After their works were criticized by the public, the Pre-Raphaelites were not very **sanguine** about their art. Fortunately, they never lost hope or confidence.

(H) The accomplished poets of the group included the Rossettis, George Meredith (1828–1909), William Morris (1834–1896), and Algernon Swinburne (1837–1909). These writers may have addressed unconventional subjects, but their works were intelligent and well-crafted—far from **doggerel**.

(I) Their works were **proffered** to the public in various volumes. Pre-Raphaelite poets, except for Christina Rossetti, offered overtly romantic verse.

(J) George Meredith was a **facile**, adroit writer who wrote novels as well as refreshing poetry.

EXERCISE 3   *Sentence Completion* ✍

Directions. For each of the following items, circle the letter of the choice that best completes the meaning of the sentence or sentences.

21. Many people enjoy reading _____ because it takes little thought to read light, sing-song verse.

(A) decorum
(B) guile
(C) doggerel
(D) ascetic
(E) seraphs

22. _____ people probably avoid sad, mournful poetry and prefer poetry about hopeful, cheerful characters and events.

(A) Seraphic
(B) Ascetic
(C) Facile
(D) Sanguine
(E) Amorphous

23. Styles in art are constantly changing. Some modern art has moved so far from realism that it is _____, without definite shape or form.

(A) decorous
(B) facile
(C) sanguine
(D) seraphic
(E) amorphous

24. Different people appreciate different kinds of art. Some prefer earthy, natural paintings, others like rather frilly, _____ scenes of floating cherubs, while still others enjoy modern abstract works.

(A) sanguine
(B) seraphic
(C) ascetic
(D) proferred
(E) amorphous

25. People with _____ know how to behave in art galleries. They speak quietly and don't touch any of the art works.

(A) guile
(B) decorum
(C) protégés
(D) ascetics
(E) doggerel

26. It is a mark of _____ to know what kind of poetry a friend might enjoy. It would be impolite to _____ an unsuitable kind of poetry.

(A) decorum . . . proffer
(B) doggerel . . . blazon
(C) guile . . . admonish
(D) amorphousness . . . proffer
(E) protégé . . . lampoon

27. Writers can lose faith in their work and believe it is _____, not profound. Eventually, however, most determined writers regain their confidence and feel _____ again.

(A) guileful . . . seraphic
(B) ascetic . . . amorphous
(C) sanguine . . . guileful
(D) facile . . . sanguine
(E) amorphous . . . ascetic

28. Because many artists and poets are poor, they live _____ lives. The lack of clutter and distractions enables them to be more _____ workers, able to exercise their talents easily.

(A) sanguine . . . amorphous
(B) ascetic . . . facile
(C) facile . . . seraphic
(D) seraphic . . . ascetic
(E) amorphous . . . guileful

29. Writers and poets are often _____ of influential people who help and support them until their _____ works are accepted.

(A) ascetics . . . sanguine
(B) seraphs . . . ascetic
(C) protégés . . . proffered
(D) protégés . . . guileful
(E) doggerel . . . seraphic

30. Although the Pre-Raphaelite movement lasted only a few years, its open, natural style—its lack of _____—and its optimistic, _____ outlook strikes a happy note in the history of art.

(A) decorum . . . guileful
(B) doggerel . . . amorphous
(C) guile . . . sanguine
(D) ascetics . . . seraphic
(E) protégés . . . guileful

MAKING NEW WORDS YOUR OWN

Lesson 6 | CONTEXT: Literary Figures
The Space Stories of Doris Lessing

Doris Lessing (b. 1919), one of the most important British novelists of this century, began her series of "space fiction," known as *Canopus in Argos: Archives,* in 1979. The five books in the series are *Shikasta; The Marriages Between Zones Three, Four and Five; The Sirian Experiments; The Making of the Representative for Planet 8;* and *Documents Relating to the Sentimental Agents in the Volyen Empire.* A major premise of the series is that good beings and malevolent beings in space influence events on earth.

In the following exercises, you will have the opportunity to expand your vocabulary by reading about the space stories of Doris Lessing. Below are ten vocabulary words that will be used in these exercises.

dogma	inveigle	nonentity	scurrilous	tacit
exhort	nondescript	parsimonious	sundry	vociferous

EXERCISE 1 *Mapping*

Directions. In the item below, a vocabulary word is provided and used in a sentence. Take a guess at the word's meaning and write it in the box labeled **Your Guess**. Then look the word up in your dictionary and write the definition in the box labeled **Definition**. In the **Other Forms** box, write as many other forms of the word, such as adjective and noun forms, as you can think of or find in your dictionary.

Then, following the same procedure, draw your own map for each of the nine remaining vocabulary words. Use a separate sheet of paper.

1.

dogma →

Dear Janet,
    I know that you have a strong set of personal beliefs, but I wish that you had a more open mind and could be tolerant of other people's beliefs. For instance, I am sure that some of the ideas expressed by British writer Doris Lessing in her space series would conflict with your **dogma**, but I think you should be exposed to them anyway.

Your Guess:

Other Forms:

Definition:

2.

exhort ➡️ I **exhort** you to read at least one of Lessing's books. I'd like to know what you think of the philosophical views presented in her science fiction. If you read just one book, you may not need my further urgings to read the others.

3.

inveigle ➡️ I became so interested in the series that I **inveigled** my mother to buy copies of the books for me for my birthday. "You're a great mom," I flattered her, "and you've always been so good about encouraging my love of reading." My trick worked—sort of. She ended up buying me three of the five books.

4.

nondescript ➡️ Frankly, I think some of the characters in the series are rather **nondescript.** They don't have distinctive characteristics and are therefore hard to describe. But they serve important functions in the books.

5.

nonentity ➡️ I think that Lessing deliberately makes some of her characters **nonentities** because they are of little importance as individuals. What Lessing wants her readers to see is that human destiny is in the control of these alien beings, who act as outside forces. She is less interested in developing their characters.

6.

parsimonious ➡️ I'd like to buy you a copy of *Shikasta*, but I can't right now. It's not that I am **parsimonious**—as you know, I'm usually generous with my money—but I loaned all my money to my brother so he could buy a new bicycle.

7.

scurrilous ➡️ My brother can be rather **scurrilous**. I told him that if he didn't use any indecent language for two weeks, I would lend him the money. So far, he has kept his promise. It's been peaceful around here without his vulgar talk.

8.

sundry ➡️ Anyway, the story of my brother and his bicycle is only one of **sundry** things that I wanted to tell you about. While many items are on my list, I am most interested in discussing Doris Lessing's space stories.

9.

tacit ➡️ My brother and I have never talked openly about borrowing and reading each other's books. We've just always had a **tacit** agreement to share our books. He's now reading the second book in Lessing's science fiction series.

10.

vociferous ➡️ I hope that you will like the series as much as he does. He wanted the second book before I even finished reading it. In fact, he became **vociferous**, shouting at me and trying to grab the book from my hands. He can be really loud and demanding at times.

EXERCISE 2 *Context Clues* ✍

Directions. Scan the definitions in Column A. Then think about how the boldface words are used in the sentences in Column B. To complete the exercise, match each definition in Column A with the correct vocabulary word from Column B. Write the letter of your choice on the line provided; then write the vocabulary word on the line preceding the definition.

COLUMN A	COLUMN B

COLUMN A

_____ **11.** word: _____
adj. implied or understood without being expressed openly; unspoken

_____ **12.** word: _____
adj. not having individual characteristics; lacking in distinctive qualities; drab; hard to describe

_____ **13.** word: _____
adj. various; miscellaneous

_____ **14.** word: _____
v. to win over with trickery or flattery; to entice; to coax with deceitful talk; to dupe

_____ **15.** word: _____
n. a belief or set of beliefs held to be true, especially by a church or other authority; a doctrine

_____ **16.** word: _____
adj. given to the use of abusive, indecent, or vulgar language; foulmouthed

_____ **17.** word: _____
adj. too economical; stingy; miserly

_____ **18.** word: _____
v. to urge strongly; to advise or warn earnestly; to admonish

_____ **19.** word: _____
n. a person or thing of little or no importance; something that does not exist or that exists only in the imagination

_____ **20.** word: _____
adj. loud and noisy; clamorous; demanding

COLUMN B

(A) Try to coax or **inveigle** the librarian to reserve for you a copy of *The Marriages Between Zones Three, Four and Five.* You may have to pretend that you need it for a class.

(B) You may not want my advice, but I **exhort** you to reserve a copy since the book is so popular.

(C) Find a nice, quiet place, away from **vociferous** people, to read about the romance of Queen Al-Ith from Zone Three and King Ben Ata from Zone Four.

(D) The **nondescript** Providers, the rulers of the cosmos who don't have distinctive qualities, order Al-Ith and Ben Ata to marry and unite the two zones.

(E) Zone Three is a lovely, peaceful place. Zone Four is a militaristic, crude place where soldiers use **scurrilous** language. The contrast between sweetness and vulgarity is pretty jarring.

(F) Despite the **sundry** differences in their societies— and believe me, there are too many to count— Al-Ith and Ben Ata discover that they are compatible.

(G) A **tacit** bond, the sort of closeness that doesn't need to be expressed in words, develops between Al-Ith and Ben Ata.

(H) This is my favorite book in the series because it focuses on characters that seem real rather than on **nonentities** who could exist only in the imagination.

(I) Problems develop, but they are not the usual domestic ones, such as conflicts between a generous husband and a stingy, **parsimonious** wife.

(J) The Providers order Ben Ata to abandon Al-Ith and to marry the queen of Zone Five. All of these characters clearly live by a **dogma**, or doctrine, that is foreign to our society. I can't imagine following their beliefs.

EXERCISE 3 *Sentence Completion* ✍

Directions. For each of the following items, circle the letter of the choice that best completes the meaning of the sentence or sentences.

21. I don't find it difficult to consider _____ that are different from my own beliefs.
    (A) exhortations
    (B) nonentities
    (C) inveiglements
    (D) dirges
    (E) dogmas

22. The fifth book, *Documents Relating to the Sentimental Agents in the Volyen Empire*, is about an older agent teaching a young agent how to avoid becoming the victim of words, whether decent or _____.
    (A) nondescript
    (B) tacit
    (C) scurrilous
    (D) sundry
    (E) parsimonious

23. In this book there is a trial in which the Volyen state is accused of _____ the people, of completely deceiving them.
    (A) dogmatizing
    (B) inveigling
    (C) broaching
    (D) exhorting
    (E) subjugating

24. The complicated plot deals with forms of tyranny, those that are expressed and obvious as well as those that are _____.
    (A) sundry
    (B) nondescript
    (C) vociferous
    (D) tacit
    (E) parsimonious

25. Lessing tries to show us that societies decay when the people become too self-centered. I suppose that being _____ with money is a mark of self-centeredness. My miserly sister wouldn't lend my brother even five dollars for his bicycle.
    (A) scurrilous
    (B) nondescript
    (C) parsimonious
    (D) vociferous
    (E) sundry

26. Among Lessing's various, or _____, ideas is the belief that earth has lost the "substance-of-we-feeling." Sometimes she expresses the idea openly and sometimes _____, or implicitly.
    (A) sundry . . . tacitly
    (B) scurrilous . . . scurrilously
    (C) nondescript . . . parsimoniously
    (D) vociferous . . . dogmatically
    (E) parsimonious . . . scurrilously

27. The creatures in the fourth novel clearly are _____ that exist only in Lessing's imagination. These imaginary beings are strongly warned that their planet is dying and then are _____ to make plans to leave.
    (A) dogmas . . . exhorted
    (B) exhortations . . . inveigled
    (C) inveiglements . . . dogmatized
    (D) dogmas . . . inveigled
    (E) nonentities . . . exhorted

28. Is the dying planet _____? No, Lessing makes the planet real and distinctive by providing various and _____ descriptions.
    (A) tacit . . . parsimonious
    (B) parsimonious . . . vociferous
    (C) scurrilous . . . nondescript
    (D) nondescript . . . sundry
    (E) vociferous . . . scurrilous

29. Lessing's fans can be quite vocal, even _____, in support of her. And they're not at all _____ when it comes to buying her books.
    (A) parsimonious . . . scurrilous
    (B) vociferous . . . parsimonious
    (C) nondescript . . . sundry
    (D) sundry . . . tacit
    (E) vociferous . . . nondescript

30. I _____ you to read Lessing's science fiction, but others may urge you to read her realistic novels, such as *The Golden Notebook*. I hope you won't think I am _____ you to read her books when I say that they appeal to very intelligent people like you.
    (A) exhort . . . broaching
    (B) inveigle . . . exhorting
    (C) exhort . . . inveigling
    (D) broach . . . exhorting
    (E) inveigle . . . broaching

Name _____ Date _____ Class _____

MAKING NEW WORDS YOUR OWN

Lesson 7 | CONTEXT: Literary Figures
Old English: A Foreign Language

My grandparents live in England, and when they visit us, there is always good-natured talk about the English language. They contend that Americans don't speak real English at all. What they said made me wonder: What is real English, and where did it come from? I decided to ask Dr. Hobson, a family friend who teaches the history of the English language at our local college. She told me that English has been spoken in England for only fifteen hundred of the island's more than fifty-thousand-year history.

In the following exercises, you will have the opportunity to expand your vocabulary by reading about the languages of England before the English language evolved. Below are ten vocabulary words that will be used in these exercises.

broach	erudite	gratuitous	predispose	truism
charlatan	extol	immutable	prerogative	venerate

EXERCISE 1 | Mapping

Directions. In the item below, a vocabulary word is provided and used in a sentence. Take a guess at the word's meaning and write it in the box labeled **Your Guess**. Then look the word up in your dictionary and write the definition in the box labeled **Definition**. In the **Other Forms** box, write as many other forms of the word, such as adjective and noun forms, as you can think of or find in your dictionary.

Then, following the same procedure, draw your own map for each of the nine remaining vocabulary words. Use a separate sheet of paper.

1.

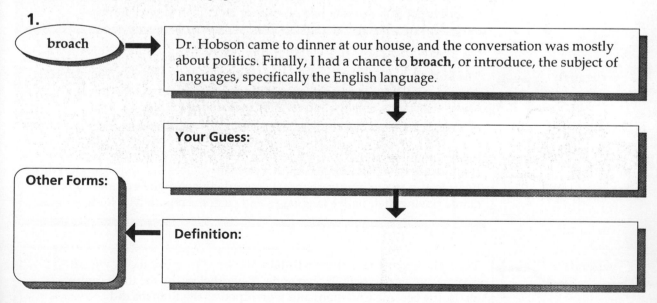

broach → Dr. Hobson came to dinner at our house, and the conversation was mostly about politics. Finally, I had a chance to **broach,** or introduce, the subject of languages, specifically the English language.

Your Guess:

Other Forms:

Definition:

2.

charlatan →

Dr. Hobson is no **charlatan**. She has expert knowledge of the history of the English language.

3.

erudite →

She was taught by many **erudite** professors and has herself become a learned teacher. When I asked her about the origins of English, she told me that the language is closely related to German.

4.

extol →

My grandparents may **extol** English as it is spoken in England, but the English they praise is actually a mixture of several languages, including Latin and French.

5.

gratuitous →

The changes in the English language were not **gratuitous**, or without cause or justification. They came about as a result of the island's conquests by Romans, Danes, Normans, and the Dutch who drove out the native Celts, Picts, and Scots.

6.

immutable →

But none of the languages brought to Britain by these invading groups was **immutable**. Each one changed somewhat—sometimes a great deal—as it came into contact with other languages.

7.

predispose →

Britain seemed **predisposed** to conquest by seafaring adventurers. It was susceptible mainly because it was a small island with no central government. Julius Caesar's forces invaded three times, and later the forces of the emperor Claudius put Britain under Roman rule for more than three centuries.

8.

prerogative →

The Romans considered it their **prerogative** to Romanize their surroundings. They regarded it as their right to build roads, water systems, and cities and towns with baths, temples, and theaters so that they could feel at home.

9.

truism →

It is a **truism** that the Romans improved many places that they conquered, but it is also an obvious truth that the people they conquered rarely appreciated having their native languages and customs replaced by Roman ones.

10.

venerate →

The Celts and others native to Britain preferred to speak their own languages and **venerate** their own gods. Nevertheless, by the third century A.D. some became Christians and worshiped as the Romans did.

EXERCISE 2 *Context Clues* ✍

Directions. Scan the definitions in Column A. Then think about how the boldface words are used in the sentences in Column B. To complete the exercise, match each definition in Column A with the correct vocabulary word from Column B. Write the letter of your choice on the line provided; then write the vocabulary word on the line preceding the definition.

COLUMN A

_____ **11.** word: _____

adj. freely given or obtained; unearned; uncalled for; without justification or cause

_____ **12.** word: _____

n. a right or privilege belonging to a particular person or class; any exclusive privilege

_____ **13.** word: _____

v. to regard with deep respect, honor, or esteem; to revere

_____ **14.** word: _____

n. a statement the truth of which is obvious or well known

_____ **15.** word: _____

adj. having or displaying extensive knowledge; learned; scholarly

_____ **16.** word: _____

n. a person who falsely claims to possess expert knowledge or skill; a quack; an impostor

_____ **17.** word: _____

v. to praise highly

_____ **18.** word: _____

v. to mention for the first time; to introduce a subject; to start a discussion of

_____ **19.** word: _____

v. to create or possess a tendency or preference in advance; to make susceptible

_____ **20.** word: _____

adj. never changing; unchangeable; unalterable

COLUMN B

(A) Just as the Romans felt it was their right to move into Britain when they wanted to, they thought it was their **prerogative** to move out of Britain in A.D. 410.

(B) Within fifty years of the Romans' departure, the Teutonic invasions of Britain began. Dr. Hobson said that it is a **truism,** an obvious truth, that these invasions changed the course of Britain's history.

(C) She went on to say that the different Teutonic groups—the Saxons, Jutes, and Angles—seemed **predisposed** to fighting. They preferred a warlike way of life to a peaceful one.

(D) These conquerors and settlers from northern Europe did not **venerate** the same gods that the Romans revered.

(E) With **gratuitous** military action, the Teutons invaded Britain and destroyed Roman architecture and influence without justification.

(F) The thought of such wanton destruction depressed me. Seeing my reaction, Dr. Hobson introduced a new topic and **broached** the subject of the origin of the name *England*.

(G) It is a form of the word *Angle*—in Old English, *Engle*. That alteration in spelling shows that language is not **immutable,** that it does indeed change.

(H) The **erudite** Dr. Hobson informed me that *England* comes from the word *English,* and not the other way around. I was impressed by how much she knew about the subject.

(I) The English language that developed after the invasions is far different from the English my grandparents now **extol,** or praise.

(J) I hope my grandparents do not consider me a **charlatan** when I show them how well informed I have become about the English language—my sources are well respected and I am not faking my knowledge.

EXERCISE 3 *Sentence Completion* 👈

Directions. For each of the following items, circle the letter of the choice that best completes the meaning of the sentence or sentences.

21. The impressively knowledgeable Dr. Hobson, _____ scholar, then showed me some of the letters that were in the Old English alphabet but that are not used now.

(A) an immutable
(B) an abject
(C) an erudite
(D) a truistic
(E) a gratuitous

22. It is _____ that Old English, the form of English used from A.D. 450 to 1150, is a dead language, since it's obvious that no one uses it anymore.

(A) a charlatan
(B) a truism
(C) a prerogative
(D) an extollment
(E) a veneration

23. It would be _____ to say that it's a waste of time to study a language that's no longer in existence. Still, I know that many people do make such unjustified statements.

(A) erudite
(B) immutable
(C) omniscient
(D) gratuitous
(E) phlegmatic

24. Dr. Hobson said no language is _____ because all languages change as new words are created and adopted.

(A) immutable
(B) venerated
(C) gratuitous
(D) sanguine
(E) erudite

25. Therefore, it is useless to _____ a language, expecting that the features one esteems the most will remain the same forever.

(A) broach
(B) exhort
(C) predispose
(D) proffer
(E) venerate

26. English seemed especially _____ to change, and many of the changes were _____, in the sense that they developed freely.

(A) venerated . . . immutable
(B) predisposed . . . gratuitous
(C) extolled . . . erudite
(D) broached . . . facile
(E) exhorted . . . predisposed

27. Dr. Hobson then _____ the subject of the Normans, a conquering people who considered it their right, or _____, to invade England in 1066.

(A) predisposed . . . prerogative
(B) extolled . . . truism
(C) broached . . . prerogative
(D) venerated . . . charlatan
(E) extolled . . . erudition

28. The Norman Conquest was not _____, or praised, by England's inhabitants. It did not take an _____ person to know that life would never be the same; anyone, learned or not, could see change coming.

(A) broached . . . immutable
(B) predisposed . . . erudite
(C) lampooned . . . abject
(D) extolled . . . erudite
(E) predisposed . . . amorphous

29. I introduced, or _____, the subject of the Normans, who evidently considered it their right, or _____, to replace Old English with French.

(A) extolled . . . charlatan
(B) venerated . . . truism
(C) broached . . . prerogative
(D) predisposed . . . veneration
(E) venerated . . . predisposition

30. Today we still use many French words, such as _____, which means "an impostor." English has never been _____ in England or America, but has continued to change.

(A) prerogative . . . erudite
(B) charlatan . . . immutable
(C) extollment . . . bellicose
(D) truism . . . gratuitous
(E) veneration . . . nondescript

MAKING NEW WORDS YOUR OWN

Lesson 8   **CONTEXT:** Literary Figures

Rudyard Kipling: At Home on Four Continents

Rudyard Kipling (1865–1936) is my favorite author. Kipling lived an interesting and varied life. He lived in India, England, America, and Rhodesia, and he wrote about all of those places. My whole family likes his writing. My father says that he tries to live up to the advice in Kipling's poem "If," and my mother is still delighted by the *Jungle Books*, which are classics of children's literature. To me, the appeal of Kipling's writing is that there's something for readers of every age.

In the following exercises, you will have the opportunity to expand your vocabulary by reading about Rudyard Kipling's life and writing. Below are ten vocabulary words that will be used in these exercises.

absolve	antipodes	infringe	ostensible	specious
antipathy	indigent	nettle	retroactive	subjugate

EXERCISE 1   *Mapping* ✍

Directions. In the item below, a vocabulary word is provided and used in a sentence. Take a guess at the word's meaning and write it in the box labeled **Your Guess**. Then look the word up in your dictionary and write the definition in the box labeled **Definition**. In the **Other Forms** box, write as many other forms of the word, such as adjective and noun forms, as you can think of or find in your dictionary.

Then, following the same procedure, draw your own map for each of the nine remaining vocabulary words. Use a separate sheet of paper.

1.

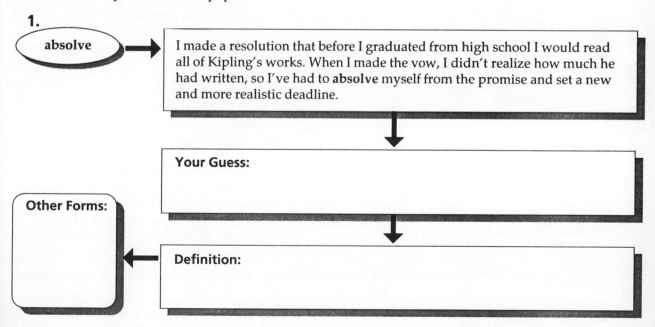

absolve → I made a resolution that before I graduated from high school I would read all of Kipling's works. When I made the vow, I didn't realize how much he had written, so I've had to **absolve** myself from the promise and set a new and more realistic deadline.

Your Guess:

Other Forms:

Definition:

2.

antipathy →

Some of my friends have an **antipathy** for reading, but I love it. Maybe if they read something exciting, like Kipling's *Captains Courageous* or *Kim*, they would develop a liking for books.

3.

antipodes →

Kipling was born in India but later lived in Vermont. Those points on the globe are in different hemispheres, but they are not true **antipodes**. They are not directly opposite each other, though they are so far away from each other that it seems like they could be.

4.

indigent →

Kipling's parents lived in India, where his father was the principal of an art school. I don't know how much money Kipling's father made, but I know that the family was not **indigent**. In fact, they had enough money to send Kipling to England for schooling when he was five.

5.

infringe →

Kipling was miserable in England because the retired naval officer and his wife with whom Kipling lived neglected and mistreated him. His parents did not realize that the couple had **infringed** on the agreement to provide proper child care.

6.

nettle →

Although the abusive couple **nettled** Kipling, he had to live with the irritation until he was twelve. At that time he was sent to United Services College, where he performed in plays and began writing poetry.

7.

ostensible →

When he was seventeen, Kipling returned to India, **ostensibly** to edit a newspaper. In reality he spent much of his time writing stories for it.

8.

retroactive →

Kipling's stories and poems were published in India and became popular with travelers, some of whom brought them to England. When he returned to England in 1889, it must have seemed to Kipling that his fame was **retroactive:** He had become famous in England months before he even arrived there.

9.

specious →

In England, Kipling went to pubs, barracks rooms, and music halls to listen to songs. He thought many of the lyrics were **specious;** they sounded good on the surface but lacked meaning and truth. He wrote new lyrics for some of these songs and published them as *Barracks Room Ballads* in 1892.

10.

subjugate →

Kipling loved to travel and was never able to **subjugate** his wanderlust, except for brief periods of time. Even after he married and supposedly submitted to a more settled life in Vermont, he returned to England briefly to gather material for his novel *Captains Courageous*.

EXERCISE 2 *Context Clues* ✍

Directions. Scan the definitions in Column A. Then think about how the boldface words are used in the sentences in Column B. To complete the exercise, match each definition in Column A with the correct vocabulary word from Column B. Write the letter of your choice on the line provided; then write the vocabulary word on the line preceding the definition.

COLUMN A

_____ **11.** word: _____

v. to violate or disregard a law or an agreement; to trespass; to break in on

_____ **12.** word: _____

adj. seemingly desirable, reasonable, or true but not really so; having a deceptively good appearance; plausible

_____ **13.** word: _____

adj. outwardly professed; apparent; seeming

_____ **14.** word: _____

v. to declare free from guilt and blame; to set free from a promise or an obligation

_____ **15.** word: _____

v. to subdue; to conquer; to force to submit

_____ **16.** word: _____

n. any two places at directly opposite points on the earth; two opposite things

_____ **17.** word: _____

adj. applying to events that are past

_____ **18.** word: _____

n. a strong dislike; an aversion

_____ **19.** word: _____

n. a spiny or stinging plant *v.* to sting with, or as if with, a nettle; to cause sharp annoyance; to irritate

_____ **20.** word: _____

adj. poor; needy

COLUMN B

(A) Kipling viewed Eastern and Western philosophies and lifestyles as complete opposites. He commented on the **antipodes** of Asian and European cultures in "The Ballad of East and West."

(B) Kipling did not consider it a **specious** statement to say that "Oh, East is East, and West is West, and never the twain shall meet. . . ." To him, the statement was utterly true and reasonable.

(C) Kipling's interest in children's stories was not a **retroactive** desire stemming from unfinished business in his own childhood; it grew from his desire to make up stories for his own children.

(D) In the story "The Elephant's Child," a young elephant is constantly punished for asking questions. He asks the Kolokolo Bird, who is sitting in a sharp **nettle**, to help him. The Kolokolo Bird looks down at him from its perch in the spiny plant.

(E) The Kolokolo Bird appears to help the little elephant, but his **ostensibly** friendly advice really places the elephant child in danger, for the Kolokolo Bird sends him to visit the Crocodile.

(F) So far in the story, the other animals have failed to **subjugate** the little elephant's curiosity and questioning, which seems to have no end. They don't know how to subdue such inquisitiveness.

(G) They think that his never-ending questions **infringe** on their right to live in peace and quiet, trespassing on their privacy.

(H) All the animals have an **antipathy** for the Elephant Child's curiosity, but he finds ways to get even for their dislike and mistreatment of him.

(I) Eventually, when the little elephant comes home with something all of his relatives want, they **absolve** him, no longer blaming him for his curiosity.

(J) The popularity of this story and others in *Just So Stories* brought Kipling a good income, so he was never **indigent**. In fact, he was probably among the most financially successful authors of his day.

EXERCISE 3 Sentence Completion ✍

Directions. For each of the following items, circle the letter of the choice that best completes the meaning of the sentence or sentences.

21. Kipling held political views that were popular with many other British people at the time. For example, he did not think imperialism _____ on native people's rights, violating their freedoms.
    (A) nettled
    (B) subjugated
    (C) absolved
    (D) admonished
    (E) infringed

22. He spent time in Rhodesia each summer for eight years and seemed to have no _____ for colonial policies there. He apparently saw nothing to violently dislike.
    (A) retroactivity
    (B) infringement
    (C) antipathy
    (D) antipode
    (E) subjugation

23. Kipling felt that the benefits Europeans brought to native peoples they conquered compensated for the _____ of their cultures.
    (A) speciousness
    (B) subjugation
    (C) antipathy
    (D) absolvement
    (E) retroactivity

24. Kipling had more than a seeming, or _____, interest in native cultures; his interest was real and evident.
    (A) indigent
    (B) antipodal
    (C) antipathetic
    (D) ostensible
    (E) absolvent

25. Many imperialists at the time felt that it was natural for Europeans to be affluent and for native peoples to be _____.
    (A) indigent
    (B) antipodal
    (C) ostensible
    (D) specious
    (E) retroactive

26. Some people see Kipling's poem "The White Man's Burden" as _____ the colonial powers of guilt for _____, or trespassing, on native people's rights.
    (A) subjugating . . . absolving
    (B) infringing . . . subjugating
    (C) absolving . . . infringing
    (D) nettling . . . absolving
    (E) subjugating . . . nettling

27. The cruel deeds of the past can't be undone _____; we can't change the past. But we must realize that no one has the right to _____, or forcefully subdue, another human being.
    (A) antipathetically . . . nettle
    (B) retroactively . . . subjugate
    (C) indigently . . . absolve
    (D) speciously . . . infringe
    (E) ostensibly . . . absolve

28. Some of Kipling's views may _____ people now, and their irritation is understandable. Still, there is no reason to develop _____ for all of Kipling's writing.
    (A) subjugate . . . an absolvent
    (B) absolve . . . a retroactivity
    (C) infringe . . . a speciousness
    (D) absolve . . . an infringement
    (E) nettle . . . an antipathy

29. Kipling's writings are not _____, but are of genuine value. He was awarded the Nobel Prize in literature in 1907, which is more than an _____ honor: it is a very real one.
    (A) subjugated . . . absolvent
    (B) retroactive . . . antipathetic
    (C) specious . . . ostensible
    (D) indigent . . . antipodal
    (E) nettlesome . . . indigent

30. Kipling thought the East and West were _____, or opposite, in nature, yet his enjoyable, informative stories and poems have surely lessened the _____ people sometimes feel for different cultures.
    (A) indigent . . . retroactivity
    (B) antipathetic . . . subjugation
    (C) antipodal . . . antipathy
    (D) specious . . . infringement
    (E) retroactive . . . speciosity

MAKING NEW WORDS YOUR OWN

Lesson 9 — CONTEXT: Literary Figures
Should Women Write?

Pearl S. Buck (1892–1973), Alice Walker (b. 1944), Jane Austen (1775–1817)—the list of great women writers of the past and present could go on and on. In today's literary world there certainly is no debate about women's capability to be writers. However, there was such a debate in the eighteenth century. English writer Maria Edgeworth (1767–1849), who herself would become a famous and respected novelist, presented both sides of the debate in *Letters to Literary Ladies* (1795).

In the following exercises, you will have the opportunity to expand your vocabulary by reading about Maria Edgeworth and the debate over "literary ladies." Below are ten vocabulary words that will be used in these exercises.

abnegation	eulogy	extraneous	poignant	sonorous
copious	euphony	mundane	progeny	tenure

EXERCISE 1 — *Mapping* ✍

Directions. In the item below, a vocabulary word is provided and used in a sentence. Take a guess at the word's meaning and write it in the box labeled **Your Guess**. Then look the word up in your dictionary and write the definition in the box labeled **Definition**. In the **Other Forms** box, write as many other forms of the word, such as adjective and noun forms, as you can think of or find in your dictionary.

Then, following the same procedure, draw your own map for each of the nine remaining vocabulary words. Use a separate sheet of paper.

1.

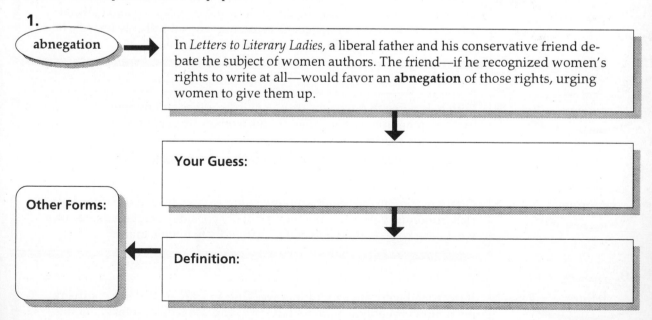

abnegation → In *Letters to Literary Ladies*, a liberal father and his conservative friend debate the subject of women authors. The friend—if he recognized women's rights to write at all—would favor an **abnegation** of those rights, urging women to give them up.

Your Guess:

Other Forms:

Definition:

2.

copious →

The father, modeled after Edgeworth's own father, provides **copious** reasons why women should be respected as authors. Among the extensive evidence he cites is the fact that women have produced significant works on natural history, education, and other subjects.

3.

eulogy →

In reading the friend's "An Attack on Literary Ladies," one gathers that he thinks women should never lift their pens, not even to write a **eulogy** honoring a deceased friend or relative.

4.

euphony →

Edgeworth certainly was capable of good writing and of using words in pleasant-sounding combinations. Don't you like the **euphony** of her title *Letters to Literary Ladies*?

5.

extraneous →

From what I've read of the book so far, the two men in *Letters to Literary Ladies* keep to the topic—whether women should be writers—and avoid **extraneous** subjects. They do not stray from their main topic.

6.

mundane →

The friend implies that women should confine their interests to the **mundane** pursuits of domestic life. When women venture away from these ordinary activities, he says, they may harm themselves and others.

7.

poignant →

The father has several **poignant** comments. Particularly pointed is his argument that women should be given the same educational and cultural advantages that men are given. Considering women's disadvantages, he marvels "that so much has been affected " by women.

8.

progeny →

Both men agree that women are meant to be wives and mothers and to care for their **progeny**, but the father thinks women are capable of much more than simply rearing children.

9.

sonorous →

One can imagine the friend actually telling women his theories in a deep, rich, **sonorous** voice: ". . . We [men] usually consider a certain degree of weakness, both of mind and body, as friendly to female grace."

10.

tenure →

If the friend were alive today and working as a supervisor in a company, his **tenure** probably would not last very long. He would quickly lose his position and would likely be replaced with someone whose views more closely mirror the father's.

EXERCISE 2 *Context Clues* ✍

Directions. Scan the definitions in Column A. Then think about how the boldface words are used in the sentences in Column B. To complete the exercise, match each definition in Column A with the correct vocabulary word from Column B. Write the letter of your choice on the line provided; then write the vocabulary word on the line preceding the definition.

COLUMN A

_____ **11.** word: _____
adj. ordinary; commonplace; of this world (rather than the world beyond)

_____ **12.** word: _____
n. a speech or piece of writing in praise of a person or thing, especially to honor one who has recently died; a tribute; praise

_____ **13.** word: _____
n. children; offspring; descendants

_____ **14.** word: _____
adj. abundant; plentiful; full of information; wordy

_____ **15.** word: _____
n. the holding of an office; the length of time for which a position is held; the permanence of position granted to teachers, civil service employees, and others

_____ **16.** word: _____
n. agreeableness of sound; pleasant combination of sounds in spoken words

_____ **17.** word: _____
adj. giving out, capable of producing, or having a deep, rich sound

_____ **18.** word: _____
n. self-denial; a giving up or a renunciation of rights

_____ **19.** word: _____
adj. painfully felt; emotionally touching or moving; pointed; sharp

_____ **20.** word: _____
adj. coming from outside; foreign; not necessary; irrelevant

COLUMN B

(A) The story of Maria Edgeworth's life would make a **poignant** novel. I am always emotionally touched by true success stories.

(B) Edgeworth's father was an inventor and educator who had twenty-one **progeny**. Maria was his second child.

(C) Maria's childhood was not **mundane;** in fact, it was far from ordinary. Most children do not have the opportunity to grow up on an estate and be taught by their fathers.

(D) On the family estate in Ireland, Richard Edgeworth's lessons to his daughter were **copious**. She quickly absorbed the abundance of information.

(E) I imagine that a **sonorous** bell rang at the start of the Edgeworth children's lessons, its deep, rich sound filling the estate.

(F) Richard Edgeworth apparently believed in strength through the expansion of individual rights rather than the **abnegation** of rights. He did not believe that people should be made to renounce their rights.

(G) He exposed Maria to essential ideas from England as well as **extraneous** ideas from foreign lands, such as those of French philosophy.

(H) Although Richard Edgeworth was not a university professor with **tenure**, his lack of a professional position did not diminish the fact that he was an excellent teacher.

(I) Don't you think he has a nice-sounding name? I really like the **euphony** of his full name, Richard Lovell Edgeworth.

(J) I wonder if Maria wrote a **eulogy** about her father after his death. Even if she didn't, her career itself was a tribute to him and his inspiration.

EXERCISE 3 *Sentence Completion* ✍

Directions. For each of the following items, circle the letter of the choice that best completes the meaning of the sentence or sentences.

21. Our English teacher, Ms. Carbone, gave us _____ information about Maria Edgeworth's life and works. I'd never taken so many notes!

(A) sonorous
(B) mundane
(C) extraneous
(D) copious
(E) eulogistic

22. Most of the information was necessary and relevant, but I thought much of the material about Ireland's early history was _____.

(A) euphonious
(B) extraneous
(C) sonorous
(D) eulogistic
(E) copious

23. I didn't question her judgment, however. Our teacher's _____ here has lasted for thirty years; she must know her job very well in order to have kept it for so long.

(A) eulogy
(B) progeny
(C) tenure
(D) abnegation
(E) euphony

24. Ms. Carbone told us about the _____, ordinary lives of the Irish people portrayed in Edgeworth's novel *Castle Rackrent* (1800).

(A) copious
(B) sonorous
(C) tenured
(D) extraneous
(E) mundane

25. Rackrent is a great name for a castle, I think, because the sound is so _____. Others may not agree, but I think the sound of the name is pleasing.

(A) euphonious
(B) copious
(C) poignant
(D) mundane
(E) extraneous

26. Personally, I can't imagine having twenty-one _____, as Edgeworth's father did. I hope there were _____ amounts of food around to feed so many children!

(A) tenures . . . poignant
(B) eulogies . . . mundane
(C) euphonies . . . sonorous
(D) progeny . . . copious
(E) abnegations . . . extraneous

27. Any _____ written following Edgeworth's death should have mentioned her work during the Irish potato famine of 1847. The _____ story of the Irish people's suffering moved me deeply.

(A) euphony . . . copious
(B) abnegation . . . sonorous
(C) eulogy . . . poignant
(D) progeny . . . extraneous
(E) tenure . . . mundane

28. Later I was similarly moved by Edgeworth's _____ comments about her father, who had taught her to defend her rights as a woman rather than to accept _____ of them.

(A) sonorous . . . a tenure
(B) extraneous . . . a eulogy
(C) mundane . . . a progeny
(D) sonorous . . . a euphony
(E) poignant . . . an abnegation

29. The school bell, its tone flat rather than deep and _____, put an end to my note taking. I wished I could hear Edgeworth's tributes to her father as well as the _____ to her.

(A) copious . . . progenies
(B) sonorous . . . eulogies
(C) poignant . . . euphonies
(D) mundane . . . abnegations
(E) extraneous . . . euphonies

30. Edgeworth did not have any _____ of her own. She wrote _____, however, and her many books could be called her offspring.

(A) tenure . . . eulogistically
(B) eulogies . . . sonorously
(C) abnegations . . . poignantly
(D) progeny . . . copiously
(E) euphonies . . . euphoniously

MAKING NEW WORDS YOUR OWN

Lesson 10 **CONTEXT:** Literary Figures

Jane Austen: Laughing at Herself and Others

Jane Austen (1775–1817), whom some scholars consider the world's greatest female writer, once said she couldn't write a serious romance. She explained that she needed to be able to "relax into laughing at myself" and others. In the six novels for which she is famous, including *Sense and Sensibility* (1811) and *Pride and Prejudice* (1813), Austen quite wittily and comically describes the lives of upper-middle-class girls in England at the end of the eighteenth century. She laughs especially at husband-hunting young ladies, their scheming mothers, self-important clergymen, and arrogant aristocrats.

In the following exercises, you will have the opportunity to expand your vocabulary by reading about the life and writings of Jane Austen. Below are ten vocabulary words that will be used in these exercises.

ascribe	engender	homily	idiosyncrasy	introvert
elegy	hackneyed	humdrum	inconsequential	paragon

EXERCISE 1 *Mapping*

Directions. In the item below, a vocabulary word is provided and used in a sentence. Take a guess at the word's meaning and write it in the box labeled **Your Guess**. Then look the word up in your dictionary and write the definition in the box labeled **Definition**. In the **Other Forms** box, write as many other forms of the word, such as adjective and noun forms, as you can think of or find in your dictionary.

Then, following the same procedure, draw your own map for each of the nine remaining vocabulary words. Use a separate sheet of paper.

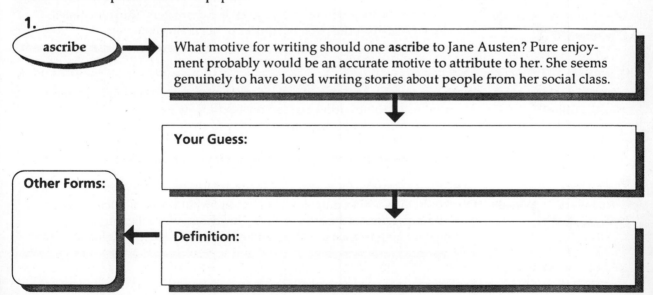

1.

ascribe → What motive for writing should one **ascribe** to Jane Austen? Pure enjoyment probably would be an accurate motive to attribute to her. She seems genuinely to have loved writing stories about people from her social class.

Your Guess:

Other Forms:

Definition:

2.

elegy ➤ A narrator's lively, bright tone shines in each of Austen's novels. Austen obviously delighted in "sitting room" society, with its clever conversations and amusing characters. You won't find any **elegies**—sad and mournful lyrics—among Austen's writings!

3.

engender ➤ Austen's young protagonists are always hoping that their looks and social graces will **engender** successful results in marital contests. Sometimes the desired effects are produced, and the happy young women become engaged.

4.

hackneyed ➤ The character descriptions in Austen's novels are fresh and original, not **hackneyed**. In *Pride and Prejudice,* for example, Mrs. Bennet is described as "a woman of mean understanding, little information, and uncertain temper."

5.

homily ➤ Of course, Austen has much to say about the men and women who moved in her social class, but she did not use **homilies** to do so. You won't have to struggle through long, moralizing passages in Austen's novels; instead, you'll find sharp, revealing dialogue.

6.

humdrum ➤ Don't get the idea that Austen's "sitting room" plots are **humdrum** just because they mainly revolve around young ladies trying to find suitable husbands. In Austen's novels, such events are not commonplace and trivial: They are shrewd, calculated hunts with plenty of humor, excitement, and variety.

7.

idiosyncrasy ➤ Austen is especially gifted in bringing out her characters' **idiosyncrasies**. She cleverly satirizes the personal quirks of her main characters.

8.

inconsequential ➤ While reading Austen's novels, one never knows what seemingly **inconsequential** social information may become extremely important. A supposedly minor detail can perhaps hold the key to a young lady's future marriage and fortune.

9.

introvert ➤ Obviously, the sociable, outgoing young ladies within Austen's fictional world have the best chance of attracting suitable husbands, while the **introverts** among the young women are often ignored because of their shy, retiring ways.

10.

paragon ➤ Darcy, one of the main characters in *Pride and Prejudice,* is regarded as a **paragon** by the men, but he is not viewed as a model of perfection by the women, who dislike his pride.

EXERCISE 2   *Context Clues*

Directions. Scan the definitions in Column A. Then think about how the boldface words are used in the sentences in Column B. To complete the exercise, match each definition in Column A with the correct vocabulary word from Column B. Write the letter of your choice on the line provided; then write the vocabulary word on the line preceding the definition.

COLUMN A

_____ **11.** word: _____

adj. used too often; stale from overuse; trite; clichéd

_____ **12.** word: _____

n. a model of excellence or perfection; a perfect example of something

_____ **13.** word: _____

v. to assign (as to a cause); to attribute; to think of as coming from or belonging to someone

_____ **14.** word: _____

adj. unimportant; petty; trivial

_____ **15.** word: _____

adj. without variety or excitement; monotonous; dull; commonplace

_____ **16.** word: _____

v. to bring into being; to produce; to cause

_____ **17.** word: _____

n. a personal peculiarity that is an identifying trait; a quirk

_____ **18.** word: _____

n. a sad or mournful poem or song, often about someone who is dead

_____ **19.** word: _____

n. a person who looks inward; a shy, quiet person

_____ **20.** word: _____

n. a sermon, especially on something in the Bible; a long, often dull, moralizing talk or writing

COLUMN B

(A) Austen's novels **engendered,** or caused, much interest in Austen herself, but she avoided literary circles and publicity.

(B) Although a private person, Austen apparently was not an **introvert,** because she was lively and outgoing among family and friends.

(C) What some people would regard as **humdrum** domestic duties occupied much of Austen's time. I wonder if she found them as monotonous as my friends and I would.

(D) We might not **ascribe** an interest in acting to Austen, but such an interest was very much a part of her character.

(E) She performed in home theatrical shows. Do you think this experience was important, or was it **inconsequential** to Austen as a novelist?

(F) Austen received much of her education from her father, a teacher and minister. I imagine that he was a serious, learned man who wrote long, scholarly **homilies** on Bible stories.

(G) Austen considered her older sister Cassandra to be a **paragon** of talent. She especially regarded Cassandra as a model comedy writer.

(H) The family may have regarded Austen's habit of writing in the sitting room as a peculiarity, but they tolerated this **idiosyncrasy.**

(I) No one could complain that Austen was writing **hackneyed** stories, because her work was never trite or unoriginal.

(J) Cassandra wrote lovingly, even poetically, of her sister, Jane. Do you know if Cassandra or another family member ever wrote an **elegy** to mourn Jane Austen's death in 1817?

EXERCISE 3 Sentence Completion ✍

Directions. For each of the following items, circle the letter of the choice that best completes the meaning of the sentence or sentences.

21. I don't think that Austen would have wanted anyone to write _____ about her, because she was not a mournful person. If anything, I think she would want to be memorialized in a comic poem or story.
(A) an elegy
(B) a paragon
(C) an idiosyncrasy
(D) an introvert
(E) an inconsequentiality

22. Because I consider Austen to be _____ of an accomplished author, I am using her as a model for my own writing career.
(A) an elegy
(B) a homily
(C) an introvert
(D) a paragon
(E) an idiosyncrasy

23. Austen lets readers know her ideas about moral values without writing _____ that bore readers. She knows how to make her point without writing sermons.
(A) paragons
(B) homilies
(C) hackneys
(D) idiosyncrasies
(E) elegies

24. Don't make the mistake of considering Austen's earlier writings to be totally _____; there's much in them that has value and substance.
(A) ascribable
(B) introverted
(C) inconsequential
(D) elegiac
(E) idiosyncratic

25. Austen's early work *Love and Freindship* (her spelling) contains a few clichéd, overused ideas, but the work as a whole is not _____.
(A) elegiac
(B) omniscient
(C) farcical
(D) introverted
(E) hackneyed

26. What I like about Austen is that she can make _____, or trivial, conversations sound really interesting and not _____ and dull at all.
(A) elegaic . . . humdrum
(B) homiletic . . . inconsequential
(C) ascribable . . . idiosyncratic
(D) inconsequential . . . humdrum
(E) introverted . . . hackneyed

27. Only such _____ of writing talent, a model novelist, could communicate people's personal peculiarities, or _____, so well.
(A) a paragon . . . idiosyncrasies
(B) an introvert . . . elegies
(C) an elegy . . . homilies
(D) an idiosyncrasy . . . paragons
(E) a paragon . . . elegies

28. Some people cannot decide if Austen was an extrovert or _____, or whether Austen thought her life was _____ or exciting.
(A) a homily . . . hackneyed
(B) a paragon . . . idiosyncratic
(C) an introvert . . . humdrum
(D) an elegy . . . ascribable
(E) an introversion . . . hackneyed

29. Reading Austen's novels _____, or brought about, my interest in researching _____ among supposedly shy authors who write forceful and sometimes controversial books.
(A) engendered . . . paragon
(B) ascribed . . . elegy
(C) broached . . . homily
(D) venerated . . . idiosyncrasy
(E) engendered . . . introversion

30. I _____ my interest in Jane Austen to an English teacher who attributed his own initial interest to a seemingly _____ fact: His last name, too, was Austen.
(A) engender . . . hackneyed
(B) ascribe . . . elegiac
(C) nettle . . . humdrum
(D) ascribe . . . inconsequential
(E) extol . . . introverted

MAKING NEW WORDS YOUR OWN

Lesson 11   CONTEXT: History and Society

The First British Artists

The history of art in Great Britain began long before the first paintings were hung in London's Tate Gallery. Some fifteen thousand years ago, artists of the Old Stone Age made bone engravings. In the New Stone Age, or Neolithic period, which began around 2000 B.C., artists carved great stone tombs. Stonehenge could be considered the greatest artistic monument of the Neolithic and Early Bronze ages. Neolithic artists also made pots, jewelry, and woodcarvings. The Celts, who invaded Britain in the fifth century B.C., used bronze and gold for works of art such as mirrors, helmets, and necklaces.

In the following exercises, you will have the opportunity to expand your vocabulary by reading about prehistoric art in Great Britain. Below are ten vocabulary words that will be used in these exercises.

aberration	candor	dearth	herculean	retrospect
adjudge	corroborate	diurnal	ludicrous	salient

EXERCISE 1   Mapping ✍

Directions. In the item below, a vocabulary word is provided and used in a sentence. Take a guess at the word's meaning and write it in the box labeled **Your Guess**. Then look the word up in your dictionary and write the definition in the box labeled **Definition**. In the **Other Forms** box, write as many other forms of the word, such as adjective and noun forms, as you can think of or find in your dictionary.

Then, following the same procedure, draw your own map for each of the nine remaining vocabulary words. Use a separate sheet of paper.

1.

aberration → My parents say that my decision to become an art historian is an **aberration**, for there have been five generations of medical doctors in my family. I am departing from that tradition to study prehistoric British art.

Your Guess:

Other Forms:

Definition:

2.

If the law had any jurisdiction over my career, I think my parents would take my decision to court and let the court **adjudge** what I should do. Mom and Dad aren't too impressed with Irish tomb carvings!

3.

"If I may speak frankly," I told them, "I much prefer examining the gold shields of Celtic warriors or even the bronze masks of their horses to examining patients." I don't think my parents appreciated my **candor**.

4.

"You see, I'm really good in art history, and I'm lousy in science," I said. To **corroborate** the truth of this, I reminded them of my poor grades in science and my excellent grades in art history. Surely that evidence would confirm my position.

5.

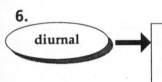

I had thought about studying Old Stone Age art in Britain, but there really is a **dearth** of artifacts from that time period. It wouldn't be very interesting to study just a few bone engravings.

6.

"I've been a doctor for forty years, and I'm still interested in my **diurnal** rounds at the hospital," Dad said. I replied, "I'm glad you enjoy your daily rounds, but if I had to do the same thing every day, I would rather take a daily walk through a museum!"

7.

I want to study the tomb carvings at New Grange, Ireland. It must have been a demanding, **herculean** task to move those stones that form the tombs because the stones are so massive and heavy.

8.

"The image of you hiking all over Ireland and peering at old tombs is **ludicrous**," Mom said, laughing to herself over the ridiculous picture in her mind.

9.

In **retrospect**, I know that I should not have told both my parents at once about my career decision. In looking back on the scene, I also see that I should have told them more about the value of studying prehistoric art.

10.

Most people can comment on the **salient** features of an artwork, even something as old as a wooden figure from the sixth century B.C. But I am fascinated by the features that aren't so noticeable, for they may help unlock the secrets of prehistoric cultures.

EXERCISE 2 *Context Clues* 🖐

Directions. Scan the definitions in Column A. Then think about how the boldface words are used in the sentences in Column B. To complete the exercise, match each definition in Column A with the correct vocabulary word from Column B. Write the letter of your choice on the line provided; then write the vocabulary word on the line preceding the definition.

COLUMN A	COLUMN B

COLUMN A

_____ **11.** word: _____

v. to support or strengthen an idea or a statement; to attest to the truth of; to confirm

_____ **12.** word: _____

n. a departure from the usual course; a deviation; an abnormal development

_____ **13.** word: _____

adj. extremely demanding or difficult; requiring or having great courage or strength, like that possessed by Hercules

_____ **14.** word: _____

n. a contemplation or survey of things that happened in the past

_____ **15.** word: _____

n. a scarcity, as of food; a lack; too small a supply of something

_____ **16.** word: _____

adj. standing out; easily seen or noticed; conspicuous; noticeable; prominent

_____ **17.** word: _____

v. to decree or decide by law; to pass sentence

_____ **18.** word: _____

adj. occurring every day; daily; occurring during the daytime

_____ **19.** word: _____

n. openness; saying what one really thinks; frankness; impartiality

_____ **20.** word: _____

adj. amusingly absurd; ridiculous

COLUMN B

(A) I once had a weird dream that I was sent to court in order for a jury to decide whether I was worthy of being sent to England to study Stonehenge. In the dream, the court **adjudged** that I was indeed qualified to research ancient British art.

(B) I don't think about my own past a lot, but in **retrospect**, I decided to study prehistoric British art because of that dream.

(C) I actually ended up going to Stonehenge the summer after I graduated from high school. Stonehenge is a gigantic **aberration**, an abnormal grouping of stones on the Salisbury Plain that is totally different from anything else around it.

(D) Can you imagine the **herculean** effort required to drag the fifty-ton sandstone blocks into place?

(E) There are many theories about the meaning and purpose of Stonehenge, but there is little physical evidence to **corroborate**, or confirm, these theories.

(F) Stonehenge may have been a temple to which Neolithic people made **diurnal** visits, perhaps to watch the sun rise every morning.

(G) There is a **dearth** of artistic markings on the stones, but a few still remain—carvings of a dagger and depictions of bronze axe heads, for example.

(H) These markings are difficult to see; they are not among Stonehenge's most **salient** features.

(I) Do you think it is **ludicrous** that people come from all over the world to see Stonehenge? I certainly do not—there is nothing absurd about admiring a work of art!

(J) As an art historian, what do I really think of Stonehenge? With complete **candor** I can say that it is magnificent.

EXERCISE 3 *Sentence Completion*

Directions. For each of the following items, circle the letter of the choice that best completes the meaning of the sentence or sentences.

21. The Neolithic potter noticed that his village had a _____ of bowls and drinking mugs. This shortage concerned him.
    (A) candor
    (B) salience
    (C) retrospect
    (D) dearth
    (E) corroboration

22. As he made his pots, he thought about his past. He realized that, in _____, he had enjoyed learning from the old potters.
    (A) aberration
    (B) dearth
    (C) retrospect
    (D) salience
    (E) corroboration

23. Some people say it is _____ to decorate the cups, but I don't think it is ridiculous, the potter thought to himself.
    (A) diurnal
    (B) herculean
    (C) salient
    (D) aberrational
    (E) ludicrous

24. The potter felt that if he ever had to stand before the village lawmakers and defend himself, he would be _____ a good and useful member of the community.
    (A) capitulated
    (B) adjudged
    (C) emanated
    (D) corroborated
    (E) engendered

25. The potter didn't like any _____ from his routine. But, although the potter would not tolerate any departure from his normal course, many thought it was _____ to be so absurdly serious about a schedule.
    (A) retrospect . . . salient
    (B) candor . . . diurnal
    (C) dearth . . . ludicrous
    (D) corroboration . . . salient
    (E) aberration . . . ludicrous

26. Digging the clay sometimes took a superhuman, _____, effort. Also, sometimes there was a scarcity, or _____, of good clay.
    (A) diurnal . . . retrospect
    (B) salient . . . candor
    (C) retrospective . . . aberration
    (D) herculean . . . dearth
    (E) ludicrous . . . candor

27. His son _____, or supported, his father's claim that digging clay is hard work. The boy was glad the chore was weekly and not _____; he would hate to have to perform the task each day.
    (A) corroborated . . . aberrational
    (B) adjudged . . . herculean
    (C) corroborated . . . diurnal
    (D) nettled . . . ludicrous
    (E) adjudged . . . salient

28. The potter toiled _____, never missing a day of work. He exhibited almost superhuman abilities, working with _____ diligence.
    (A) diurnally . . . retrospective
    (B) ludicrously . . . diurnal
    (C) saliently . . . aberrational
    (D) ludicrously . . . corroborative
    (E) diurnally . . . herculean

29. The potter liked his work to have _____ characteristics: prominent markings that would make it possible for people to tell it was his work.
    (A) salient
    (B) ludicrous
    (C) herculean
    (D) diurnal
    (E) retrospective

30. The potter and his son were frank and open with each other. This _____, the son would realize one day in _____, benefited their relationship.
    (A) retrospect . . . candor
    (B) candor . . . retrospect
    (C) dearth . . . aberration
    (D) aberration . . . dearth
    (E) retrospect . . . dearth

MAKING NEW WORDS YOUR OWN

Lesson 12 | CONTEXT: History and Society

England: Welcome to the Roman Empire

There's an old saying that Rome wasn't built in a day—and neither was the Roman Empire. At its height, the Roman Empire included North Africa, Asia Minor, much of the Mediterranean, and a large portion of Europe—including Britain. The Romans began building in England in the middle of the first century A.D. Roman occupation of England continued for almost four hundred years. During that time, Roman customs and styles combined with native Celtic traditions. Roman civilization transformed England in many ways, especially in the areas of architecture and art. Some examples of Roman-influenced art and architecture survive and are our most vivid reminders that England was once part of the Roman Empire.

In the following exercises, you will have the opportunity to expand your vocabulary by reading about the Roman occupation of England. Below are ten vocabulary words that will be used in these exercises.

artifice	captivate	configuration	extant	refute
augury	chicanery	deduce	proponent	scrupulous

EXERCISE 1   *Mapping*

Directions. In the item below, a vocabulary word is provided and used in a sentence. Take a guess at the word's meaning and write it in the box labeled **Your Guess**. Then look the word up in your dictionary and write the definition in the box labeled **Definition**. In the **Other Forms** box, write as many other forms of the word, such as adjective and noun forms, as you can think of or find in your dictionary.

Then, following the same procedure, draw your own map for each of the nine remaining vocabulary words. Use a separate sheet of paper.

1.

artifice →

In 55 and 54 B.C., the Roman army, under Julius Caesar's command, invaded England. Caesar was a clever soldier and no doubt knew many **artifices** to trick and ultimately defeat an enemy, but the Britons were not difficult to subdue.

Your Guess:

Other Forms:

Definition:

2.

augury → Caesar did not conquer all of Britain because he ran out of time and money. Some Britons may have practiced **augury**, pointing to various signs and omens that they believed predicted that the Romans would return to the island and finish what Caesar had begun.

3.

captivate → Roman builders and artists probably **captivated** the Britons who, used to simple wooden huts, would have been fascinated by the stone and brick buildings erected by the Romans.

4.

chicanery → The Romans may have used some **chicanery** in gathering the Britons' support for their projects, such as the building of forts. The Britons may have been tricked by the Romans' cleverly worded deceptions, but, no matter how the Romans enlisted the Britons' help, it is certain that the Britons enabled their invaders to accomplish a great deal.

5.

configuration → Modern scholars and historians can tell the general **configurations** of Roman villas in England because the remains of foundations suggest the outlines of these buildings and the manner in which they were arranged.

6.

deduce → By studying these foundations, scholars can **deduce** what the villas looked like and how tall they were. By examining surviving fragments of artwork, scholars can also infer how the villas were decorated.

7.

extant → You may be surprised to learn that some fragments of fresco paintings from Roman villas in England are **extant**. The most famous of those still in existence are at the mansion at Fishbourne, near Chichester.

8.

proponent → The Romans were great **proponents** of road building and built the first roads in Britain. They advocated the construction of roads so that soldiers could move quickly from one fort to another.

9.

refute → It is doubtful that any scholar could **refute** the statement that the Romans transformed the Britons' society. There certainly is proof that the first towns in England formed along the roads built by the Romans.

10.

scrupulous → Wealthy Romans—and Britons who imitated the Roman style—covered their floors with mosaics. Artists had to be very **scrupulous** when creating mosaics because placing small stones in cement to form designs is exacting work.

EXERCISE 2 · Context Clues ✍

Directions. Scan the definitions in Column A. Then think about how the boldface words are used in the sentences in Column B. To complete the exercise, match each definition in Column A with the correct vocabulary word from Column B. Write the letter of your choice on the line provided; then write the vocabulary word on the line preceding the definition.

COLUMN A	**COLUMN B**

COLUMN A

_____ **11.** word: _____

n. a skill; a clever device; a sly or artful trick; trickery

_____ **12.** word: _____

n. the position or arrangement of parts or elements of something; a shape; an outline

_____ **13.** word: _____

adj. giving strict attention to what is right or proper; exact and careful

_____ **14.** word: _____

v. to infer by reasoning; to conclude from known facts and principles

_____ **15.** word: _____

v. to prove that someone or something is false or incorrect; to disprove

_____ **16.** word: _____

v. to catch the attention of, by beauty or excellence; to enchant; to fascinate; to charm; to attract

_____ **17.** word: _____

n. a person who supports a cause or idea; someone who makes a proposition; an advocate

_____ **18.** word: _____

adj. still in existence; not extinct, lost, or destroyed

_____ **19.** word: _____

n. the use of clever talk or trickery to deceive or evade

_____ **20.** word: _____

n. the practice of foretelling the future from signs and omens; an omen or a sign

COLUMN B

(A) I marvel at the **artifices** used by the clever Roman artists who skillfully created life-size bronze busts.

(B) A bronze head of the emperor Claudius, who defeated the Britons, shows **scrupulous** attention to proper proportions. The three-dimensional portrait is so exactly and carefully made, in fact, that it almost seems like a real face.

(C) Unlike many other Roman rulers, who were known for using clever talk to deceive their subjects, Claudius is not known for **chicanery**.

(D) From looking at the bronze head of Claudius, a viewer can **deduce** that Roman art was realistic. He or she might also infer that the Romans appreciated simplicity and directness.

(E) It would be difficult to **refute**, or disprove, the evidence that early English sculptors were influenced by Roman artists.

(F) The stone relief of the hideous monster Medusa, carved at Bath by an early English artist, still **captivates** visitors. The image is fascinating and unforgettable.

(G) The arrangement of the locks of hair tangled with snakes around Medusa's face is an especially interesting **configuration**.

(H) We're fortunate that the stone relief is still **extant** and that it wasn't destroyed after the Romans withdrew from Britain.

(I) Some people may be opposed to spending money to uncover Roman artifacts in England, but I am a strong **proponent** of such efforts.

(J) If I were a believer in such things, I would look for signs and omens and use **augury** to predict what wonderful discoveries may be found in the future!

EXERCISE 3 — Sentence Completion ☞

Directions. For each of the following items, circle the letter of the choice that best completes the meaning of the sentence or sentences.

21. My friend Blythe, who believes in omens, said that all the _____ indicated that this was the year he should go to England to see the Roman ruins.
    (A) artifices
    (B) chicaneries
    (C) configurations
    (D) proponents
    (E) auguries

22. Blythe is a person of many _____, and he used his skills to earn money for the trip.
    (A) deductions
    (B) configurations
    (C) artifices
    (D) auguries
    (E) chicaneries

23. Still, Blythe ended up borrowing money from relatives, asking them frankly and honestly for the money rather than using _____ to trick them into lending him some.
    (A) augury
    (B) proponents
    (C) deduction
    (D) chicanery
    (E) configuration

24. Once Blythe arrived in England, he was charmed by English customs and villages and was totally _____ by the town of Bath. It was intensely fascinating to him.
    (A) deduced
    (B) captivated
    (C) configured
    (D) refuted
    (E) inundated

25. He especially liked seeing the _____ of the Roman baths there and carefully noted the arrangement of all the rooms, trying to imagine what it would have looked like centuries before.
    (A) configuration
    (B) proponent
    (C) augury
    (D) chicanery
    (E) scrupulosity

26. From the layout, or _____, of the baths, Blythe was able to _____ the Romans' bathing procedures. He made other inferences about Roman social practices.
    (A) chicanery . . . deduce
    (B) configuration . . . captivate
    (C) proponent . . . refute
    (D) configuration . . . deduce
    (E) artifice . . . captivate

27. "It's amazing that the baths are _____," he wrote. "Even Romans skilled in the practice of _____ could not have predicted that the baths would last so long."
    (A) scrupulous . . . chicanery
    (B) configurational . . . artifice
    (C) extant . . . augury
    (D) refutable . . . proponent
    (E) deducible . . . configuration

28. In the museum at Bath, Blythe examined the precise, exacting work of _____ Roman artists and studied other _____ artifacts that had survived from Roman times.
    (A) refutable . . . artificial
    (B) extant . . . scrupulous
    (C) scrupulous . . . deducible
    (D) extant . . . refutable
    (E) scrupulous . . . extant

29. "These beautiful sculptures _____ your comment that Roman artists were not skilled," Blythe wrote to me. "Admit that I have proven you wrong. Besides, you would be just as _____ and fascinated as I am if you were here."
    (A) captivate . . . deducible
    (B) refute . . . captivated
    (C) deduce . . . refutable
    (D) refute . . . scrupulous
    (E) captivate . . . extant

30. "I am _____ of firsthand observation," he wrote. "I highly recommend that you come see the _____, or shape, of the Roman temple area at Bath."
    (A) a chicanery . . . augury
    (B) an augury . . . proponent
    (C) a configuration . . . artifice
    (D) a proponent . . . configuration
    (E) an artifice . . . chicanery

MAKING NEW WORDS YOUR OWN

Lesson 13 CONTEXT: History and Society
Lexicography: The Passion of Samuel Johnson

One of the major figures in the history of lexicography, the compilation of dictionaries, is Samuel Johnson (1709–1784). In 1746, at the age of thirty-six, Johnson began an enormous task—writing the first major English dictionary. During the next nine years, Johnson wrote definitions for more than 40,000 words and selected 114,000 quotations from the finest English writing on various academic subjects. His *Dictionary of the English Language* was a monumental achievement. It was the model for all English dictionaries to come for more than a century.

In the following exercises, you will have the opportunity to expand your vocabulary by reading about the personality and work of English lexicographer and writer Samuel Johnson. Below are ten vocabulary words that will be used in these exercises.

civility	exhilaration	germane	obsequious	precocious
connoisseur	foible	gregarious	patrimony	punctilious

EXERCISE 1 Mapping

Directions. In the item below, a vocabulary word is provided and used in a sentence. Take a guess at the word's meaning and write it in the box labeled **Your Guess**. Then look the word up in your dictionary and write the definition in the box labeled **Definition**. In the **Other Forms** box, write as many other forms of the word, such as adjective and noun forms, as you can think of or find in your dictionary.

Then, following the same procedure, draw your own map for each of the nine remaining vocabulary words. Use a separate sheet of paper.

1.

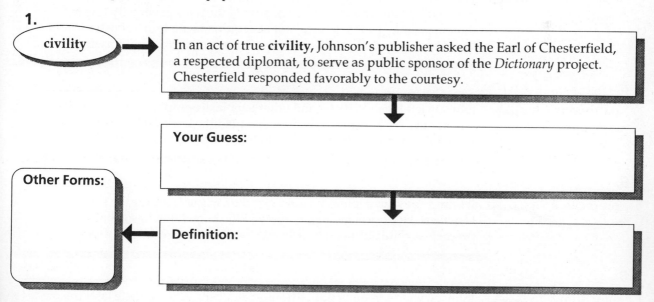

civility ⟶ In an act of true **civility**, Johnson's publisher asked the Earl of Chesterfield, a respected diplomat, to serve as public sponsor of the *Dictionary* project. Chesterfield responded favorably to the courtesy.

Your Guess:

Other Forms:

Definition:

2.
connoisseur →

You could say that Johnson became a **connoisseur** of words as he compiled the *Dictionary*. He certainly became an expert on word meanings, usage, and history.

3.
exhilaration →

As work on the *Dictionary* began, the **exhilaration** must have been great in Johnson's "dictionary workshop," located in the garret of his house. One reason for Johnson's high spirits was the hope that the *Dictionary* would establish his reputation.

4.
foible →

Johnson's strengths as well as his faults have been well documented in various biographies. One **foible** that he had to overcome while working on the *Dictionary* was impatience.

5.
germane →

The fact that France, Italy, and Spain had already produced great dictionaries was **germane** to Johnson's project. It was pertinent because Johnson acted partly in the interest of national pride: He wanted England's dictionary to equal or surpass those of the other countries.

6.
gregarious →

Johnson was **gregarious,** and his friendly, sociable manner brought him many friends. While compiling the *Dictionary*, Johnson borrowed books from his friends and marked passages he liked in the books with a black lead pencil.

7.
obsequious →

The six assistants whom Johnson employed for the *Dictionary* project were very poor when they were hired. Despite Johnson's generosity toward these men, they probably were not **obsequious** with him. Johnson would have discouraged any flattering, fawning behavior toward himself.

8.
patrimony →

Johnson left Noah Webster and other later lexicographers an impressive **patrimony**. We know that Webster accepted the legacy because he borrowed thousands of definitions from Johnson's *Dictionary*.

9.
precocious →

It is impressive that Johnson worked on the *Dictionary* during the prime of his life, not at the close of his literary career. Who knows: If Johnson had been a **precocious** child, he might have begun the dictionary at the age of ten!

10.
punctilious →

Johnson was extremely **punctilious** about facts. When people later quizzed him about the details of compiling the *Dictionary*, Johnson gave exact answers so questioners would understand the procedures he had followed.

EXERCISE 2   *Context Clues*

Directions. Scan the definitions in Column A. Then think about how the boldface words are used in the sentences in Column B. To complete the exercise, match each definition in Column A with the correct vocabulary word from Column B. Write the letter of your choice on the line provided; then write the vocabulary word on the line preceding the definition.

COLUMN A

_____ **11.** word: _____
adj. outgoing; sociable

_____ **12.** word: _____
n. high spirits; invigoration; excitement

_____ **13.** word: _____
n. an inheritance from one's father or ancestors; any heritage or legacy

_____ **14.** word: _____
adj. too ready to please, praise, or obey; servile; fawning

_____ **15.** word: _____
n. politeness; courtesy; a polite action

_____ **16.** word: _____
adj. closely related to the matter at hand; pertinent; to the point

_____ **17.** word: _____
adj. paying attention to the fine details of etiquette; meticulous; scrupulous; very exact

_____ **18.** word: _____
n. a minor weakness or fault; a minor but persistent personal failing; a shortcoming

_____ **19.** word: _____
n. someone who is an expert in some field, especially in art or in matters of taste

_____ **20.** word: _____
adj. showing unusually early development; mature or advanced for one's age

COLUMN B

(A) A greatly appreciated **patrimony** left by my father's great-grandfather is a copy of Johnson's two-volume *Dictionary of the English Language.* Our family was fortunate to inherit it.

(B) My father, who is an expert in lexicography as well as a **connoisseur** of rare books, keeps the dictionary in a safe.

(C) My father was a **precocious** child and recalls memorizing definitions from the dictionary at the age of four.

(D) I know more stories about my father's childhood, but they are not about lexicography and therefore would not be **germane** to this topic.

(E) My mother says that my father's only **foible** is talking about dictionaries too much. I don't think this is a serious shortcoming at all!

(F) He is very **gregarious**, and in social groups his outgoing tendencies are evident—he talks to complete strangers about dictionaries and literature.

(G) His **exhilaration** about the subject, especially about Johnson's achievements, adds to my excitement about dictionaries.

(H) Fortunately, at parties my father is **punctilious**, and, politely following the rules of etiquette, he always asks his listeners if they would like to hear about dictionaries. He does not want to bore anyone.

(I) It is an act of **civility** to ask, and listeners seem to appreciate his politeness. Of course, they usually respond that they would like to hear what he has to say.

(J) Some of the people are a little **obsequious**, and I'm not sure they really mean it when they praise his knowledge of dictionaries. They seem a little too eager to please him.

EXERCISE 3 *Sentence Completion* ✍

Directions. For each of the following items, circle the letter of the choice that best completes the meaning of the sentence or sentences.

21. "I'd like to know more about Johnson," Gwen said. "Was he always _____, or was he outgoing only as he got older?"
    - (A) obsequious
    - (B) germane
    - (C) punctilious
    - (D) precocious
    - (E) gregarious

22. "In his later years he became _____ of conversation," Mrs. Baker said. "He considered conversation an art form, and he was an expert at it."
    - (A) a civility
    - (B) a patrimony
    - (C) a connoisseur
    - (D) an exhilaration
    - (E) a foible

23. "He apparently found _____ in conversations with other great men. Such talks lifted his spirits and made him happy, especially after his wife's death."
    - (A) foible
    - (B) exhilaration
    - (C) patrimony
    - (D) connoisseur
    - (E) civility

24. "What kind of _____ did Johnson leave his children?" Jesse asked. "Was it a large inheritance?"
    - (A) civility
    - (B) foible
    - (C) exhilaration
    - (D) patrimony
    - (E) connoisseur

25. "He didn't have any children," Mrs. Baker replied with _____. She always tried to answer questions politely.
    - (A) civility
    - (B) patrimony
    - (C) connoisseur
    - (D) precociousness
    - (E) exhilaration

26. "This question may be too far off the subject and not _____," Gwen said, "but was Johnson's biographer James Boswell as _____ as the sociable Johnson?"
    - (A) gregarious . . . germane
    - (B) punctilious . . . obsequious
    - (C) germane . . . gregarious
    - (D) obsequious . . . punctilious
    - (E) precocious . . . germane

27. "Please, let's stay on the subject for now," Mrs. Baker said _____. She was a very precise person. "Let's talk about Johnson as an expert, or _____, of words."
    - (A) gregariously . . . foible
    - (B) precociously . . . civility
    - (C) obsequiously . . . patrimony
    - (D) precociously . . . exhilaration
    - (E) punctiliously . . . connoisseur

28. "Your discussions are always so good," Gwen said _____, trying to hide her embarrassment by flattering Mrs. Baker. "They always create _____, a sense of excitement."
    - (A) punctiliously . . . civility
    - (B) obsequiously . . . exhilaration
    - (C) precociously . . . connoisseur
    - (D) gregariously . . . foible
    - (E) obsequiously . . . patrimony

29. Jesse said, "I've read that one of Johnson's _____ was impatience, but how could he have had such a shortcoming and yet have been so _____, so scrupulous, about the *Dictionary*?"
    - (A) patrimonies . . . precocious
    - (B) civilities . . . germane
    - (C) connoisseurs . . . gregarious
    - (D) foibles . . . punctilious
    - (E) patrimonies . . . civil

30. "I'm just sure Johnson was _____ as a child," Gwen said, "because he was such a genius as an adult. We shouldn't criticize him for his minor faults, or _____."
    - (A) precocious . . . foibles
    - (B) germane . . . civilities
    - (C) punctilious . . . foibles
    - (D) obsequious . . . patrimonies
    - (E) germane . . . connoisseurs

MAKING NEW WORDS YOUR OWN

Lesson 14 **CONTEXT:** History and Society

William Wilberforce: Britain's Antislavery Crusader

Last Tuesday during Quiz Bowl practice, our coach asked if we could name the greatest British activist for the abolition of slavery in the 1800s. Although no one on the team knew that it was William Wilberforce (1759–1833), the question launched a discussion about the abolition of slavery. Mr. Tucker, our coach and history teacher, told us that the British abolished slavery almost thirty years before the American Civil War even began. He also told us about the life of William Wilberforce.

In the following exercises, you will have the opportunity to expand your vocabulary by reading about William Wilberforce and his passionate fight against slavery. Below are ten vocabulary words that will be used in these exercises.

affront	capitulate	guffaw	magnanimous	propitious
buffoon	effusion	indulgent	munificent	querulous

EXERCISE 1 *Mapping* 👈

Directions. In the item below, a vocabulary word is provided and used in a sentence. Take a guess at the word's meaning and write it in the box labeled **Your Guess**. Then look the word up in your dictionary and write the definition in the box labeled **Definition**. In the **Other Forms** box, write as many other forms of the word, such as adjective and noun forms, as you can think of or find in your dictionary.

Then, following the same procedure, draw your own map for each of the nine remaining vocabulary words. Use a separate sheet of paper.

1.

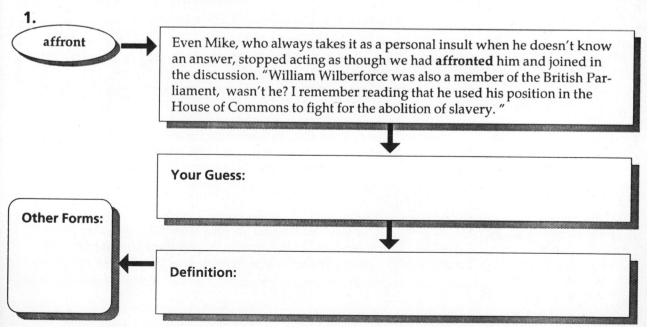

affront → Even Mike, who always takes it as a personal insult when he doesn't know an answer, stopped acting as though we had **affronted** him and joined in the discussion. "William Wilberforce was also a member of the British Parliament, wasn't he? I remember reading that he used his position in the House of Commons to fight for the abolition of slavery."

Your Guess:

Other Forms:

Definition:

2.

buffoon →

"Wilberforce is a great name—let's have a contest to see who can say it five times fast," said Charlie in his usual joking manner. He loved to act the part of our team's **buffoon**.

3.

capitulate →

"Very funny," said Mr. Tucker. "But I would be more impressed if you could simply learn who he was and what he accomplished. He was one of the leaders of the Clapman Sect, the social reform group that forced Parliament in 1807 to **capitulate**, or give in, to their demand for the abolition of the slave trade."

4.

effusion →

"I didn't know Britain abolished slavery that early," said Kay. Mr. Tucker answered her, but in the **effusion**, or pouring forth, of discussion, I could barely hear him say that only the slave trade was abolished in the British colonies; people who were already slaves were not freed.

5.

guffaw →

In the meantime, Charlie was clowning around with some of the other team members. I could hear him **guffawing** at his own humor. The coach ignored his loud laughter. "The distinction I was making," Mr. Tucker continued, "for those who did not hear me, is that slaves who were purchased before 1807 were not set free."

6.

indulgent →

"Slaveholders at that time thought that they were being **indulgent** with their slaves if they treated them well. The owners felt that they would be seen as far too lenient if they set the slaves free," Mr. Tucker continued.

7.

magnanimous →

"Wilberforce was a **magnanimous** man; his efforts were noble and unselfish. He worked with fierce dedication to abolish slavery. In 1823, he sponsored the establishment of the Anti-Slavery Society," continued Mr. Tucker.

8.

munificent →

"Wilberforce's **munificent** attitude came from the teachings of evangelical Christianity, which preached generosity and love toward all. He began his abolition work soon after his 1784 conversion to evangelism."

9.

propitious →

"Many people at the time did not find the idea of abolishing slavery **propitious**," Mr. Tucker continued. "But despite the fact that many did not look favorably on his beliefs, Wilberforce worked tirelessly for his cause."

10.

querulous →

"But didn't slaves provide valuable labor to the colonies?" asked Mike, **querulous** as always. Mike can never resist taking issue with other people's arguments.

EXERCISE 2 · Context Clues ✍

Directions. Scan the definitions in Column A. Then think about how the boldface words are used in the sentences in Column B. To complete the exercise, match each definition in Column A with the correct vocabulary word from Column B. Write the letter of your choice on the line provided; then write the vocabulary word on the line preceding the definition.

<table>
<tr><td>

COLUMN A

_____ **11.** word: _____
n. a pouring forth; an unrestrained expression of feeling in talking or writing

_____ **12.** word: _____
adj. complaining; faultfinding; peevish

_____ **13.** word: _____
adj. very lenient; not strict enough; making allowances

_____ **14.** word: _____
n. an open, intentional insult; *v.* to insult openly; to offend

_____ **15.** word: _____
adj. favorable; favorably inclined

_____ **16.** word: _____
adj. extremely generous; very liberal and lavish in giving

_____ **17.** word: _____
n. a loud or coarse burst of laughter; a horselaugh; *v.* to laugh loudly or coarsely

_____ **18.** word: _____
v. to surrender on certain terms; to give up; to yield; to stop resisting

_____ **19.** word: _____
n. a person who amuses people with tricks, pranks, and jokes; a clown

_____ **20.** word: _____
adj. noble in spirit; generous in forgiving; unselfish; rising above petty, mean concerns

</td><td>

COLUMN B

(A) Mike's question about slave labor in the colonies began another **effusion** of comments, and soon everyone was bursting forth with ideas and questions.

(B) Mr. Tucker answered that slavery is never a **propitious** condition. It is always wrong to keep people in the unfavorable state of bondage, he stated firmly.

(C) Joy, whose great-great-grandparents were slaves, said that the slaves' masters were not **indulgent**. In fact, they were usually very strict.

(D) "I take it as an **affront** that you would say that about slavery," she told Mike. "Even if you didn't mean it that way, it still sounded insulting."

(E) "Lucky for you, I'm **magnanimous** enough to forgive you," Joy continued.

(F) "Yeah, but not lucky for us—it robs us of the entertaining spectacle of seeing you clobber him," said Charlie with a loud **guffaw** that broke the tension. Other team members started to laugh.

(G) "I didn't mean anything by it," said Mike in a **querulous** tone that plainly showed he was still peevish.

(H) "So what finally happened to Wilber Horse?" asked Charlie, never missing a chance to be a **buffoon** and make us laugh.

(I) "He died a month before Parliament **capitulated** completely, surrendering to his demands and abolishing the slave trade," Mr. Tucker replied.

(J) "It's a shame that he was not alive when Parliament abolished slavery," said Joy. "Wilberforce was **munificent**, generously giving so much time and energy to the cause."

</td></tr>
</table>

EXERCISE 3 *Sentence Completion* ✍

Directions. For each of the following items, circle the letter of the choice that best completes the meaning of the sentence or sentences.

21. "Wilberforce's ____ paid off in the end," said Mr. Tucker. "His generosity to the cause of abolition was not wasted."
(A) affront
(B) munificence
(C) effusion
(D) guffaw
(E) buffoon

22. "Yeah, he died," said Charlie, trying to be funny as usual with his ____. "What a great payoff."
(A) indulgence
(B) capitulation
(C) effusion
(D) buffoonery
(E) magnanimity

23. "His dedication to the abolition of slavery was obvious in the ____ letters and speeches that he wrote. His torrent of writing and speechmaking spread to other countries," said Mr. Tucker.
(A) indulgent
(B) querulous
(C) effusive
(D) buffoonish
(E) propitious

24. "Most people began to view his work more ____. They developed a more favorable opinion of abolition," Mr. Tucker continued.
(A) querulously
(B) effusively
(C) irrevocably
(D) munificently
(E) propitiously

25. "Britain's ____ to Wilberforce's demands influenced slavery elsewhere. It set a precedent for other governments to give in to abolitionists' demands and abolish slavery."
(A) buffoonery
(B) effusion
(C) capitulation
(D) querulousness
(E) affrontery

26. "Venezuela and Mexico ____ in 1810, soon after Britain outlawed the slave trade," said Mr. Tucker. "They gave in to the abolitionists and worked with ____, or noble spirit, to stop slavery."
(A) capitulated . . . magnanimity
(B) affronted . . . buffoonery
(C) guffawed . . . indulgence
(D) capitulated . . . effusion
(E) guffawed . . . querulousness

27. "In 1817, Spain took ____ step and outlawed slavery. But this favorable action was weakened by the government's ____ in making allowances for those who continued to buy and sell slaves."
(A) an indulgent . . . buffoonery
(B) a querulous . . . munificence
(C) a buffoonish . . . affront
(D) a propitious . . . indulgence
(E) an effusive . . . guffaw

28. Charlie spoke seriously, without ____. "They should have punished people who wouldn't give in or ____ to the new law."
(A) capitulating . . . guffaw
(B) affronting . . . capitulate
(C) guffawing . . . capitulate
(D) indulging . . . propitiate
(E) guffawing . . . affront

29. "Don't take that as an ____," he added quickly to Joy. "I wasn't trying to offend you. I know I spend a lot of time being a ____ and clowning around, but this time I'm serious."
(A) affront . . . buffoon
(B) indulgence . . . guffaw
(C) affront . . . querulousness
(D) effusion . . . capitulation
(E) indulgence . . . magnanimity

30. "I'm not ____," said Joy. "I didn't complain, did I? I think it's great to have ____, unrestrained discussion about slavery."
(A) buffoonish . . . an indulgent
(B) propitious . . . a munificent
(C) magnanimous . . . an effusive
(D) indulgent . . . a magnanimous
(E) querulous . . . an effusive

MAKING NEW WORDS YOUR OWN

Lesson 15 **CONTEXT:** History and Society

Advancing the Flags

In the late nineteenth century, people in Great Britain, Germany, Italy, and other European countries were excited by the phrase "advance of the flag." The phrase stood for a country's pride in expanding its powers beyond its own borders. Such expansion is known as imperialism. For reasons of national pride, prestige, and economic gain, European countries sought colonies and power bases in other parts of the world. Africa was a prime target of European imperialism—and an example of imperialism at its most aggressive.

In the following exercises, you will have the opportunity to expand your vocabulary by reading about European imperialism before World War I. Below are ten vocabulary words that will be used in these exercises.

abeyance	homogeneous	inscrutable	perfidious	primordial
discrepancy	illicit	inundate	pervade	sumptuous

EXERCISE 1 *Mapping*

Directions. In the item below, a vocabulary word is provided and used in a sentence. Take a guess at the word's meaning and write it in the box labeled **Your Guess**. Then look the word up in your dictionary and write the definition in the box labeled **Definition**. In the **Other Forms** box, write as many other forms of the word, such as adjective and noun forms, as you can think of or find in your dictionary.

Then, following the same procedure, draw your own map for each of the nine remaining vocabulary words. Use a separate sheet of paper.

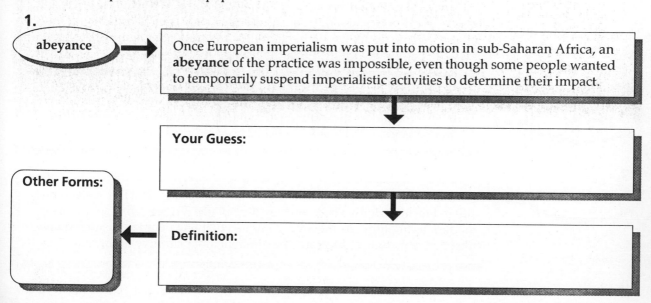

1.

abeyance → Once European imperialism was put into motion in sub-Saharan Africa, an **abeyance** of the practice was impossible, even though some people wanted to temporarily suspend imperialistic activities to determine their impact.

Your Guess:

Other Forms:

Definition:

2.

discrepancy →

Governments led citizens to believe that imperialism was good for the underdeveloped countries of Africa, but often a **discrepancy** existed between propaganda and the facts. The public, however, was unaware of any such inconsistency.

3.

homogeneous →

Africa was an enormous region inhabited by many distinct peoples. These groups did not have uniform governments or customs and therefore could not be called **homogeneous**. It was easy for them to be divided into colonies.

4.

illicit →

Although many of the imperialistic practices were unfair and inhumane, they may not actually have been **illicit** because formal laws often did not exist or apply in the new colonies.

5.

inscrutable →

The motives for European expansion should not be **inscrutable** to any of today's students who are aware of current events. They probably don't find it hard to understand that many countries practice imperialism today for exactly the same reasons countries did in the nineteenth century: greed.

6.

inundate →

European countries seeking more wealth, land, and power **inundated** Africa after 1870. The native Africans were completely overwhelmed, and Europeans had Africa divided within twenty-five years.

7.

perfidious →

Imperialistic countries used all kinds of methods, including military force, to gain control of African regions. The European military forces were mostly loyal to their countries, but there were some **perfidious** soldiers. Of course, some of these soldiers may have been truly treacherous people, but others were no doubt considered faithless and traitorous simply because they sympathized with the people they were conquering.

8.

pervade →

Through force and treaties, European countries **pervaded**, or penetrated, the "Dark Continent," which previously had been mostly isolated from the world.

9.

primordial →

African societies seemed **primordial** to the Europeans. The Europeans considered them primitive because they did not use written languages or have modern technology. At the time, it seemed that few people considered the idea that Africans might simply be different, not primitive or inferior.

10.

sumptuous →

Many imperialists were not at all interested in the welfare of African societies. They sought only the profits from raw materials, investments, and markets needed to maintain their own **sumptuous**, luxurious life styles.

EXERCISE 2 *Context Clues* ✍

Directions. Scan the definitions in Column A. Then think about how the boldface words are used in the sentences in Column B. To complete the exercise, match each definition in Column A with the correct vocabulary word from Column B. Write the letter of your choice on the line provided; then write the vocabulary word on the line preceding the definition.

COLUMN A

_____ **11.** word: _____
adj. deliberately faithless; treacherous

_____ **12.** word: _____
adj. forbidden by law; improper; unauthorized

_____ **13.** word: _____
n. an inconsistency; a contradiction; a difference

_____ **14.** word: _____
v. to cover by overflowing; to flood; to overwhelm (as if by a flood)

_____ **15.** word: _____
adj. costly; magnificent; luxurious; lavish

_____ **16.** word: _____
adj. mysterious or obscure; hard to grasp; not easily understood

_____ **17.** word: _____
n. a temporary suspension of an activity; a state of being put aside for future action

_____ **18.** word: _____
adj. from earliest times; primitive; fundamental; original

_____ **19.** word: _____
adj. of the same kind or nature; composed of similar or identical parts or elements; uniform

_____ **20.** word: _____
v. to extend all over; to spread or be diffused throughout

COLUMN B

(A) David Livingstone (1813–1873), a Scottish missionary and physician, explored the **inscrutable**, mysterious interior of Africa. His original reason for going to South Africa in 1840 was to be a medical missionary, but other interests later replaced this goal.

(B) Livingstone must have been fascinated by the **primordial** landscape of Africa. It must have seemed to him like the world as it existed at the beginning of time.

(C) He explored many lakes and rivers, as well as areas that the lakes and rivers sometimes **inundated** after heavy rains.

(D) Livingstone and his wife, Mary, had **homogeneous** natures. Their values and interests were similar, and they shared the excitement of traveling into areas unknown to Europeans.

(E) While exploring Africa, the Livingstones did not stay in **sumptuous** houses. The tents and huts they lived in were neither magnificent nor costly.

(F) The young Livingstone became distressed by the African slave trade. Slave trading, he discovered, was **illicit** in some countries but legal in others.

(G) He called, not for a mere **abeyance** of the slave trade, but for a permanent stop to it.

(H) Some articles contain **discrepancies** in facts about Livingstone, and these contradictions can be confusing.

(I) All contact with Livingstone was lost for several years. Fellow explorer Henry Stanley (1841–1904) was sent to find Livingstone in 1869, and finally found him in 1871. Stanley proved himself to be a loyal, not **perfidious**, friend by carrying on Livingstone's work after the Scottish explorer's death.

(J) The African explorations of Stanley and Livingstone helped make possible the imperialism that eventually **pervaded** sub-Saharan Africa. One wonders what the two explorers would have thought of the consequences of their explorations.

EXERCISE 3 *Sentence Completion* ✍

Directions. For each of the following items, circle the letter of the choice that best completes the meaning of the sentence or sentences.

21. Can you even begin to understand the enormous greed of King Leopold II of Belgium (1835–1909)? I find his greed _____ —as difficult to grasp as a puzzle without a solution.
(A) homogeneous
(B) primordial
(C) inscrutable
(D) perfidious
(E) illicit

22. Leopold's greed evidently spread throughout Belgium and also eventually _____ his so-called "Congo Free State."
(A) homogenized
(B) reviled
(C) corroborated
(D) vindicated
(E) pervaded

23. Although Leopold's activities were often improper, they were not _____ because the major powers in 1885 legally recognized the Congo Free State as being under his rule.
(A) primordial
(B) illicit
(C) homogeneous
(D) sumptuous
(E) perfidious

24. There was nothing to keep Leopold's exploitation of the Congo in _____, much less permanently put an end to it.
(A) pervasion
(B) sumptuousness
(C) discrepancy
(D) abeyance
(E) inundation

25. Leopold employed agents who had uniform, _____ goals—goals identical to his own. Like Leopold, these agents did not hesitate to force natives to work for them.
(A) homogeneous
(B) illicit
(C) primordial
(D) sumptuous
(E) inscrutable

26. Since _____ times, before history began, the native peoples had never known such cruelty as now _____, or extended throughout, their land.
(A) perfidious . . . pervaded
(B) homogeneous . . . inundated
(C) primordial . . . pervaded
(D) illicit . . . homogenized
(E) sumptuous . . . inundated

27. Leopold would have done anything, whether lawful or _____, for personal gain. Few of his subjects dared any treacherous, or _____, acts against him.
(A) sumptuous . . . inscrutable
(B) homogeneous . . . primordial
(C) illicit . . . perfidious
(D) inscrutable . . . illicit
(E) perfidious . . . homogeneous

28. Leopold's motives may not be _____ or mysterious if you understand the importance of the Congo's rubber trees. He was able to make millions of dollars by _____, or flooding, the export market with rubber.
(A) homogeneous . . . pervading
(B) primordial . . . homogenizing
(C) sumptuous . . . inundating
(D) primordial . . . pervading
(E) inscrutable . . . inundating

29. I'm sure that Leopold lived in a _____ palace, lavishly decorated, with the fragrance of expensive perfumes _____ every room.
(A) primordial . . . reviling
(B) sumptuous . . . pervading
(C) perfidious . . . inundating
(D) sumptuous . . . homogenizing
(E) pervasive . . . inundating

30. Between these two books there is _____ about the Congo's exact size. The contradictory figures temporarily suspended my research: I put my studies in _____ until I could verify which book was correct.
(A) an abeyance . . . discrepancy
(B) a sumptuousness . . . inscrutability
(C) a perfidy . . . discrepancy
(D) a discrepancy . . . abeyance
(E) an inundation . . . pervasion

MAKING NEW WORDS YOUR OWN

Lesson 16 | CONTEXT: History and Society
St. Joan and Bernard Shaw

What does Joan of Arc (1412–1431), the young French girl who led an army to victory over the English at Orléans and who was later burned at the stake for witchcraft, have in common with Bernard Shaw (1856–1950), one of Ireland's most famous dramatists? Shaw wrote a play based on Joan's life, titled *Saint Joan*, that was first produced three years after her canonization as a saint. The discussion about Shaw's life, the play, and St. Joan's life is about to begin in my English class. Please sit in.

In the following exercises, you will have the opportunity to expand your vocabulary by reading about St. Joan and Bernard Shaw. Below are ten vocabulary words that will be used in these exercises.

chastise	deplore	emanate	intercede	obnoxious
demagogue	detriment	harbinger	irrevocable	prevaricate

EXERCISE 1 — Mapping ✍

Directions. In the item below, a vocabulary word is provided and used in a sentence. Take a guess at the word's meaning and write it in the box labeled **Your Guess**. Then look the word up in your dictionary and write the definition in the box labeled **Definition**. In the **Other Forms** box, write as many other forms of the word, such as adjective and noun forms, as you can think of or find in your dictionary.

Then, following the same procedure, draw your own map for each of the nine remaining vocabulary words. Use a separate sheet of paper.

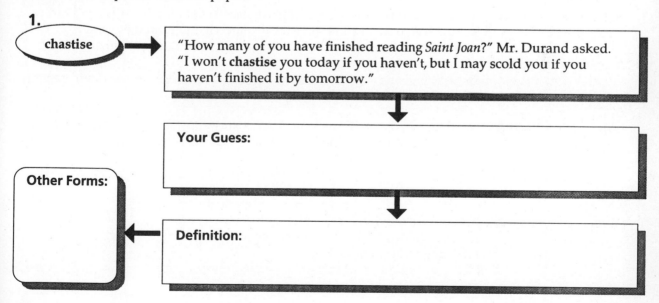

1.

chastise → "How many of you have finished reading *Saint Joan*?" Mr. Durand asked. "I won't **chastise** you today if you haven't, but I may scold you if you haven't finished it by tomorrow."

Your Guess:

Other Forms:

Definition:

2.

demagogue ➤ "I don't mean to be a **demagogue**—isn't that what you said a rabble-rouser is called?—but I read the play in the time you gave us, and I don't think it's fair to give others more time," said Alan, our unofficial class upstart.

3.

deplore ➤ "How many others **deplore** my decision?" Mr. Durand asked. "Or do you approve of my decision and agree that we can use the time today to talk generally about Shaw and *Saint Joan*?"

4.

detriment ➤ "I'm sure there is no **detriment**, or harm, done to those studious few who have read the entire play and the play's outstanding preface. Now, you should know that Shaw received the Nobel Prize for literature in 1925."

5.

emanate ➤ "We may wonder how so many great plays issued from just one man, but just think of all the plays that **emanated** from the mind of Shakespeare. Of course, Shaw, always a self-promoter, probably would have rated himself above Shakespeare."

6.

harbinger ➤ "Didn't Shaw's plays **harbinger** a change in modern drama?" Janell asked. "His were the first plays to indicate that 'the action is in the language . . . not in the unrolling of plot.'"

7.

intercede ➤ Alan, true to form, started arguing with Janell about her question, and Mr. Durand had to step in and settle the dispute. He **interceded** by saying, "Shaw didn't develop that type of drama, but he certainly did his share to popularize it."

8.

irrevocable ➤ "Mr. Durand, do you think Joan of Arc's story appealed to Shaw because her fate was so **irrevocable**?" Ima asked. "I mean, being burned at the stake is pretty final."

9.

obnoxious ➤ "That's an **obnoxious** idea," Earl said, obviously offended. "It wasn't Saint Joan's death but her life that interested and inspired Shaw—and that led to her being named a saint."

10.

prevaricate ➤ Earl said he had read *Saint Joan* four times and that he admired Joan's determination to do what she thought was right for her country and church. Personally, I think he was lying, at least about reading the play four times. I know from past experience that he sometimes **prevaricates**.

EXERCISE 2   *Context Clues* ✍

Directions. Scan the definitions in Column A. Then think about how the boldface words are used in the sentences in Column B. To complete the exercise, match each definition in Column A with the correct vocabulary word from Column B. Write the letter of your choice on the line provided; then write the vocabulary word on the line preceding the definition.

COLUMN A

_____ **11.** word: _____

v. to announce; to indicate what will follow; *n.* a forerunner; a herald; a precursor

_____ **12.** word: _____

v. to issue from; to originate from

_____ **13.** word: _____

n. a leader who stirs up people by appealing to their emotions; a rabble-rouser

_____ **14.** word: _____

v. to tell a lie; to evade the truth

_____ **15.** word: _____

n. damage; harm; injury; anything that causes damage or injury

_____ **16.** word: _____

adj. very disagreeable; highly offensive; hateful

_____ **17.** word: _____

v. to punish; to criticize severely; to scold

_____ **18.** word: _____

adj. not capable of being retracted, recalled, or withdrawn; unalterable

_____ **19.** word: _____

v. to feel very sorry about; to regret deeply; to lament; to disapprove of

_____ **20.** word: _____

v. to plead, or petition, on another's behalf; to act as a mediator in a dispute

COLUMN B

(A) "Mr. Durand, since Joan was a leader who really stirred up people by appealing to their emotions, wasn't she really a **demagogue**?" Alan asked smugly.

(B) "I don't know about that. But she certainly was a **harbinger** for a new day for France," Mr. Durand replied. "Dressed in armor, she was an imposing herald of change."

(C) "It seems that courage just poured out of her. She was like a solitary light **emanating** from an otherwise dark house," remarked Ima.

(D) "In his play, does Shaw make you **deplore** Joan's death?" Mr. Durand asked. "If so, why do you regret her fate and feel sorry for her?"

(E) "People shouldn't have killed her just because they found her **obnoxious** and disagreed with her ways," Earl said. "Personally, I don't see why people found her actions so offensive."

(F) "It is more complicated than that," Mr. Durand said. "She was a **detriment** to the English, who were afraid she would cause even greater damage to them in the future."

(G) "The English could have simply **chastised** her," Janell said. "But I guess a severe reprimand would never have stopped her."

(H) "During the play's trial scene, I kept wishing someone would **intercede** and speak on Joan's behalf," Ima said.

(I) "When she was questioned, she should have **prevaricated**, or been evasive, to save herself," Earl said. "I know I would have been tempted to lie to save myself."

(J) "What happened is history," Alan said, "and it can't be altered. The past is **irrevocable**."

EXERCISE 3 *Sentence Completion* ✍

Directions. For each of the following items, circle the letter of the choice that best completes the meaning of the sentence or sentences.

21. "Some people," Mr. Durand said, "thought Bernard Shaw was too outspoken and offensive and therefore _____."
 (A) irrevocable
 (B) demagogic
 (C) obnoxious
 (D) emanative
 (E) detrimental

22. "If he had been a political leader, Shaw most certainly would have been a rabble-rousing _____, inciting people to action. I like to think that if he had been present at Joan's trial, he would have done everything he could to drum up popular support for her."
 (A) demagogue
 (B) harbinger
 (C) prevaricator
 (D) detriment
 (E) chastiser

23. "People were captivated by Shaw's wit and unusual ideas. Some saw him as a precursor, or _____, of social change."
 (A) demagogue
 (B) harbinger
 (C) deplorer
 (D) detriment
 (E) chastisement

24. "Did he identify with Saint Joan?" asked a voice _____ from the back of the room.
 (A) chastising
 (B) prevaricating
 (C) interceding
 (D) emanating
 (E) deploring

25. "That's a good question, Janell," Mr. Durand said. Abruptly, he changed the subject and _____ Alan for not paying attention. Alan blushed at the criticism.
 (A) pervaded
 (B) interceded
 (C) chastised
 (D) emanated
 (E) prevaricated

26. "A playwright is just a _____ because he writes lies—fictional stories," Alan said. "I think Shaw sounds very disagreeable, almost _____."
 (A) demagogue . . . irrevocable
 (B) harbinger . . . obnoxious
 (C) detriment . . . demagogic
 (D) chastiser . . . irrevocable
 (E) prevaricator . . . obnoxious

27. "Your views are a _____ to yourself, Alan, not an injury to anyone else," Mr. Durand said. "You should try to understand the ethical ideas _____ from Shaw's mind."
 (A) harbinger . . . chastising
 (B) demagogue . . . harbingering
 (C) prevarication . . . prevaricating
 (D) deplorer . . . interceding
 (E) detriment . . . emanating

28. "I deeply regret—yes, I _____—your inability to see that Shaw and Saint Joan believed strongly in certain values and ideas for which they sometimes were severely criticized or _____."
 (A) prevaricate . . . deplored
 (B) deplore . . . prevaricated
 (C) intercede . . . emanated
 (D) deplore . . . chastised
 (E) emanate . . . interceded

29. Earl decided to _____ on Alan's behalf and ask Mr. Durand to ease up on him. "Please remember, Mr. Durand, that Alan enjoys his image as _____; he thinks it's his role to stir up the class."
 (A) harbinger . . . a detriment
 (B) deplore . . . an emanation
 (C) intercede . . . a demagogue
 (D) emanate . . . a harbinger
 (E) chastise . . . a prevaricator

30. Mr. Durand replied, "Your role is not _____, Alan; it can be changed. To avoid further _____, I'd suggest that you start paying better attention."
 (A) obnoxious . . . emanation
 (B) irrevocable . . . chastisement
 (C) emanative . . . demagogue
 (D) demagogic . . . prevarication
 (E) detrimental . . . intercession

MAKING NEW WORDS YOUR OWN

Lesson 17 | CONTEXT: History and Society
India: The Jewel of the British Empire

Last summer, I traveled to London with my history club. While we were there, we visited several museums and saw photographs and documents from India. One museum guide explained that India was a British colony from the late 1700s until 1947. He also told us that India was once called the "jewel of the British empire" because of its size and resources. Unlike many of Britain's other colonies, India retained very little of its independence during the years of British control.

In the following exercises, you will have the opportunity to expand your vocabulary by reading about India under British rule. Below are ten vocabulary words that will be used in these exercises.

anarchy	commodious	extricate	menial	pestilence
cajole	ethnology	impair	nadir	rampant

EXERCISE 1 *Mapping*

Directions. In the item below, a vocabulary word is provided and used in a sentence. Take a guess at the word's meaning and write it in the box labeled **Your Guess**. Then look the word up in your dictionary and write the definition in the box labeled **Definition**. In the **Other Forms** box, write as many other forms of the word, such as adjective and noun forms, as you can think of or find in your dictionary.

Then, following the same procedure, draw your own map for each of the nine remaining vocabulary words. Use a separate sheet of paper.

1.

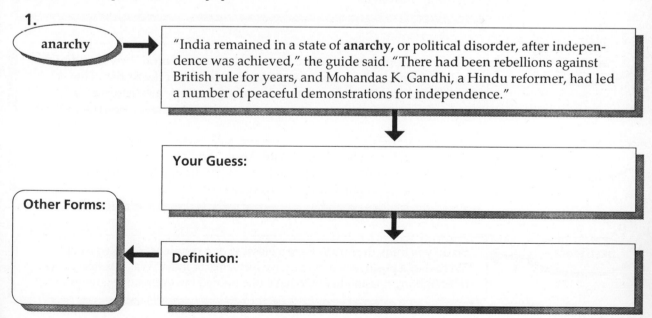

anarchy

"India remained in a state of **anarchy**, or political disorder, after independence was achieved," the guide said. "There had been rebellions against British rule for years, and Mohandas K. Gandhi, a Hindu reformer, had led a number of peaceful demonstrations for independence."

Your Guess:

Other Forms:

Definition:

2.

cajole →

He continued: "Although Gandhi was a great leader, he was sent to prison many times. The British government did not want to be **cajoled** into giving up India. Britain resisted the idea of being coaxed into action by the Indians, whom they considered inferior."

3.

commodious →

"Did the British treat the Indians badly?" asked James.
"Well," answered the guide, "there was serious inequality. While the British lived in **commodious** houses, the Indians did not have spacious homes. Many Indians lived in great poverty."

4.

ethnology →

"If you would like to know more about India," said the guide, "there is a great amount of writing on the subject in the field of **ethnology,** the branch of anthropology that deals with various races of people and their origins, distribution, characteristics, and cultures."

5.

extricate →

The guide seemed to want to talk all day, so we eventually had to **extricate** ourselves from the museum. But the information was so interesting that I hated to tear myself away from the discussion.

6.

impair →

In the bus we continued to discuss India. Anthony said that fighting between different religious groups and kingdoms had **impaired** India's ability to prevent British colonialism. "India was weakened by its own infighting," he told us.

7.

menial →

"The conditions for the Indians were awful," said Kamul. "My grandfather told stories about his parents working as **menials** for the British. The British thought that the Indians were only fit to be domestic servants."

8.

nadir →

"But that isn't the whole story," said Amy. "You're just talking about the **nadir** of colonialism. Forcing people into servitude is definitely the lowest point, but some Indians held government posts."

9.

pestilence →

"So do you think the British were a blessing or a **pestilence**?" asked Katie. "Were they a positive or a destructive influence in India? Was it better to have states fighting one another or to have one unified but oppressive government?"

10.

rampant →

"Those are hard questions," said Anthony. "Ever since the British left, there has been **rampant** fighting in India. The widespread Hindu and Muslim conflict seems to be getting worse instead of better."

EXERCISE 2 *Context Clues* ✍

Directions. Scan the definitions in Column A. Then think about how the boldface words are used in the sentences in Column B. To complete the exercise, match each definition in Column A with the correct vocabulary word from Column B. Write the letter of your choice on the line provided; then write the vocabulary word on the line preceding the definition.

COLUMN A	COLUMN B

COLUMN A

_____ **11.** word: _____
v. to release from an entanglement or a difficulty; to set free

_____ **12.** word: _____
adj. of or suited to a servant; *n.* a domestic servant

_____ **13.** word: _____
adj. growing without check or restraint; flourishing; widespread

_____ **14.** word: _____
v. to persuade by pleasant words; to coax with flattery and insincere talk; to wheedle

_____ **15.** word: _____
n. a contagious and often fatal disease that spreads rapidly; an illness of epidemic proportions; a destructive or evil influence or factor

_____ **16.** word: _____
n. the absence of government or law; political disorder

_____ **17.** word: _____
n. the point in the celestial sphere directly below the observer and opposite the zenith; the lowest possible point

_____ **18.** word: _____
n. the branch of anthropology that deals with various races of people, their origins, distribution, characteristics, and cultures

_____ **19.** word: _____
v. to make worse; to damage or weaken

_____ **20.** word: _____
adj. roomy; spacious

COLUMN B

(A) A few days after my return from London, I went to the **commodious** public library and settled myself in the roomy interior to do my research on India.

(B) From one book I learned that Britain took control of India during the **rampant**, unrestrained fighting of the Seven Years' War.

(C) In 1773, the East India Company **cajoled**, or persuaded, the British Parliament to put it in control of India.

(D) The company acted as an unofficial government agency and prevented **anarchy** by providing law and order throughout India during the turbulent time.

(E) From the start the British believed that the Indians should do only **menial** tasks and work as servants.

(F) Their attitude spread like a **pestilence**, and, like such a fatal disease, it dispirited the Indians.

(G) Discouragement **impaired** the Indians' attempts to rebel. Many Indians believed that they deserved servitude, and this belief weakened them.

(H) Some Indians, however, managed to receive an education, which **extricated** them, or freed them, from the feeling of inferiority.

(I) According to the field of **ethnology**, which deals with cultures, these educated Indians believed they deserved a better life.

(J) They came to view British rule as the **nadir**, or lowest point, of Indian history.

EXERCISE 3 *Sentence Completion* ✍

Directions. For each of the following items, circle the letter of the choice that best completes the meaning of the sentence or sentences.

21. The educated Indians began to _____ other Indians to fight against the British. In time, they persuaded many others to join their cause.
   (A) extricate
   (B) impair
   (C) cajole
   (D) affront
   (E) chastise

22. In 1885, the educated Indians formed the Hindu National Congress in an attempt to _____, or remove, themselves from British rule.
   (A) extricate
   (B) cajole
   (C) guffaw
   (D) impair
   (E) pervade

23. They wanted Indians to act no longer as _____, or servants, to the British.
   (A) ethnologies
   (B) menials
   (C) anarchies
   (D) impairments
   (E) pestilences

24. These views, however, were not as _____ as some Indians had hoped. The views did not spread rapidly through the lower classes.
   (A) commodious
   (B) extricable
   (C) menial
   (D) pestilent
   (E) rampant

25. The British were not just _____, or a destructive influence, however. They also did some important work in India.
   (A) an anarchy
   (B) a cajolement
   (C) a pestilence
   (D) an ethnology
   (E) a nadir

26. One _____ who wrote a book on Indian culture said the British saved India from a state of near _____, or lawlessness.
   (A) anarchy . . . impairment
   (B) cajolement . . . pestilence
   (C) rampancy . . . extrication
   (D) ethnologist . . . anarchy
   (E) ethnologist . . . commodiousness

27. He said the British _____ India from civil war, freeing India from the lowest point, or _____, of humanity.
   (A) cajoled . . . anarchy
   (B) extricated . . . nadir
   (C) impaired . . . pestilence
   (D) extricated . . . cajolement
   (E) impaired . . . ethnology

28. "Speaking _____, or with regard to culture and race, the most _____, harmful characteristic of British rule was their attitude of superiority toward the Indians."
   (A) ethnologically . . . pestilent
   (B) anarchically . . . commodious
   (C) menially . . . impaired
   (D) pestilently . . . rampant
   (E) cajolingly . . . commodious

29. The British _____ their own success by refusing to give up the _____ belief that they were superior. This widespread belief weakened their ability to rule educated Indians.
   (A) cajoled . . . commodious
   (B) impaired . . . menial
   (C) extricated . . . rampant
   (D) cajoled . . . pestilent
   (E) impaired . . . rampant

30. The educated Indians believed that if they worked hard, they, too, should have _____, or spacious, homes. They also believed they should no longer be treated as _____, or servants, to the British.
   (A) rampant . . . commodiousness
   (B) menial . . . rampancy
   (C) impaired . . . pestilence
   (D) commodious . . . menials
   (E) extricable . . . nadirs

MAKING NEW WORDS YOUR OWN

Lesson 18 ## CONTEXT: History and Society
Nothing to Fear: The British in World War II

Last summer when my family took a trip to Arizona, we stopped in Phoenix to stay with my great-uncle Derek. One night, after my parents had gone to bed, Derek took out his old scrapbooks and told me stories about his years in the British army. When he was nineteen, he fell in love with and married a young British woman, and the couple settled in England. Shortly after their marriage, World War II began, and Derek left his new home in Cropshire in November 1939 to join the army.

In the following exercises, you will have the opportunity to expand your vocabulary by reading about the British in World War II. Below are ten vocabulary words that will be used in these exercises.

cadaverous	elocution	maim	restitution	subversion
consign	incorrigible	residual	strident	virulent

EXERCISE 1 *Mapping*

Directions. In the item below, a vocabulary word is provided and used in a sentence. Take a guess at the word's meaning and write it in the box labeled **Your Guess**. Then look the word up in your dictionary and write the definition in the box labeled **Definition**. In the **Other Forms** box, write as many other forms of the word, such as adjective and noun forms, as you can think of or find in your dictionary.

Then, following the same procedure, draw your own map for each of the nine remaining vocabulary words. Use a separate sheet of paper.

1.

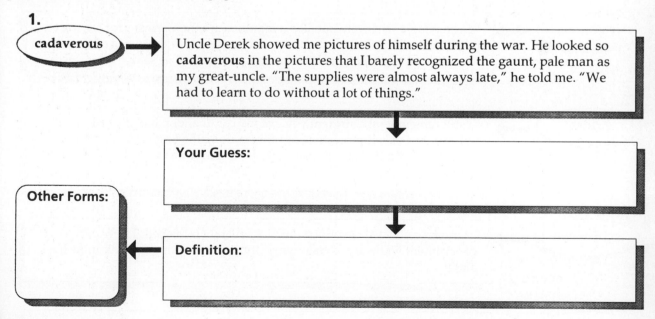

cadaverous → Uncle Derek showed me pictures of himself during the war. He looked so **cadaverous** in the pictures that I barely recognized the gaunt, pale man as my great-uncle. "The supplies were almost always late," he told me. "We had to learn to do without a lot of things."

Your Guess:

Other Forms:

Definition:

2.

(consign) ➡️ "I was **consigned** to a base near the English Channel," he said. "When France fell to Germany in 1940, Britain was left exposed to attack. I often wished that I had not been assigned to such a dangerous place."

3.

(elocution) ➡️ "Luckily," he continued, "Winston Churchill became Britain's prime minister just after France fell to Germany. His inspiring **elocution** kept our morale up. His style of public speaking was determined and rousing, full of conviction that we could defeat the Nazis."

4.

(incorrigible) ➡️ "Unlike the previous prime minister, Neville Chamberlain, Churchill realized that Hitler was **incorrigible:** Churchill knew that treaties would not reform Hitler, who was driven by ruthless ambition."

5.

(maim) ➡️ "At first," he said, "most of the British were against the war. Millions of people had been **maimed** or killed in World War I, and the images of wounded soldiers were still fresh in the minds of many British citizens."

6.

(residual) ➡️ "But when Hitler invaded Poland and then Belgium, the Netherlands, Luxembourg, and France, the **residual** horrors of World War I faded. The British became more concerned about a new invasion than about the lingering pain of the previous war."

7.

(restitution) ➡️ "Even people who were initially sympathetic to the Germans for having to pay heavy **restitution,** or compensation, to the rest of the world after World War I realized that Hitler had to be stopped," he said.

8.

(strident) ➡️ "I still remember the **strident** voice of my commander, harshly calling out our orders. For self-protection, our forces along the English Channel were assigned to eliminate the French navy to keep it from falling into German hands."

9.

(subversion) ➡️ "Anyone convicted of **subversion** was severely punished. The British government was wary of Nazi sympathizers attempting to undermine its plans."

10.

(virulent) ➡️ Uncle Derek pulled out a letter from a friend who had been accused of treason. "As you can imagine, Joe was extremely upset by the **virulent** accusation," said Uncle Derek. "He was angered by the intensely bitter and spiteful attack on his character."

EXERCISE 2 *Context Clues* ✍

Directions. Scan the definitions in Column A. Then think about how the boldface words are used in the sentences in Column B. To complete the exercise, match each definition in Column A with the correct vocabulary word from Column B. Write the letter of your choice on the line provided; then write the vocabulary word on the line preceding the definition.

COLUMN A	COLUMN B

_____ **11.** word: _____
adj. remaining; *n.* a remainder left over after the completion of a process

_____ **12.** word: _____
adj. very poisonous or harmful; deadly; intensely bitter or spiteful

_____ **13.** word: _____
adj. having or making a harsh sound; shrill

_____ **14.** word: _____
v. to deliver; to deliver as goods to be sold; to send; to hand over; to assign to an undesirable position or place

_____ **15.** word: _____
n. the art of public speaking; a style or manner of public speaking or reading

_____ **16.** word: _____
n. the overthrowing or undermining of something established, such as a government

_____ **17.** word: _____
adj. corpselike; pale and ghostly; thin and gaunt

_____ **18.** word: _____
n. a person who will not be reformed; *adj.* incapable of being corrected or reformed; persistently bad

_____ **19.** word: _____
n. the return of what has been lost or taken away; compensation for any loss or damage

_____ **20.** word: _____
v. to wound or injure seriously; to disable in some way; to mutilate; to cripple

(A) "This is Joe," said Uncle Derek, pointing to a picture of a man who was so gaunt that he was almost corpselike. His **cadaverous** face seemed to stare at me from the old photograph.

(B) "Joe was **maimed** during an attack, and the wound left him permanently crippled," Uncle Derek said.

(C) "Even after the wound healed, the **residual,** or remaining, pain was extremely severe."

(D) "Joe devoted himself to **elocution**," said Uncle Derek. "Following the example of Churchill, he inspired us with his speeches."

(E) "I am sure the officers regretted their spiteful attacks on his character. There had been no cause for their **virulent** words, and now it was too late to take them back."

(F) "During the bombing of London, Joe was in charge of **consigning,** or delivering, goods to the soldiers," Uncle Derek continued.

(G) "Hitler hoped the bombing would cause a **subversion** of our defense, but our plans were not undermined."

(H) "The British saw Hitler as an **incorrigible**," said Uncle Derek. "They began to see that he was incapable of reform."

(I) "For many British, the **strident** sounds of air-raid sirens became a shrill reminder of their determination to win the war."

(J) "People rallied together. Hope for a peaceful future was the only **restitution** they had to compensate for the deaths of those they loved," he said.

EXERCISE 3 Sentence Completion ✍

Directions. For each of the following items, circle the letter of the choice that best completes the meaning of the sentence or sentences.

21. "The United States soon began delivering goods to the British army," said Uncle Derek. "The _____ of these goods helped Britain resist Hitler's aggression."
    (A) virulence
    (B) subversion
    (C) consignment
    (D) elocution
    (E) incorrigible

22. "Still, these goods and Churchill's skill as _____ were not enough. Supplies and speechmakers were important, but Britain needed a strong military."
    (A) a consignment
    (B) an incorrigible
    (C) a virulence
    (D) an elocutionist
    (E) a cadaver

23. "Britain was able to _____ some German attacks by undermining the Germans' plans at sea," he said.
    (A) maim
    (B) consign
    (C) capitulate
    (D) subvert
    (E) extricate

24. "But the Germans damaged and disabled many British ships and aircraft through frequent and heavy bombing. And, of course, countless soldiers were similarly _____ in these attacks."
    (A) consigned
    (B) maimed
    (C) subverted
    (D) guffawed
    (E) cajoled

25. "Luckily, the British did not depend on the _____ weaponry of World War I. This left-over war machinery was important, but not as useful as new military equipment."
    (A) strident
    (B) subversive
    (C) virulent
    (D) incorrigible
    (E) residual

26. "Soon," he said, "the harsh, _____ sounds of air raids were less frequent, and fewer people were killed or _____ by bombs."
    (A) strident . . . maimed
    (B) incorrigible . . . consigned
    (C) residual . . . cajoled
    (D) elocutionary . . . maimed
    (E) cadaverous . . . subverted

27. "Churchill began using his _____ skills to make moving speeches about post-war plans," said Uncle Derek. "He promised that the British would defeat the _____ Hitler and his persistent evil."
    (A) residual . . . strident
    (B) subversive . . . virulent
    (C) elocutionary . . . incorrigible
    (D) consignable . . . cadaverous
    (E) virulent . . . cadaverous

28. "There could never be sufficient _____ for the lingering grief of losing loved ones, but Hitler's defeat provided some compensation for the survivors' _____ sorrow."
    (A) cadaver . . . maimed
    (B) subversion . . . virulent
    (C) stridence . . . elocutionary
    (D) restitution . . . residual
    (E) cadaver . . . strident

29. A _____ sound—the shrill ringing of the alarm clock—startled me. "We're both going to look gaunt and _____ from staying up all night," Uncle Derek said.
    (A) residual . . . consignable
    (B) strident . . . cadaverous
    (C) maimed . . . strident
    (D) subversive . . . virulent
    (E) residual . . . incorrigible

30. Although tired from the _____ effects of having stayed up all night, we went for a morning walk in the desert. Uncle Derek pointed out several poisonous snakes whose _____ bites could be deadly.
    (A) residual . . . virulent
    (B) incorrigible . . . subversive
    (C) consignable . . . elocutionary
    (D) residual . . . cadaverous
    (E) subversive . . . strident

Name _____ Date _____ Class _____

MAKING NEW WORDS YOUR OWN

Lesson 19   ## CONTEXT: History and Society
Mary Astell's Serious Proposal

"Happy retreat!" writes Mary Astell (1668–1731) in her book *A Serious Proposal to Ladies* (1694). Just what kind of retreat did Astell have in mind? She proposed the creation of a special place where single women could withdraw from society and become educated. Astell recognized that English society at the time did not value the education of women and actually barred women from educational advantages. Believing strongly that "women are [as] capable of learning as men are," Astell proposed a retreat in which women could acquire "useful knowledge" and "right ideas."

In the following exercises, you will have the opportunity to expand your vocabulary by reading about Mary Astell and *A Serious Proposal to Ladies*. Below are ten vocabulary words that will be used in these exercises.

calumny	dissent	litigation	recant	saline
contingency	impassive	mollify	retaliate	sedentary

EXERCISE 1   *Mapping*

Directions. In the item below, a vocabulary word is provided and used in a sentence. Take a guess at the word's meaning and write it in the box labeled **Your Guess**. Then look the word up in your dictionary and write the definition in the box labeled **Definition**. In the **Other Forms** box, write as many other forms of the word, such as adjective and noun forms, as you can think of or find in your dictionary.

Then, following the same procedure, draw your own map for each of the nine remaining vocabulary words. Use a separate sheet of paper.

1.

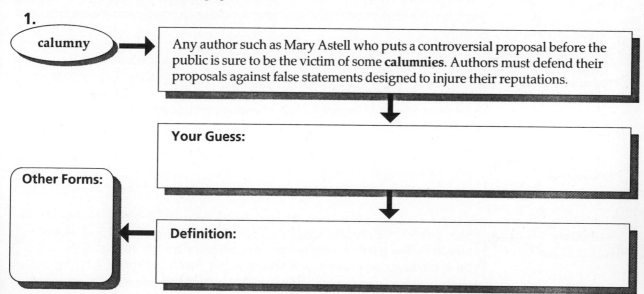

calumny → Any author such as Mary Astell who puts a controversial proposal before the public is sure to be the victim of some **calumnies**. Authors must defend their proposals against false statements designed to injure their reputations.

Your Guess:

Other Forms:

Definition:

2.

(contingency) →

Astell probably did not imagine that her retreat could prepare women for every **contingency** in society. Even the most thorough education could not prepare students for absolutely anything that might happen in their lives.

3.

(dissent) →

Astell **dissented** from society's established beliefs concerning the capabilities of women. In her proposal, she suggested that men would resent her refusal to conform to traditional beliefs.

4.

(impassive) →

Astell did not expect women to lead **impassive,** or emotionless, lives, but she did want women to be able to control their emotions and to accomplish worthy goals that went beyond "trifles and gaieties and secular affairs."

5.

(litigation) →

Through her writing, Astell tried to correct society's discrimination against women. At that time, complaints of discrimination against women could not be settled with **litigation** because there were no laws protecting women's rights.

6.

(mollify) →

In her proposal, Astell made no attempt to **mollify,** or pacify, readers who might be angered by her belief that women's minds should be filled "with a stock of solid and useful knowledge."

7.

(recant) →

Astell had definite, strong opinions about the abilities of women. I would be surprised to learn that she ever **recanted** any of those opinions, even though some readers thought she should retract them.

8.

(retaliate) →

Astell did not want to **retaliate** against men for denying advantages to women. She was more interested in improving opportunities for women than in getting even with men for denying women these advantages.

9.

(saline) →

Like a **saline,** or salty, solution stinging an open wound, Astell's ideas probably stung some people.

10.

(sedentary) →

She spoke out against the traditional belief that women should lead **sedentary** lives. She felt that most women did not enjoy merely sitting all the time, reading, embroidering, or talking about "froth and trifles."

EXERCISE 2 Context Clues ✍

Directions. Scan the definitions in Column A. Then think about how the boldface words are used in the sentences in Column B. To complete the exercise, match each definition in Column A with the correct vocabulary word from Column B. Write the letter of your choice on the line provided; then write the vocabulary word on the line preceding the definition.

COLUMN A

_____ **11.** word: _____
adj. of or relating to salt; salty

_____ **12.** word: _____
v. to take back formally or publicly; to withdraw or retract an opinion expressed in the past

_____ **13.** word: _____
n. a possible happening; a chance event; something that depends on chance or uncertain conditions

_____ **14.** word: _____
n. the carrying on of a lawsuit; a lawsuit

_____ **15.** word: _____
v. to return an injury for an injury; to get even

_____ **16.** word: _____
n. a false statement made to injure someone's reputation; slander

_____ **17.** word: _____
adj. used to sitting much of the time; moving little and rarely; staying in one place

_____ **18.** word: _____
adj. not feeling or showing emotion

_____ **19.** word: _____
v. to differ in opinion; to disagree; *n.* the refusal to conform to the beliefs of an established authority, such as church or state; a difference of opinion

_____ **20.** word: _____
v. to soothe the temper of; to appease; to pacify

COLUMN B

(A) Jay's mother, an attorney, cited an excerpt from Mary Astell's book in a **litigation** she filed for a client.

(B) The case involved a woman who was upset by the **calumny** she swore was uttered against her by her employer. She sued him for his slanderous statement.

(C) Since the employer would not publicly admit to being wrong and would not **recant** his slanderous comments, the woman had to go to court.

(D) The employer said the woman was just trying to get even with him for reducing her work hours. But it was not her intention to **retaliate**.

(E) "My client does not agree with her employer's attitude toward women," Jay's mother wrote. "In fact, she strongly **dissents**."

(F) "She will not be **mollified** by soothing but empty words. As Mary Astell said, women have 'the faculty of thinking.'"

(G) According to Jay's mother, cases of alleged slander are never presented **impassively;** they always involve strong emotions.

(H) She was rarely **sedentary** as she researched and prepared the case. She was always on the go.

(I) She tried to prepare for every **contingency** because she didn't know exactly what might occur during the trial.

(J) Jay's mother urged her client not to cry during the trial. In an attempt at humor, she told the woman that the only **saline** liquid she would allow in her presence was her client's **saline** contact lens rinse, not salty tears.

EXERCISE 3 — Sentence Completion ✍

Directions. For each of the following items, circle the letter of the choice that best completes the meaning of the sentence or sentences.

21. The class discussion about Astell's proposal was lengthy. Some of the students were tired of being _____ for so long, and they fidgeted in their seats.
    (A) saline
    (B) calumnious
    (C) sedentary
    (D) contingent
    (E) retaliative

22. Most of the students agreed with Astell that women should read more than novels and romances, but Yvonne _____. She made her disagreement very plain.
    (A) mollified
    (B) consigned
    (C) retaliated
    (D) recanted
    (E) dissented

23. Yvonne said she was old-fashioned and would just as soon drink _____ water from the ocean as accept Astell's ideas.
    (A) impassive
    (B) saline
    (C) calumnious
    (D) sedentary
    (E) contingent

24. "You're from the Stone Age!" Greg yelled angrily, but Yvonne sat _____, not showing her feelings.
    (A) impassively
    (B) contingently
    (C) calumniously
    (D) clandestinely
    (E) solicitously

25. "I'm not paying attention to any _____ from you because I know you delight in making me look bad," Yvonne said.
    (A) contingency
    (B) retaliation
    (C) litigation
    (D) calumny
    (E) impassiveness

26. However, Yvonne tried to _____ by insulting Greg. Her attack surprised Mr. Hansen, and he handled his confusion by putting on a bland, almost _____ expression.
    (A) dissent . . . saline
    (B) recant . . . calumnious
    (C) mollify . . . saline
    (D) dissent . . . retaliatory
    (E) retaliate . . . impassive

27. "Class, I thought I had prepared my lesson for every _____, but I didn't expect a fight," Mr. Hansen said. "_____ is okay, but don't fight over your disagreements."
    (A) calumny . . . Litigation
    (B) dissent . . . Contingency
    (C) contingency . . . Dissension
    (D) retaliation . . . Calumny
    (E) litigation . . . Salinization

28. "Yvonne, you don't have to _____ or withdraw your views. But some people may react as though you had poured a very salty or _____ solution on an open wound!"
    (A) mollify . . . dissentient
    (B) recant . . . saline
    (C) dissent . . . calumnious
    (D) litigate . . . impassive
    (E) recant . . . retaliatory

29. The discussion jumped to current _____ about women's rights. "Would Astell have _____ from or agreed with the motives behind these lawsuits?" Mr. Hansen asked.
    (A) contingencies . . . retaliated
    (B) dissents . . . recanted
    (C) litigation . . . dissented
    (D) calumnies . . . mollified
    (E) salinization . . . dissented

30. "Astell would not be _____, or appeased, as long as society imposed a 'cloud of ignorance' over women," Amy said. "Her willingness to _____, her refusal to conform, should inspire women today."
    (A) mollified . . . dissent
    (B) dissented . . . mollify
    (C) retaliated . . . recant
    (D) recanted . . . retaliate
    (E) retaliated . . . dissent

MAKING NEW WORDS YOUR OWN

Lesson 20 | CONTEXT: History and Society
The Letters of Lady Mary Wortley Montagu

As a letter writer, Lady Mary Wortley Montagu (1689–1762) should be an inspiration to all of us today. Lady Montagu, a socially prominent, learned English author, lived during a time in which people corresponded extensively through personal letters. Almost nine hundred of Lady Montagu's letters are in print. In amusing and lively correspondence with her husband, daughter, and sister, Lady Montagu recorded nearly all the major events of her life. Among her letters are many describing adventures in Turkey during the two years that her husband was England's ambassador to Constantinople.

In the following exercises, you will have the opportunity to expand your vocabulary by reading about Lady Mary Wortley Montagu. Below are ten vocabulary words that will be used in these exercises.

auspices	clandestine	hiatus	solicitous	vestige
austerity	foment	obese	temerity	vindicate

EXERCISE 1 Mapping

Directions. In the item below, a vocabulary word is provided and used in a sentence. Take a guess at the word's meaning and write it in the box labeled **Your Guess**. Then look the word up in your dictionary and write the definition in the box labeled **Definition**. In the **Other Forms** box, write as many other forms of the word, such as adjective and noun forms, as you can think of or find in your dictionary.

Then, following the same procedure, draw your own map for each of the nine remaining vocabulary words. Use a separate sheet of paper.

1.

auspices → A series of programs about great letter writers and the art of letter writing was presented recently under the **auspices** of the city's library board, which had never supported such a project before. The first program focused on Lady Mary Wortley Montagu.

Your Guess:

Other Forms:

Definition:

2.

Lady Montagu was a colorful character who enjoyed the benefits and privileges of being a wealthy and prominent aristocrat. Her life was not one of **austerity,** but one of lavishness and self-gratification.

3.

Her father, Evelyn Pierrepont, the duke of Kingston, disapproved of her courtship with Edward Wortley Montagu. The couple **clandestinely** eloped, probably after a number of equally secret meetings.

4.

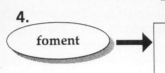

Lady Montagu did not **foment** national rebellions, but she did stir up a lot of controversy. She was educated and outspoken in a time when women were supposed to be neither.

5.

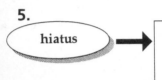

The program instructor read aloud one of the letters Lady Montagu had written while living in Turkey. I would have preferred to hear the entire letter without interruption, but there were several **hiatuses** in the instructor's presentation.

6.

Some of us at the program naturally wondered what Lady Montagu looked like—whether she was thin or **obese,** for example—but the instructor had never seen a picture of her and did not know.

7.

The instructor was **solicitous** to turn the discussion to information with which she was more familiar, especially concerning Lady Montagu's activities at the center of a London literary circle. We shared her eagerness.

8.

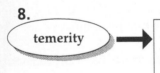

Some people of her time criticized what they considered Lady Montagu's **temerity** in publicly displaying her education. Lady Montagu realized that her actions and opinions were often considered recklessly bold.

9.

Lady Montagu wrote that "there is hardly a character in the world more despicable, or more liable to universal ridicule, than that of a learned woman." Do you detect a **vestige,** or trace, of sarcasm in her comment?

10.

Lady Montagu, who wrote that she had an innate passion for learning, often had to **vindicate** her interest in acquiring knowledge. She justified an interest in reading by stating, "No entertainment is so cheap as reading, nor any pleasure so lasting."

EXERCISE 2 *Context Clues* ✍

Directions. Scan the definitions in Column A. Then think about how the boldface words are used in the sentences in Column B. To complete the exercise, match each definition in Column A with the correct vocabulary word from Column B. Write the letter of your choice on the line provided; then write the vocabulary word on the line preceding the definition.

COLUMN A

_____ **11.** word: _____
v. to clear of suspicion or blame; to justify or support

_____ **12.** word: _____
adj. extremely overweight

_____ **13.** word: _____
n. reckless boldness; rashness; foolhardiness

_____ **14.** word: _____
n. severe simplicity; severity of appearance, attitude, or manner; harsh self-discipline; economy or thrift

_____ **15.** word: _____
v. to foster trouble, rebellion, or strife; to stir up; to incite

_____ **16.** word: _____
adj. showing concern or worry; anxiously concerned; eager

_____ **17.** word: _____
n. approval and support; patronage

_____ **18.** word: _____
n. a space where something is missing; any break in continuity

_____ **19.** word: _____
adj. concealed, usually for a forbidden purpose; secret; covert

_____ **20.** word: _____
n. a slight remnant; a trace of something that no longer exists; a bit; a trace

COLUMN B

(A) There was a twenty-minute intermission during the library program. We were told that the discussion about Lady Montagu would resume after the **hiatus**.

(B) I didn't want to stand around and eat fatty snacks during the intermission. After all, I don't want to become **obese**.

(C) I needed to talk to my friend Leslie in secret. While no one was noticing us, we went upstairs for a **clandestine** meeting.

(D) I had heard that Leslie had been **fomenting** trouble by getting the library board angry.

(E) I wanted to give Leslie a chance to **vindicate** herself of the charges if she was not to blame.

(F) Leslie explained, "I want future series to be held under the **auspices** of the Literary Guild, which is eager to support programs like this."

(G) "The library board has little money and must practice **austerity**, but the Literary Guild is well financed now," she said.

(H) "I'm concerned about the **vestige**, or trace, of hostility that still exists between the library board and the Literary Guild," she said.

(I) I couldn't believe my own **temerity** in speaking to Leslie, but my boldness didn't seem to upset her.

(J) Leslie was unexpectedly **solicitous** toward me, concerned that I had been worried about her talks with the board.

EXERCISE 3 *Sentence Completion* ✍

Directions. For each of the following items, circle the letter of the choice that best completes the meaning of the sentence or sentences.

21. When we resumed the meeting, the instructor discussed Lady Montagu's _____ and said some people accused her of recklessness.
    (A) temerity
    (B) hiatus
    (C) auspices
    (D) vestige
    (E) austerity

22. She read a rather strange letter in which Lady Montagu was _____ about her granddaughter, apparently worried about the girl's future.
    (A) clandestine
    (B) solicitous
    (C) temerarious
    (D) obese
    (E) hiatal

23. Lady Montagu apparently did not have even a slight trace, or _____, of hope that her granddaughter could ever get married.
    (A) hiatus
    (B) austerity
    (C) auspice
    (D) temerity
    (E) vestige

24. "I hope the problem wasn't that the girl was too thin or too fat," Dorothy said. "Whether a person is skinny or _____, he or she should be judged on character, not on physical appearance."
    (A) solicitous
    (B) clandestine
    (C) austere
    (D) obese
    (E) vestigial

25. In the letter, Lady Montagu tries to _____, or support, her claim that learning will make the girl content and happy.
    (A) foment
    (B) dissent
    (C) vindicate
    (D) impair
    (E) recant

26. Perhaps the girl and her mother went off in secret for _____ meetings. Away from the family, the concerned mother would _____ discuss Lady Montagu's letter.
    (A) obese . . . austerely
    (B) hiatal . . . vestigially
    (C) clandestine . . . solicitously
    (D) solicitous . . . austerely
    (E) obese . . . solicitously

27. "Was Lady Montagu trying to _____ trouble between her daughter and granddaughter?" Dorothy asked. "She sounds rash; it took _____ to write such a letter."
    (A) foment . . . austerity
    (B) vindicate . . . vestige
    (C) recant . . . hiatus
    (D) dissent . . . auspice
    (E) foment . . . temerity

28. "Lady Montagu should have helped the granddaughter, putting her under her _____," Leslie said. "Do you find _____, or trace, of real love in the letter?"
    (A) austerities . . . a temerity
    (B) auspices . . . a vestige
    (C) vestiges . . . an austerity
    (D) hiatuses . . . an auspice
    (E) austerities . . . a hiatus

29. "Some people suspect that the granddaughter had a severe attitude, _____ that scared away suitors. But perhaps I'm only trying to _____ Lady Montagu, hoping to make her seem less hardhearted," the instructor said.
    (A) an austerity . . . vindicate
    (B) a vestige . . . foment
    (C) a hiatus . . . dissent
    (D) an auspice . . . vindicate
    (E) a temerity . . . foment

30. "There may have been _____ of some years since Lady Montagu last saw her granddaughter. The lapse of time may have clouded her judgment," I said, _____ that Lady Montagu not be unfairly criticized.
    (A) a vestige . . . obese
    (B) a temerity . . . clandestine
    (C) a hiatus . . . solicitous
    (D) an austerity . . . temerarious
    (E) an auspice . . . hiatal

MAKING NEW WORDS YOUR OWN

Lesson 21 | CONTEXT: Science and Technology

From Alchemy to Chemistry: The Development of Science in England

Scientific research and the resulting discoveries play an important part in shaping the modern world, yet science as we know it today is a fairly recent development. Modern British chemistry, for example, dates only from about the seventeenth century. Chemistry has its roots in alchemy, an early form of chemistry practiced during the Middle Ages. The primary aims of alchemy were to change base metals into gold and to find a substance that would cure all ailments and prolong life. The development of chemistry from alchemy illustrates the evolving role of science in England from the fifteenth through the twentieth centuries. Because the different branches of science were not distinct until the 1600s, the term chemist is used here to refer to someone who studies both chemistry and related disciplines.

In the following exercises, you will have the opportunity to expand your vocabulary by reading about the development of science in England. Below are ten vocabulary words that will be used in these exercises.

differentiate	empirical	officious	renounce	testimonial
disparity	facetious	quiescent	scathing	treatise

EXERCISE 1 *Mapping*

Directions. In the item below, a vocabulary word is provided and used in a sentence. Take a guess at the word's meaning and write it in the box labeled **Your Guess**. Then look the word up in your dictionary and write the definition in the box labeled **Definition**. In the **Other Forms** box, write as many other forms of the word, such as adjective and noun forms, as you can think of or find in your dictionary.

Then, following the same procedure, draw your own map for each of the nine remaining vocabulary words. Use a separate sheet of paper.

1.

differentiate →

Paracelsus (1493–1541), a Swiss scholar, helped to **differentiate**, or distinguish, chemistry from alchemy. He rejected the alchemist's traditional search for a way to turn base metal into gold; instead, as a modern chemist might do, he identified chemical reactions that could cure diseases.

Your Guess:

Other Forms:

Definition:

2.

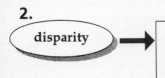

A great **disparity**, or inequality, exists between the recognition given to Mary Boyle (c. 1626–1678), a little-known scientist, and her brother, the famous chemist Robert Boyle (1627–1691).

3.

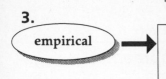

The English physician William Harvey (1578–1657), by performing various experiments, **empirically** demonstrated that blood circulation begins in the heart.

4.

Satirist Jonathan Swift's witty depiction of the Academy of Projectors in *Gulliver's Travels* is very **facetious**, showing misguided scientists attempting to extract sunshine from cucumbers.

5.

The Italian author and chemist Primo Levi (1919–1987) satirized British chemists through his comic portrayal of the character Caselli, a meddlesome, **officious** servant to an English professor of chemistry.

6.

British chemists today cannot remain **quiescent**, or inactive, in the face of industrial pollution; their contributions are necessary to help solve such environmental problems.

7.

Seventeenth-century scientists, such as Harvey and Boyle, pursued scientific inquiry for its own sake. But scientists today, concerned with the practical application of their work, have **renounced**, or turned their backs on, this approach to research.

8.

Robert Boyle had to defend his first important work against **scathing** criticism. It is remarkable that Boyle persisted in his efforts when faced with such harsh judgment of his work.

9.

Two men received the Nobel Prize for their roles in the discovery of the structure of the DNA molecule. But a woman, Rosalind Franklin (1920-1958), received little **testimonial**, or tribute, for her contribution to the discovery.

10.

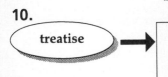

A. Sayre's **treatise** *Rosalind Franklin and DNA: A Vivid View of What It Is Like to be a Gifted Woman in an Especially Male Profession* (1975), which is in our library's collection, is an extensive discussion of Rosalind Franklin's case.

EXERCISE 2   Context Clues ✍

Directions. Scan the definitions in Column A. Then think about how the boldface words are used in the sentences in Column B. To complete the exercise, match each definition in Column A with the correct vocabulary word from Column B. Write the letter of your choice on the line provided; then write the vocabulary word on the line preceding the definition.

COLUMN A	COLUMN B

_____ **11.** word: _____

n. inequality; difference; unlikeness

_____ **12.** word: _____

v. to give up; to abandon; to cast off something; to disown; to repudiate

_____ **13.** word: _____

adj. too ready to please, praise, or obey; meddlesome; offering unwanted or unneeded advice or comments

_____ **14.** word: _____

adj. harsh or caustic; extremely severe or bitter

_____ **15.** word: _____

adj. joking; said in fun; meant to be amusing

_____ **16.** word: _____

adj. based on experiment and observation; based entirely on practical experience rather than theory

_____ **17.** word: _____

v. to make or become different; to tell the difference between; to note differences

_____ **18.** word: _____

n. a formal, written discussion of a subject

_____ **19.** word: _____

n. inactivity; quietness; stillness

_____ **20.** word: _____

n. a recommendation of a person or product; a tribute to a person's accomplishments

(A) Robert Boyle's **treatise** *The Skeptical Chemist* (1661), widely read in its day, paved the way for the science of modern chemistry.

(B) We can **differentiate** chemical engineering from chemistry in the following way: chemical engineering applies the principles of chemistry to industrial uses.

(C) Chemistry became possible when scientists, starting in about the sixteenth century, **renounced** their alchemical practices, turning their backs on the futile quest to turn base metals into gold.

(D) The English chemist and physicist John Dalton (1766–1844) developed theories from **empirical** evidence gathered through years of meticulous observation.

(E) The Victorian era was not a time of **quiescence** for the field of chemistry. On the contrary, there was great activity in the field, and the number of recognized chemical elements increased steadily throughout the period.

(F) Only recently has the **disparity** between women's scientific achievements and the actual recognition of these achievements been acknowledged.

(G) The statue of John Dalton in Manchester, England, is a **testimonial** to his scientific contributions.

(H) In a **scathing** criticism of Robert Boyle's atomic theory, science historian Stephen F. Mason harshly judges Boyle, claiming that Boyle failed to give a complete and accurate description of known chemical properties.

(I) When chemists publish their articles in scholarly journals, they must expect that at least one **officious** critic will make trivial or worthless comments.

(J) Princeton professor Charles Coulson Gillispie, seeing the humor in his subject, writes in a **facetious** tone about John Dalton's inexact chemical methods.

EXERCISE 3 *Sentence Completion* ✍

Directions. In each of the following items, circle the letter of the choice that best completes the meaning of the sentence or sentences.

21. Robert Boyle's appreciation for _____ observation helped establish the use of the experimental method.
(A) officious
(B) empirical
(C) quiescent
(D) scathing
(E) facetious

22. Author Trevor Levere is being _____ when he remarks jokingly that British chemist Humphrey Davy's high opinion of himself was rivaled only by his achievements.
(A) disparate
(B) facetious
(C) officious
(D) empirical
(E) quiescent

23. Chemist Dorothy Hodgkin (b. 1910) discovered a _____ between her salary and the higher salaries of her male colleagues.
(A) disparity
(B) treatise
(C) testimonial
(D) quiescence
(E) residual

24. You can _____ the discoveries of Ernest Rutherford and Henry G. J. Moseley by remembering that Rutherford found that each atom has a nucleus, while Moseley discovered that the atoms of each element have a unique number of protons.
(A) recant
(B) prevaricate
(C) renounce
(D) differentiate
(E) deplore

25. The in-depth _____ that would later be published as the *Handbook of Chemical Engineering* was first published by its author, England's George E. Davis.
(A) testimonial
(B) treatise
(C) chicanery
(D) proponent
(E) disparity

26. Hazel P. Gump's (1912–1992) professional progress was hampered by the interference of her _____, meddlesome assistant. Perhaps this explains why no memorials have been erected as _____ to Gump's contributions.
(A) officious . . . testimonials
(B) quiescent . . . treatises
(C) scathing . . . disparities
(D) facetious . . . treatises
(E) empirical . . . testimonials

27. Faced with the observable, _____ evidence of industrial pollution, British chemists could no longer be _____, or inactive.
(A) quiescent . . . facetious
(B) disparate . . . empirical
(C) empirical . . . quiescent
(D) officious . . . empirical
(E) empirical . . . disparate

28. Paracelsus made the harshly humorous, _____ comment that his shoebuckles knew more than his colleagues. This _____ observation probably brought few smiles.
(A) scathing . . . facetious
(B) facetious . . . quiescent
(C) officious . . . scathing
(D) officious . . . facetious
(E) quiescent . . . officious

29. Since England _____ its colonization of India, giving up its claim to that country in 1947, Indian scientists have been able to clearly _____ their achievements from those of British scientists.
(A) differentiated . . . renounce
(B) renounced . . . vindicate
(C) renounced . . . differentiate
(D) differentiated . . . cajole
(E) differentiated . . . prevaricate

30. Henry Moseley's experiments in physical chemistry helped scientists _____, or distinguish, the atoms of the various elements. More recent _____ studies, consisting of controlled laboratory experiments, have supported Moseley's findings.
(A) renounce . . . scathing
(B) differentiate . . . quiescent
(C) renounce . . . officious
(D) differentiate . . . empirical
(E) differentiate . . . facetious

MAKING NEW WORDS YOUR OWN

Lesson 22 | **CONTEXT: Science and Technology**

Imperialism: Technology's Child

Britain became a world power as a result of the technological advances of the Industrial Revolution. Advances in shipbuilding and the refinement of the factory system helped Britain to establish and maintain control of one of its greatest colonies: India.

At the time of colonization by Britain, Indians wore garments made inexpensively from Indian-grown cotton that was hand-spun and hand-woven into cloth, but this changed with the technological advances that occurred in the British textile industry. The British government required the export of inexpensive cotton from India to England, where cloth was manufactured by British workers. Under British rule, Indians no longer wove their own cloth but had to buy it from the British. Mohandas K. Gandhi (1869–1948) perceived the unfairness of this system. His solution was to boycott British manufacturers and encourage Indians to spin and weave their own cloth. This rejection of Western technology helped India regain its independence.

In the exercises below, you will have the opportunity to expand your vocabulary by reading about the role of technology in India's struggle for independence. Below are ten vocabulary words that will be used in these exercises.

chauvinism	devoid	inexorable	regimen	sagacity
cosmopolitan	epitome	moot	repository	tenuous

EXERCISE 1   *Mapping*

Directions. In the item below, a vocabulary word is provided and used in a sentence. Take a guess at the word's meaning and write it in the box labeled **Your Guess**. Then look the word up in your dictionary and write the definition in the box labeled **Definition**. In the **Other Forms** box, write as many other forms of the word, such as adjective and noun forms, as you can think of or find in your dictionary.

Then, following the same procedure, draw your own map for each of the nine remaining vocabulary words. Use a separate sheet of paper.

1.

(chauvinism) ➡️ In retrospect, the fierce patriotism of the colonial powers seems **chauvinistic**, as it is based on a biased belief in Western superiority.

⬇️

Your Guess:

⬇️

Other Forms: ⬅️ **Definition:**

2.

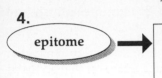

Colonization brought people of diverse cultures together, resulting in the evolution of new, more **cosmopolitan** societies.

3.

English leaders who financed early expeditions were so concerned with profit that they seemed **devoid** of conscience. Their primary consideration was capital gain, not the survival of the colonists.

4.

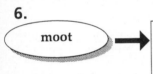

The **epitome** of British imperialism was the East India Company. This representative example of the colonial power's business interests was able to establish trading posts all along the coast of India through gifts and bribes.

5.

When internal disorder broke out in India, the British turned their trading posts into forts. This, combined with the superior military power of the English, made the British domination of India seem **inexorable** and unstoppable.

6.

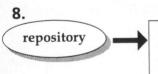

What would be the condition of the Indian economy today if colonization had never taken place? A **moot**, or debatable, question like this can never be conclusively answered.

7.

Warren Hastings, Lord Charles Cornwallis, and Richard Wellesley continued the **regimen** of British imperialism. By the beginning of the nineteenth century, the system that had been put in place enabled London to control India.

8.

The inventions and improved manufacturing techniques of the Industrial Revolution made Britain a **repository** of advanced technology; it was a storehouse for the most up-to-date technological information.

9.

sagacity

Mohandas "Mahatma" Gandhi is renowned for his **sagacity** as a leader. Gandhi's wisdom and sound judgment enabled him to lead successful campaigns of nonviolent resistance in India and South Africa.

10.

tenuous

The British were often overconfident, and it was in the places where the British considered their rule to be strongest that the Indian resistance proved British rule **tenuous**. The British were shaken to discover that their hold on India was far less substantial than they had assumed.

EXERCISE 2 · Context Clues ✍

Directions. Scan the definitions in Column A. Then think about how the words are used in the sentences in Column B. To complete the exercise, match each definition in Column A with the correct vocabulary word from Column B. Write the letter of your choice on the line provided; then write the vocabulary word on the line preceding the definition.

COLUMN A	COLUMN B

_____ **11.** word: _____

n. fanatical patriotism; biased belief in the superiority of one's own group, sex, or nation

_____ **12.** word: _____

n. a person or thing typical of an entire class; an ideal example; a summary

_____ **13.** word: _____

adj. unalterable; relentless

_____ **14.** word: _____

adj. international; beyond national boundaries; having great worldly experience; sophisticated; at home anywhere

_____ **15.** word: _____

adj. entirely without; empty; totally lacking

_____ **16.** word: _____

n. a center for storage; a place where things are put for safekeeping; a person to whom something is confided or entrusted

_____ **17.** word: _____

n. a system of government; a system for improving health

_____ **18.** word: _____

n. keen, sound judgment; mental acuteness; shrewdness

_____ **19.** word: _____

adj. thin; not substantial; flimsy

_____ **20.** word: _____

adj. debatable; arguable; unresolved; not worth further discussion or debate

(A) Mohandas "Mahatma" Gandhi challenged the seemingly **inexorable** power of British imperialism in India by condemning the relentless mechanization of industry.

(B) Gandhi prescribed a **regimen** for the Indian people that included the wearing of only hand-spun and hand-woven cloth. This prescribed system was just one of the methods the Indians used to protest British rule.

(C) The British East India Company was the **epitome** of the workings of British imperialism; it embodied all the qualities that made colonial power so relentless and all-encompassing.

(D) Gandhi's humble demeanor and the loincloth he usually wore made it easy to forget his **cosmopolitan** background. His experiences in other countries made him more worldly and sophisticated than his appearance suggested.

(E) British **chauvinism** was demonstrated in the belief that Britain was better fit to rule India than India itself was.

(F) The British port at Surat was once a **repository** of goods that were being kept safe for shipment to Europe.

(G) Although the British called the fort at Surat a factory, there was nothing in the fort to suggest that it was devoted to manufacturing; the fort was, in fact, **devoid** of industrial equipment.

(H) Gandhi's **sagacity** as a leader eventually convinced many British people of India's right to govern itself, for they recognized that Gandhi was a wise, shrewd man.

(I) Gandhi's argument for a single, unified India became **moot**; it was debated by people all over the world.

(J) After Gandhi popularized the concept of Indian independence, the British hold on India became increasingly **tenuous** and flimsy.

EXERCISE 3 *Sentence Completion*

Directions. For each of the following items, circle the letter of the choice that best completes the meaning of the sentence or sentences.

21. The British were able to maintain control of India for nearly one hundred years. Some see that as a testament to the _____, or shrewdness, of British administrators.
    (A) repository
    (B) austerity
    (C) tenuousness
    (D) sagacity
    (E) epitome

22. The British _____ in India, run according to British preferences, was often accused of being _____ of concern for the Indian people—completely lacking in consideration.
    (A) regimen . . . devoid
    (B) regimen . . . inexorable
    (C) repository . . . moot
    (D) repository . . . devoid
    (E) sagacity . . . devoid

23. The _____, or representative example, of British _____ can be found in the attitudes of British colonials. They believed absolutely in the superiority of Britain.
    (A) chauvinism . . . epitome
    (B) repository . . . sagacity
    (C) epitome . . . chauvinism
    (D) repository . . . regimen
    (E) regimen . . . sagacity

24. Gandhi had _____ education and experience, gained through university study in London, work in South Africa, and extensive travel throughout India.
    (A) an inexorable
    (B) a tenuous
    (C) a moot
    (D) a chauvinistic
    (E) a cosmopolitan

25. Many considered Gandhi a supreme example of a world leader, the _____ of a wise and just statesman whose _____ served his people well.
    (A) repository . . . regimen
    (B) repository . . . tenuousness
    (C) repository . . . chauvinism
    (D) epitome . . . sagacity
    (E) regimen . . . sagacity

26. Gandhi's treatise *Hind Swaraj* is the _____ of many of his central ideas, the accumulation of his most important thoughts.
    (A) subversion
    (B) regimen
    (C) repository
    (D) sagacity
    (E) chauvinism

27. Critics accused Gandhi of having a _____ grasp of reality. They felt that because he was anti-industrial, his practical sense must be weak and flimsy.
    (A) cosmopolitan
    (B) devoid
    (C) inexorable
    (D) moot
    (E) tenuous

28. Popular opposition to the British salt tax was made irrelevant by the Irwin-Gandhi agreement, which permitted the making of salt for personal use. Further argument or debate on the issue became _____.
    (A) tenuous
    (B) moot
    (C) inexorable
    (D) chauvinistic
    (E) cosmopolitan

29. The seemingly _____, relentless domination of India by the British became _____ when India finally achieved independence.
    (A) inexorable . . . moot
    (B) cosmopolitan . . . inexorable
    (C) moot . . . tenuous
    (D) inexorable . . . devoid
    (E) cosmopolitan . . . moot

30. Some people may have only a _____, vague understanding of the cultural diversity and _____ nature of India's cities, which include people from all parts of the world.
    (A) cosmopolitan . . . tenuous
    (B) inexorable . . . cosmopolitan
    (C) cosmopolitan . . . inexorable
    (D) tenuous . . . cosmopolitan
    (E) tenuous . . . sagacious

MAKING NEW WORDS YOUR OWN

Lesson 23 **CONTEXT:** Science and Technology

Of Chimneys and Chimney Sweeps

Most of us have been familiar with stories about chimneys since childhood. Both "good guys"—Santa Claus—and "bad guys"—the Big Bad Wolf—use chimneys. Some of us still heat our homes with wood and depend on chimneys to draw the smoke from the fireplace, stove, or furnace. We take chimneys for granted today. I learned a lot about chimneys from talking to Tom, our chimney sweep, while he was cleaning our chimney. One of the things I learned was that the first really useful chimney stacks date from the eleventh and twelfth centuries in Europe.

In the following exercises, you will have the opportunity to expand your vocabulary by reading about chimneys and chimney sweeps. Below are ten vocabulary words that will be used in these exercises.

bode	coerce	firmament	mete	mottled
burnish	esoteric	gauntlet	misnomer	terra firma

EXERCISE 1 *Mapping*

Directions. In the item below, a vocabulary word is provided and used in a sentence. Take a guess at the word's meaning and write it in the box labeled **Your Guess**. Then look the word up in your dictionary and write the definition in the box labeled **Definition**. In the **Other Forms** box, write as many other forms of the word, such as adjective and noun forms, as you can think of or find in your dictionary.

Then, following the same procedure, draw your own map for each of the nine remaining vocabulary words. Use a separate sheet of paper.

1.

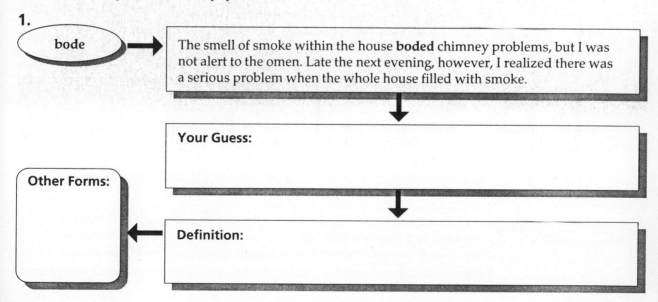

bode ➝ The smell of smoke within the house **boded** chimney problems, but I was not alert to the omen. Late the next evening, however, I realized there was a serious problem when the whole house filled with smoke.

Your Guess:

Other Forms:

Definition:

2.

(burnish) → The exterior of the wood stove in the den looked fine. I had recently polished the bronze decorations on the stove's door and legs, and the **burnish** gave the stove a glossy, new look.

3.

(coerce) → Since the problem was with the chimney, I quickly called Tom, our local chimney sweep, and asked if I could **coerce** him to come out on a cold winter's night. "When there's a problem, you don't have to force me to get moving," Tom told me.

4.

(esoteric) → Chimney sweeping had always seemed like an **esoteric** profession to me because I did not understand exactly what it involved. Tom was born in London and learned the profession there.

5.

(firmament) → I'm sure you've seen pictures of English chimney sweeps, dressed in top hats and black suits, walking across the roofs of London, their only companions the twinkling stars in the **firmament** above. I think I got my mental picture of chimney sweeps from the movie *Mary Poppins*.

6.

(gauntlet) → Tom doesn't look anything like my mental picture of a chimney sweep. I'd probably be disappointed, too, if I could see a real medieval knight because he probably wouldn't be wearing a visored helmet on his head or shiny **gauntlets** protecting his hands.

7.

(mete) → Smoke was filling the house, and I was willing to take whatever advice Tom would give me. Since I obviously had neglected the chimney, he probably would **mete** out some deserving reprimands.

8.

(misnomer) → "This chimney is a mess," Tom said after climbing up his ladder and onto the roof. "Calling this a chimney is a **misnomer** because its real name should be *smoke stopper*."

9.

(mottled) → Tom reached into the chimney and started pulling out huge, hard chunks of **mottled** soot. The dark blotches and streaks actually made an interesting design, but I was horrified that Tom was pulling the chunks out of my chimney.

10.

(terra firma) → I always get nervous if I or anyone around me is in a high place. It made me uneasy to see Tom so far off the ground. I was glad my feet were solidly on **terra firma**.

EXERCISE 2 *Context Clues* ✍

Directions. Scan the definitions in Column A. Then think about how the boldface words are used in the sentences in Column B. To complete the exercise, match each definition in Column A with the correct vocabulary word from column B. Write the letter of your choice on the line provided; then write the vocabulary word on the line preceding the definition.

COLUMN A	COLUMN B

COLUMN A

_____ **11.** word: _____
n. the expanse of the heavens; the sky

_____ **12.** word: _____
v. to be a sign or omen of; to portend

_____ **13.** word: _____
n. a long, heavy, protective glove; a metal-plated glove, part of a knight's armor

_____ **14.** word: _____
adj. marked with spots, blotches, or streaks of different colors

_____ **15.** word: _____
n. a wrong name; an error in naming a person, place, or thing

_____ **16.** word: _____
n. solid earth; firm ground

_____ **17.** word: _____
v. to polish; to make shiny by rubbing; *n.* a glossy finish; a luster

_____ **18.** word: _____
adj. intended for or understood by only a few; confidential; private

_____ **19.** word: _____
v. to give according to measure or one's judgement; to allot or distribute

_____ **20.** word: _____
v. to compel; to force; to dominate or restrain by force

COLUMN B

(A) "Your gloves don't look sturdy enough for that work," I told Tom. "What you need is a knight's metal **gauntlet**!"

(B) "These poles will do," Tom said, pointing to long instruments that he had brought with him. He must have **burnished** them because they shone.

(C) "Isn't it a **misnomer** to call you a chimney sweep?" I asked. "I mean, you don't really sweep the chimney."

(D) "Well, sweeping is cleaning, and I'm cleaning with the stiff brush on this pole," Tom replied, pausing to watch a plane streak across the **firmament** which was becoming cloudy.

(E) "I'd better hurry," he said. "Those clouds signal a change in the weather—they may **bode** more snow."

(F) Spots of soot covered Tom's face. His **mottled** face and tired expression looked comical in the moonlight.

(G) "If I could, I'd stay up on a roof all day and all night," Tom said with a sigh as he climbed down the ladder to **terra firma**.

(H) Tom motioned me to him as if he were going to give me some **esoteric** or confidential bit of knowledge.

(I) "I have some advice to **mete** out to you—burn your wood hotter and clean your chimney more often," Tom said.

(J) "I can't **coerce** you into getting your chimney cleaned regularly," he continued, "but what has happened tonight should compel you to do so."

EXERCISE 3 *Sentence Completion* ✍

Directions. For each of the following items, circle the letter of the choice that best completes the meaning of the sentence or sentences.

21. "I once started reading about how chimneys work," I told Tom, "but the information seemed _____, like it was written solely for chimney engineers."
    (A) burnished
    (B) mottled
    (C) esoteric
    (D) firmamental
    (E) gauntleted

22. "I always think of fireplaces as signs of comfort and security. Do you think chimneys always _____ comfort, Tom?"
    (A) burnish
    (B) renounce
    (C) coerce
    (D) malign
    (E) bode

23. "If they are not stopped up," Tom said, trying to _____ his dirty poles with a polishing cloth.
    (A) coerce
    (B) malign
    (C) mete
    (D) burnish
    (E) bode

24. "I may have to throw these gloves away," he said, laughing, "and maybe buy some metal plates to make _____!"
    (A) gauntlets
    (B) misnomers
    (C) firmaments
    (D) coercions
    (E) terra firma

25. "My son, Little Tom—a _____ since he is six-feet tall—is a good metalworker," Tom said.
    (A) firmament
    (B) misnomer
    (C) terra firma
    (D) burnish
    (E) gauntlet

26. "He wants to be a chimney sweep, too. I'm not _____ him to follow in my footsteps, though, anymore than I am forcing him to walk on solid ground, or _____."
    (A) meting . . . firmament
    (B) burnishing . . . misnomer
    (C) coercing . . . terra firma
    (D) meting . . . gauntlet
    (E) coercing . . . burnish

27. "Look up!" I said, pointing into the _____. "That smoke from my newly opened chimney _____ well for a warm evening indoors."
    (A) misnomer . . . coerces
    (B) burnish . . . metes
    (C) gauntlet . . . bodes
    (D) firmament . . . bodes
    (E) terra firma . . . coerces

28. I grew dizzy just looking so far above _____, which was solid beneath my feet. My last name, Skyway, is a real _____!
    (A) burnish . . . terra firma
    (B) gauntlet . . . firmament
    (C) terra firma . . . burnish
    (D) misnomer . . . gauntlet
    (E) terra firma . . . misnomer

29. Tom's clothes were _____, and I didn't know if the soot blotches would come out. I supposed he had some _____ method of cleaning soot that only chimney sweeps know.
    (A) esoteric . . . mottled
    (B) gauntleted . . . firmamental
    (C) burnished . . . gauntleted
    (D) mottled . . . esoteric
    (E) firmamental . . . mottled

30. My wife _____ out cups of hot cider for our good work in cleaning out the chimney. As we drank it, Tom pointed out to us the constellations in the _____.
    (A) meted . . . firmament
    (B) coerced . . . burnish
    (C) boded . . . misnomer
    (D) meted . . . gauntlet
    (E) boded . . . terra firma

MAKING NEW WORDS YOUR OWN

Lesson 24 │ CONTEXT: Science and Technology
Clocks: Once Upon a Time

Once upon a time, there were no clocks as we know them. Sundials and water clocks were used to mark time in the ancient world. Mechanical clocks first started to appear in the thirteenth century in Europe. Town clocks with chimes that struck the hours appeared in Europe in the late fourteenth century. Household clocks and even wristwatches were used in England and the Netherlands by the sixteenth century. By this time the balance spring had been introduced, and clocks had become much more accurate. Today, we have electric clocks, quartz clocks, and clocks run by electronic chips—all of which keep time with an accuracy undreamed of when the first mechanical clocks came into use.

Imagine a conversation in which two medieval men debate the value of a newfangled invention: the mechanical clock. What would people in the Middle Ages think of such an invention?

In the following exercises, you will have the opportunity to expand your vocabulary by reading about clocks in the Middle Ages. Below are ten vocabulary words that will be used in these exercises.

acrimonious	benevolence	desist	expound	precursor
atrophy	consternation	enigma	loquacious	voluminous

EXERCISE 1   *Mapping*

Directions. In the item below, a vocabulary word is provided and used in a sentence. Take a guess at the word's meaning and write it in the box labeled **Your Guess**. Then look the word up in your dictionary and write the definition in the box labeled **Definition**. In the **Other Forms** box, write as many other forms of the word, such as adjective and noun forms, as you can think of or find in your dictionary.

Then, following the same procedure, draw your own map for each of the nine remaining vocabulary words. Use a separate sheet of paper.

1.

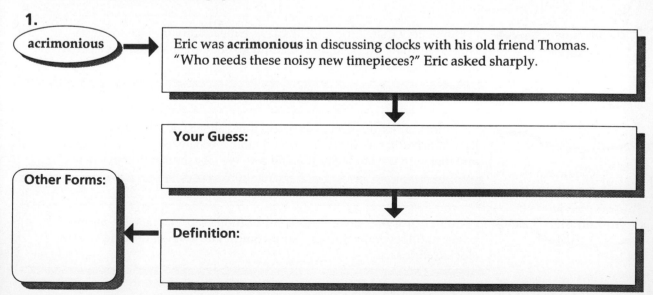

acrimonious → Eric was **acrimonious** in discussing clocks with his old friend Thomas. "Who needs these noisy new timepieces?" Eric asked sharply.

Your Guess:

Other Forms:

Definition:

2.

atrophy

"All I need to do is look at the sun in order to tell what time it is," Eric continued. "If I used a clock all the time, my mind would start to **atrophy**. It would slowly waste away from disuse."

3.

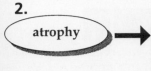
benevolence

Thomas laughed. "I am sure that you exaggerate," he said. "Don't you think that the city fathers are showing their **benevolence** in putting up a clock for the whole town? Such an act of kindness is rare, and we should be thankful for it."

4.

consternation

"I must confess, Thomas," Eric said, "that I am filled with **consternation** at their decision. I am shocked and dismayed that the city fathers think we need a clock more than new wells."

5.

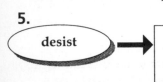
desist

"Please **desist** from protesting," Thomas said. "If you don't stop, others will follow your bad example, and there will be trouble throughout the town, all because of a clock."

6.

enigma

"Well," Eric said, "it is puzzling to me why people are fussing over this clock. Why everyone should want to know what time it is and run their lives accordingly is a real **enigma**. I can't figure it out."

7.

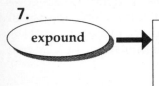
expound

"You should have come to the town meeting Tuesday night and listened to Mayor Goodman **expound** on the history and benefits of the mechanical clock," Thomas said. "He talked for a long time and even predicted that we would have clocks in our houses one day."

8.

loquacious

"I can believe that," Eric said. "I've never heard anyone else so **loquacious**; I am not surprised that he could go on and on about a topic as trivial and fleeting as clocks."

9.

precursor

"I say that clocks are **precursors** of bad times ahead," Eric continued. "I think they indicate that we'll have more and more mechanized tools in the future and that we'll use our brains less and less. We'll be the slaves of machines."

10.

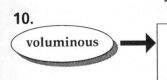
voluminous

"I don't care if the mayor posts a **voluminous** report, one with enough pages to fill several volumes. I still wouldn't be in favor of actually using clocks," Eric said.

EXERCISE 2 *Context Clues* ✍

Directions. Scan the definitions in Column A. Then think about how the boldface words are used in the sentences in Column B. To complete the exercise, match each definition in Column A with the correct vocabulary word from Column B. Write the letter of your choice on the line provided; then write the vocabulary word on the line preceding the definition.

COLUMN A	COLUMN B

_____ **11.** word: _____
n. a riddle or puzzle; something puzzling or unexplainable; a mystery

_____ **12.** word: _____
adj. very large; capable of filling volumes

_____ **13.** word: _____
n. great fear or shock that leaves one confused and bewildered; great dismay

_____ **14.** word: _____
adj. sharp or bitter in language or manner

_____ **15.** word: _____
n. something or someone that goes before and indicates what is to follow; a forerunner

_____ **16.** word: _____
v. to waste away; to wither; *n.* a wasting away, especially of a part or parts of the body

_____ **17.** word: _____
v. to interpret; to set forth or explain in detail

_____ **18.** word: _____
n. a desire to do good; an act of kindness or charity

_____ **19.** word: _____
n. to stop doing something; to cease; to abstain

_____ **20.** word: _____
adj. fond of talking; talkative

(A) "Please **expound** to me, if you can, your reasons for disliking clocks," Thomas said to Eric. "I'd like to hear the details."

(B) "If you must have help telling time, what is wrong with using a sundial?" Eric snapped. His **acrimonious** manner startled Thomas, who was not used to hearing a sharp and bitter tone from his friend.

(C) "It's no mystery: It's obvious that sundials are not practical on cloudy days," Thomas quickly replied. "Surely you can understand that people might prefer a time-telling instrument that can be used in all times and conditions. Why is this such an **enigma** to you?"

(D) "The mayor owns **voluminous** manuscripts about clocks," Eric said, "enough to fill a library. He should have much information about water clocks."

(E) "But everyone knows water clocks freeze," Thomas said in some **consternation**. He was shocked and surprised that Eric was so stubborn and single-minded on this subject.

(F) "You should **desist** from trying to think up substitutes for the mechanical clock," Thomas continued, "and cease your criticisms of clocks."

(G) "I think you should go visit the **loquacious** Mayor Goodman. As you know, he will gladly talk to you at length about clocks—or anything else, for that matter," Thomas said.

(H) "Mayor Goodman is a **precursor** of the coming mechanized world in which machines will tell us what to do," Eric said. "He's the forerunner of a way of life that I want nothing to do with."

(I) "Just as your muscles will **atrophy** if you don't exercise them," Eric continued, "your mind will weaken and waste away if you don't use it."

(J) "I appreciate your **benevolence,** Thomas," Eric said. "You are a good-hearted person who truly believes that mechanization will improve our lives. But I don't agree with your views."

EXERCISE 3 Sentence Completion ✍

Directions. For each of the following items, circle the letter of the choice that best completes the meaning of the sentence or sentences.

21. "I talked to Mayor Goodman," Eric told Thomas a few days later. "He was _____ and talked nonstop."
   (A) voluminous
   (B) acrimonious
   (C) atrophic
   (D) loquacious
   (E) precursory

22. "I think the whole town could _____ around him and become a wasteland while he was talking and he wouldn't realize it."
   (A) expound
   (B) atrophy
   (C) mete
   (D) consternate
   (E) desist

23. "He didn't convince me of anything," Eric said _____. "I'm still bitter and angry that the town is using funds to buy a clock instead of something we really need."
   (A) benevolently
   (B) enigmatically
   (C) loquaciously
   (D) impeccably
   (E) acrimoniously

24. "Goodman said he had a dream that the mechanical clock is the _____ of a tiny clock that people will be able to wear on their wrists with a band. If the clock is the forerunner of something like that, I say we're better off without it."
   (A) atrophy
   (B) enigma
   (C) precursor
   (D) consternation
   (E) benevolence

25. "My _____ was evident when he told me that," Eric said. "I told him that I really fear for civilization's future."
   (A) consternation
   (B) benevolence
   (C) atrophy
   (D) precursor
   (E) enigma

26. "I'm sure that he finds you _____," Thomas said with obvious sharpness, or _____. "You are puzzling and hard to figure out."
   (A) a consternation . . . precursor
   (B) a precursor . . . benevolence
   (C) an enigma . . . acrimoniousness
   (D) an atrophy . . . consternation
   (E) a benevolence . . . desistance

27. "Supporting statements for the town clock are _____; they could fill a great hall. But our town could _____ and die before you would accept the clock, Eric."
   (A) acrimonious . . . desist
   (B) loquacious . . . expound
   (C) enigmatic . . . desist
   (D) voluminous . . . atrophy
   (E) benevolent . . . expound

28. "What if I were to give you a mechanical clock, out of the _____ of my heart?" Thomas asked. "I suspect that you would doubt my good motives and feel that I was insulting you. Your reaction would be no _____, no mystery, to me."
   (A) consternation . . . precursor
   (B) enigma . . . atrophy
   (C) precursor . . . consternation
   (D) atrophy . . . benevolence
   (E) benevolence . . . enigma

29. "You're right, Thomas: I would stop you from giving me such a gift and also ask you to _____ from teasing me. Such an offer would seem to me to come out of ill will, not _____."
   (A) expound . . . consternation
   (B) desist . . . benevolence
   (C) atrophy . . . enigma
   (D) expound . . . precursor
   (E) desist . . . atrophy

30. "I could _____ for hours on the clock's benefits, to no avail," Thomas said, his _____ evident in his confused, bewildered expression.
   (A) desist . . . voluminosity
   (B) atrophy . . . precursor
   (C) expound . . . consternation
   (D) atrophy . . . benevolence
   (E) expound . . . precursor

MAKING NEW WORDS YOUR OWN

Lesson 25 | CONTEXT: Science and Technology

Electricity in England

"The day must come when electricity will be for everyone. . . ." declared French writer Émile Zola in *Travail* (1901). That day was just dawning in England, as well as throughout Europe and the United States. Scientists had been investigating electrical currents since around 1800. Since the 1880s, some major cities in England had been using electricity for street lights, in buildings and factories, and for transportation systems. Throughout England, electricity was still a luxury, but an electrical boom period had begun.

In the following exercises, you will have the opportunity to expand your vocabulary by reading about the development of electricity in England. Below are ten vocabulary words that will be used in these exercises.

assiduous	cessation	equanimity	inordinate	pecuniary
aver	denizen	iniquity	mercurial	tenable

EXERCISE 1 *Mapping*

Directions. In the item below, a vocabulary word is provided and used in a sentence. Take a guess at the word's meaning and write it in the box labeled **Your Guess**. Then look the word up in your dictionary and write the definition in the box labeled **Definition**. In the **Other Forms** box, write as many other forms of the word, such as adjective and noun forms, as you can think of or find in your dictionary.

Then, following the same procedure, draw your own map for each of the nine remaining vocabulary words. Use a separate sheet of paper.

1.

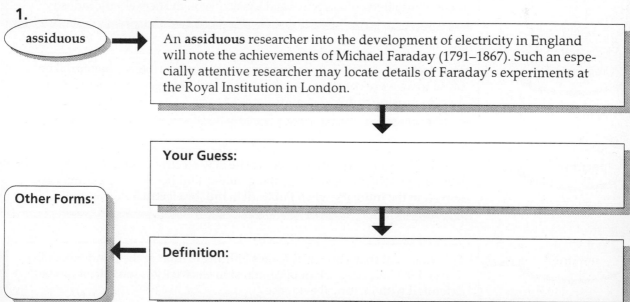

assiduous

An **assiduous** researcher into the development of electricity in England will note the achievements of Michael Faraday (1791–1867). Such an especially attentive researcher may locate details of Faraday's experiments at the Royal Institution in London.

Your Guess:

Other Forms:

Definition:

2.

aver → Historians declare that Faraday's experiments with converting electrical energy into mechanical energy in 1821 were extremely important. In these experiments, they also **aver,** Faraday demonstrated the principle of the electric motor.

3.

cessation → There was no **cessation** of Faraday's work then, however. Instead of "resting on his laurels," Faraday continued with his research. He found a way to generate a continuous electric current, thus discovering the principle of the generator.

4.

denizen → By the mid-1800s, Britain's inhabitants saw practical uses of electrical experiments by Faraday and others. For example, **denizens** around some lighthouses noticed that electric generators were producing arc lighting for the lighthouses.

5.

equanimity → Faraday must have carried out his experiments with considerable **equanimity;** one would certainly have to remain calm when working with an unknown force such as electricity.

6.

iniquity → Some people in the late 1800s and early 1900s probably viewed the development of electricity as an **iniquity,** but others, perhaps more farsighted, saw it as a blessing.

7.

inordinate → In the late 1800s, some investors in England had **inordinate** expectations for electricity. Their expectations were excessive because they did not take into account the effects of gas prices and legislation on the new electric industry.

8.

mercurial → The electric industry in its early years could be described as **mercurial** because there were constant changes as new technologies were developed to meet increasing public demands.

9.

pecuniary → Of course, **pecuniary** interests drove the new electric industry. Investors were ultimately interested in making money and became increasingly involved in the industry when public demand for electricity increased.

10.

tenable → The statement that Thomas Edison's lighting exhibit at the London Exhibition of 1882 helped spark public interest in electricity is **tenable;** it can be defended with historical evidence.

EXERCISE 2 *Context Clues* ✍

Directions. Scan the definitions in Column A. Then think about how the boldface words are used in the sentences in Column B. To complete the exercise, match the definition in Column A with the correct vocabulary word from Column B. Write the letter of your choice on the line provided; then write the vocabulary word on the line preceding the definition.

COLUMN A

_____ **11.** word: _____

n. evenness of mind or temper; calmness; composure

_____ **12.** word: _____

adj. capable of being held or defended; defensible

_____ **13.** word: _____

adj. much too great; excessive; immoderate

_____ **14.** word: _____

v. to declare to be true; to state positively

_____ **15.** word: _____

adj. concerning money; in the form of money

_____ **16.** word: _____

n. an inhabitant; a person, a plant, or an animal at home in a particular region

_____ **17.** word: _____

adj. unpredictably changeable; quick and changeable in character

_____ **18.** word: _____

adj. careful and attentive; persevering

_____ **19.** word: _____

n. sin; wickedness; injustice

_____ **20.** word: _____

n. a temporary or final ceasing; a pause or stop

COLUMN B

(A) The **denizens** around the Thames—wild animals such as birds, badgers, and hedgehogs—were affected by the construction of a huge electrical power station in southeast London.

(B) S. Z. de Ferranti (1864–1930) was the **assiduous** engineer of the station. Through careful planning and perseverance he was able to begin construction in 1888.

(C) De Ferranti's London Electric Supply Company did not take an **inordinate** amount of time to build the station; it took only two years.

(D) Historians **aver** that the venture was a failure, but they also declare that it was a partial model for future electrical stations.

(E) Your statement that customers were unhappy with disruptions of the electrical supply is **tenable**—company records support it.

(F) The company's failure did not mean a **cessation** of interest in electricity. On the contrary, interest grew.

(G) Electricity seemed to have won steady favor with the British people. The usually **mercurial** public was, for once, unchangeable and stable in its desires. As a result, power stations were common by 1903.

(H) You can imagine the **pecuniary** interests in the growing electrical industry. There was much money to be made, and profits would grow with supply and demand.

(I) Did pioneering companies in electricity proceed with **equanimity** as they expanded and consolidated? Or was their calmness and evenness of mind disrupted by greed and the promise of profits?

(J) Some **iniquities** surely occurred in the electric companies' growth period, but my resource book mentions very few instances of injustices during the boom years.

EXERCISE 3 *Sentence Completion* 👈

Directions. For each of the following items, circle the letter of the choice that best completes the meaning of the sentence or sentences.

21. Although I usually do not make strong declarations, I do _____ that the British Electrical Development Association (EDA) helped increase demand for electricity.
   (A) bode
   (B) desist
   (C) renounce
   (D) aver
   (E) quell

22. My theories about the EDA, which was formed in 1919, are completely defensible. You can look in any history book to see that they are _____.
   (A) mercurial
   (B) pecuniary
   (C) tenable
   (D) assiduous
   (E) inordinate

23. The EDA, formed by several associations, definitely had _____ interests; it wanted to increase profits from the use of electricity.
   (A) tenable
   (B) pecuniary
   (C) mercurial
   (D) assiduous
   (E) iniquitous

24. The EDA did not spend _____ amount of time deciding upon its approach. On the contrary, it quickly decided upon its consumer target.
   (A) a pecuniary
   (B) an assiduous
   (C) a mercurial
   (D) a tenable
   (E) an inordinate

25. The EDA's ads were aimed at particular _____ of regions supplied by electricity: female housekeepers.
   (A) fissures
   (B) iniquities
   (C) denizens
   (D) cessations
   (E) firmaments

26. The EDA ad campaign was unchanging rather than _____. It was based upon the _____, or defensible, theory that women wanted the most modern appliances.
   (A) pecuniary . . . assiduous
   (B) assiduous . . . mercurial
   (C) inordinate . . . iniquitous
   (D) mercurial . . . tenable
   (E) tenable . . . inordinate

27. The ads _____ that the most careful and _____ housekeepers used electric carpet cleaners, declaring this in no uncertain terms.
   (A) boded . . . tenable
   (B) averred . . . assiduous
   (C) desisted . . . assiduous
   (D) averred . . . pecuniary
   (E) averred . . . mercurial

28. The ads urged the _____ of old ways and the beginning of modern methods of housekeeping. Electricity would reduce the _____, excessive amount of time women spent cleaning house.
   (A) cessation . . . inordinate
   (B) denizen . . . assiduous
   (C) equanimity . . . tenable
   (D) iniquity . . . mercurial
   (E) tenability . . . pecuniary

29. Some ads almost seemed to _____ that electricity was the solution to a number of ills, declaring that electricity could cure all domestic and social _____—or at least the sin of bad housekeeping!
   (A) desist . . . denizens
   (B) aver . . . cessations
   (C) renounce . . . iniquities
   (D) aver . . . denizens
   (E) aver . . . iniquities

30. Did British consumers react with _____, or did they get excited? And how about the _____ aspect of the electrical boom: Did consumers save money?
   (A) iniquity . . . assiduous
   (B) denizen . . . inordinate
   (C) equanimity . . . pecuniary
   (D) cessation . . . mercurial
   (E) mercurialness . . . tenable

Name _____ Date _____ Class _____

MAKING NEW WORDS YOUR OWN

Lesson 26 | **CONTEXT:** Science and Technology

England and the Suez Canal

In January my debate team was assigned to select and then support an argument about which of the world's canals is the most important. While some of the members favored the Panama Canal, we finally decided to research and debate the importance of the Suez Canal. At our next meeting, I brought all the information that I could find, along with a map that showed how the canal connected the Mediterranean and Red seas. One of the books I found said that the canal is 190 kilometers long and 226 meters wide.

In the following exercises, you will have the opportunity to expand your vocabulary by reading about the history of the Suez Canal. Below are ten vocabulary words that will be used in these exercises.

avarice	corollary	espouse	fissure	incarcerate
conciliate	duress	extenuate	impeccable	quell

EXERCISE 1 *Mapping* ✍

Directions. In the item below, a vocabulary word is provided and used in a sentence. Take a guess at the word's meaning and write it in the box labeled **Your Guess**. Then look the word up in your dictionary and write the definition in the box labeled **Definition**. In the **Other Forms** box, write as many other forms of the word, such as adjective and noun forms, as you can think of or find in your dictionary.

Then, following the same procedure, draw your own map for each of the nine remaining vocabulary words. Use a separate sheet of paper.

1.

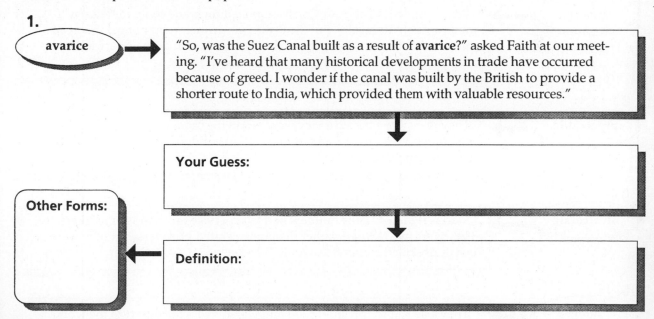

avarice → "So, was the Suez Canal built as a result of **avarice**?" asked Faith at our meeting. "I've heard that many historical developments in trade have occurred because of greed. I wonder if the canal was built by the British to provide a shorter route to India, which provided them with valuable resources."

Your Guess:

Other Forms:

Definition:

2.

(conciliate) ➤

"No," I explained. "The canal was actually built by a Frenchman, Ferdinand de Lesseps. He worked hard to **conciliate** other countries to the idea of buying stock in the project, finally winning over the Egyptian government."

3.

(corollary) ➤

"Why would the Egyptian government have resisted building the canal in the first place?" asked Mark. "I should think that its approval would have been a **corollary**, a natural consequence, of the proposal to build the canal. I've even heard that Egypt used to have a smaller canal where the Suez is now."

4.

(duress) ➤

"That's true," I said. "A canal connecting the Nile River and the Red Sea was built nearly 4,000 years ago and later abandoned. You are right that de Lesseps did not have to threaten the Egyptian government or put them under **duress** to get their financial aid."

5.

(espouse) ➤

"De Lessep's private corporation, the Suez Canal Company, also got many French investors to **espouse** the canal. Many French took up the cause in the interest of providing a shorter route between Europe and Asia."

6.

(extenuate) ➤

"Isn't there some way we can **extenuate**, or excuse, the British for their lack of interest during the early stages of the project?" asked Faith. "I can understand why they were cautious."

7.

(fissure) ➤

"Yes," I replied. "The Suez Canal shortened the trade route to India by thousands of kilometers, but the British government did not get involved until later. When the first ground was **fissured**, or broken open, for the canal, the British were still wary of the project."

8.

(impeccable) ➤

"They were wary because they were afraid the canal would hurt their railroad interests in Egypt," added Matt. "And besides, the plan for the canal was not **impeccable**, or flawless."

9.

(incarcerate) ➤

"Matt is right. First, the builders had to supervise thousands of workers. They were free laborers rather than **incarcerated** prisoners, but they were just as unskilled as convicts would have been."

10.

(quell) ➤

"They also had to transport food and water across the desert to the workers. They finally **quelled** this problem, however, putting an end to it by digging a temporary canal from the Nile into the desert and then parallel along the Suez route."

EXERCISE 2 *Context Clues*

Directions. Scan the definitions in Column A. Then think about how the boldface words are used in the sentences in Column B. To complete the exercise, match each definition in Column A with the correct vocabulary word from Column B. Write the letter of your choice on the line provided; then write the vocabulary word on the line preceding the definition.

COLUMN A	COLUMN B

COLUMN A

_____ **11.** word: _____

v. to excuse or serve as an excuse; to make the magnitude of something, such as a guilt, fault or offense, seem less

_____ **12.** word: _____

n. the use of force or threats to compel someone to act in a certain manner; coercion

_____ **13.** word: _____

v. to quiet; to put down or suppress by force; to put an end to something

_____ **14.** word: _____

v. to imprison; to confine

_____ **15.** word: _____

v. to win over; to appease; to gain good will or favor by being friendly

_____ **16.** word: _____

adj. faultless; without flaw; incapable of wrongdoing

_____ **17.** word: _____

n. something that follows once something else has been proven; a deduction; a natural consequence; a result

_____ **18.** word: _____

n. too great a desire for money and property; greed

_____ **19.** word: _____

n. a narrow or deep split, crack, or opening; *v.* to split or break open; to break into parts

_____ **20.** word: _____

v. to advocate or support a cause; to take up; to marry

COLUMN B

(A) "I can definitely see flaws in the plan," said Mark. "You're right to say that it was not **impeccable**."

(B) "Yes," I said. "There are reasons why Napoleon's engineers had **quelled**, or suppressed, his canal plans years earlier."

(C) "The engineers said that the Red and Mediterranean seas were at different levels. Under **duress**, Napoleon was forced to agree," I continued.

(D) "In his **avarice** and greed, Napoleon became convinced that it would be foolish to throw away money on the project."

(E) "But de Lesseps knew that the two seas were on the same level," I said. "He managed to win people over to his views, **to conciliate** them with his knowledge and friendliness."

(F) "As the **fissure** for the canal grew and no problems occurred with the narrow opening, more people became convinced that the project should continue."

(G) "By the time the canal opened in 1869," I informed the group, "many people had **espoused** its construction, supporting de Lesseps' efforts."

(H) "As a **corollary**, or result, the opening of the canal was a gala event. The Italian composer Verdi composed his opera *Aida* especially for the occasion."

(I) "The canal was a financial success," I concluded. "This **extenuated** Britain's doubt about the project, lessening its wariness."

(J) "But I've heard that some of Egypt's leaders were in danger of being jailed or **incarcerated** for debt," said Faith. "How could the canal have been a financial success?"

EXERCISE 3 *Sentence Completion*

Directions. For each of the following items, circle the letter of the choice that best completes the meaning of the sentence or sentences.

21. "They did fall into debt," I answered, "and as ____, a natural consequence, Britain bought Egypt's stocks in the canal."
- (A) an extenuation
- (B) a corollary
- (C) a duress
- (D) an incarceration
- (E) an avarice

22. "Britain acted ____ and, in its desire to accumulate wealth, obtained nearly half of the shares to the Suez Canal Company by 1875."
- (A) impeccably
- (B) commiseratively
- (C) ingenuously
- (D) avariciously
- (E) evanescently

23. "Who had the original charter on the canal?" asked Matt, pointing out that my explanation was not ____ because it had some flaws.
- (A) avaricious
- (B) extenuating
- (C) impeccable
- (D) quelled
- (E) conciliatory

24. "The Suez Canal Company was given a 99-year lease on the canal land and the ____, or deep crack, filled with water," I replied. "All nations were given access to the canal."
- (A) extenuation
- (B) espousal
- (C) corollary
- (D) avarice
- (E) fissure

25. "____ circumstances during the Arab-Israeli war in 1948 and 1949 served as an excuse for Egypt to close the canal to Israel," I pointed out.
- (A) Extenuating
- (B) Impeccable
- (C) Conciliatory
- (D) Avaricious
- (E) Evanescent

26. "The nations of the Middle East were unable to ____ the fighting. Because of the failure to suppress violence, another war began in 1956. As a consequence, or ____, of this war, British and French troops were sent in."
- (A) espouse . . . corollary
- (B) extenuate . . . fissure
- (C) quell . . . corollary
- (D) incarcerate . . . avarice
- (E) fissure . . . duress

27. "Did Egypt force Britain to go in under ____, by using threats and force?" asked Faith, "Or did Britain have ____ motives to make money from the war?"
- (A) espousal . . . impeccable
- (B) duress . . . avaricious
- (C) incarceration . . . conciliatory
- (D) corollary . . . extenuating
- (E) avarice . . . conciliatory

28. "Britain had once controlled Egypt and hoped to ____, to stop, Arab fighting," I replied. "When the canal was closed, residents of the area must have felt like prisoners ____ in jail."
- (A) extenuate . . . quelled
- (B) conciliate . . . espoused
- (C) fissure . . . quelled
- (D) incarcerate . . . extenuated
- (E) quell . . . incarcerated

29. "The canal was reopened in 1975, when Egypt was ____, or appeased," explained Matt, using his ____ vocabulary with characteristic flawlessness.
- (A) espoused . . . extenuating
- (B) conciliated . . . impeccable
- (C) quelled . . . avaricious
- (D) fissured . . . evanescent
- (E) extenuated . . . avaricious

30. "So today the canal joins the Red and Mediterranean seas as if they were married, or ____?" Faith asked. "I hope your knowledge makes up for, or ____, my ignorance in our debate."
- (A) conciliated . . . fissures
- (B) quelled . . . extenuates
- (C) incarcerated . . . quells
- (D) espoused . . . extenuates
- (E) extenuated . . . conciliates

MAKING NEW WORDS YOUR OWN

Lesson 27   CONTEXT: Science and Technology
Charles Dickens and Industry

Charles Dickens (1812–1870) is undoubtedly one of the most famous English writers in history. People around the world have sympathized with his characters and enjoyed his stories. But Dickens was more than simply a wonderful storyteller. He was also a social commentator who used his stories to speak out against the poverty, poor working conditions, and other social injustices of the Victorian age. One of Dickens's most fervent concerns was the changes brought by the Industrial Revolution— the machine age which Dickens viewed as retrogressive, damaging, and hardhearted.

In the following exercises, you will have the opportunity to expand your vocabulary by reading about Charles Dickens and his view of industry. Below are ten vocabulary words that will be used in these exercises.

| caricature | evanescent | gambol | maudlin | remuneration |
| commiserate | festoon | ingenuous | pallor | venal |

EXERCISE 1   *Mapping*

Directions. In the item below, a vocabulary word is provided and used in a sentence. Take a guess at the word's meaning and write it in the box labeled **Your Guess**. Then look the word up in your dictionary and write the definition in the box labeled **Definition**. In the **Other Forms** box, write as many other forms of the word, such as adjective and noun forms, as you can think of or find in your dictionary.

Then, following the same procedure, draw your own map for each of the nine remaining vocabulary words. Use a separate sheet of paper.

1.

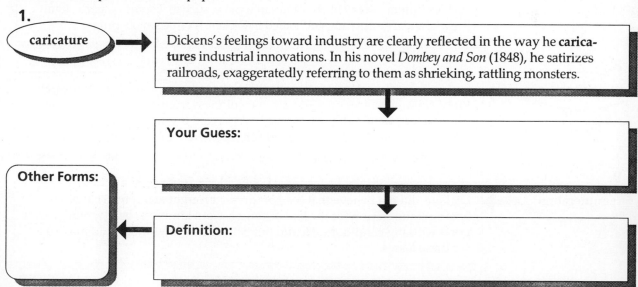

caricature

Dickens's feelings toward industry are clearly reflected in the way he **caricatures** industrial innovations. In his novel *Dombey and Son* (1848), he satirizes railroads, exaggeratedly referring to them as shrieking, rattling monsters.

Your Guess:

Other Forms:

Definition:

2.

commiserate ➤ Apparently many people **commiserated** with Dickens's viewpoint, for his books were phenomenally successful. If people had not sympathized with his opinions, they would not have been such loyal readers.

3.

evanescent ➤ Dickens's description of the construction of a railroad is equally satirical. He gives everything a sense of impermanence and confusion, describing houses that are knocked down and **evanescent** flames that vanish as soon as they appear.

4.

festoon ➤ In Dickens's world, the urban landscape is not **festooned** with things of beauty. On the contrary, it has no adornments at all and is reduced to "carcasses of ragged tenements, and fragments of unfinished walls and arches, and piles of scaffolding, and wildernesses of bricks. . . ."

5.

gambol ➤ Few children **gambol** and frolic in Dickens's books, as one might expect them to do. Instead, the wilderness of progress seems to render all people—both young and old—solemn and grave.

6.

ingenuous ➤ Dickens's descriptions are far from naive, or **ingenuous**. He was fully aware of his purpose and intended his writing to inspire changes in working and living conditions.

7.

maudlin ➤ Although critics charged that Dickens was too **maudlin**, clinging with excessive sentimentality to the past, Dickens was not alone in deploring the Industrial Revolution. Many other Victorian writers, such as Thomas Carlyle, John Ruskin, and Charles Kingsley, joined in Dickens's criticism of "progress."

8.

pallor ➤ Dickens was a master of description. He created moving images of the **pallor** of children's faces, turned pale and colorless from poverty, cruelty, and exhaustion. His 1838 book *Nicholas Nickleby* told the story of "ragged schools" in northern England where children were mercilessly abused.

9.

remuneration ➤ Dickens did not believe that the "progress" brought about by technology was a **remuneration** for the loss of compassion, kindness, beauty, and good working conditions. He did not believe that anything could make up for these losses.

10.

venal ➤ Dickens was not willing to compromise his beliefs in his writing. He was not **venal,** so he would certainly have refused bribes offered by industrialists wanting him to tone down his criticism of industry.

EXERCISE 2 *Context Clues* ✍

Directions. Scan the definitions in Column A. Then think about how the boldface words are used in the sentences in Column B. To complete the exercise, match each definition in Column A with the correct vocabulary word from Column B. Write the letter of your choice on the line provided; then write the vocabulary word on the line preceding the definition.

COLUMN A

_____ **11.** word: _____

n. a skipping or running about; *v.* to run and jump in play; to frolic

_____ **12.** word: _____

n. a payment for goods or services; a compensation for losses

_____ **13.** word: _____

n. a lack of color, particularly in the face; paleness

_____ **14.** word: _____

adj. naive; lacking sophistication; innocent; candid

_____ **15.** word: _____

adj. willing to sell one's services or influence for money; open to bribes; corruptible

_____ **16.** word: _____

adj. excessively sentimental

_____ **17.** word: _____

n. a picture or description of a person or thing in which certain features are exaggerated for a satirical effect; a ludicrous imitation *v.* to create such a picture or description

_____ **18.** word: _____

n. a string of flowers, paper or the like hung as a decoration; *v.* to decorate with such an adornment

_____ **19.** word: _____

v. to sympathize with or express sympathy for; to condole; to pity

_____ **20.** word: _____

adj. tending to disappear or fade away; fleeting; vanishing

COLUMN B

(A) Dickens did not confine his **caricatures** to industry. He also exaggerated the positive qualities of life before the machine age.

(B) In *Martin Chuzzlewit* (1843–1844), Dickens describes a delightful carriage ride, complete with four horses playfully **gamboling** in the sun.

(C) The evening is described as "mild and bright," with the **evanescent** hum of the wheels fading into the pleasant air.

(D) The harness is **festooned** with bells that tinkle on bright ribbons of decoration.

(E) The **ingenuous** man in the carriage is innocently enjoying his ride and looking forward to the beauties of London.

(F) Although some of the writing is rather **maudlin**, the reader feels that the excessive sentimentality of the episode—with its fairy-tale quality—is justified.

(G) It is easy to **commiserate** with Dickens and sympathize with his views when we realize that such carriages were replaced by dirty, mechanical trains.

(H) The carriage ride is colorful and bright. In contrast, the railroad journey is characterized by a sense of drabness and colorlessness, a **pallor** that is the legacy of industrialization.

(I) Dickens did not view the advantages brought by industry—such as speed—as sufficient **remuneration** for the loss of simple, heartfelt pleasures, such as the fairy-tale beauty of the carriage ride.

(J) Unlike many of the industrialists whom he criticized in his works, Dickens was not **venal**. His convictions and values were strong and not corruptible.

EXERCISE 3   *Sentence Completion* ✍

Directions. For each of the following items, circle the letter of the choice that best completes the meaning of the sentence or sentences.

21. One of Dickens's goals was for industry to _____, or compensate, workers and urban dwellers for illness and poor living conditions.
  (A) caricature
  (B) festoon
  (C) gambol
  (D) remunerate
  (E) commiserate

22. His novel *Nicholas Nickleby* made readers of the time _____ with the difficult lives of the school boys. This sympathy eventually led to extensive school reforms.
  (A) commiserate
  (B) caricature
  (C) festoon
  (D) gambol
  (E) remunerate

23. Dickens's *A Christmas Carol* deals with the _____ Scrooge, who has been corrupted by the values of industrial society.
  (A) evanescent
  (B) venal
  (C) ingenuous
  (D) maudlin
  (E) commiserative

24. Scrooge is incapable of sympathy for his employee, Bob Cratchit. Dickens sets up a marked contrast between the openness and _____ of Cratchit and the closed, suspicious personality of Scrooge.
  (A) gambol
  (B) festoon
  (C) evanescence
  (D) ingenuousness
  (E) pallor

25. Dickens's descriptions of Cratchit are very moving. Cratchit's skin has an unnatural _____ from working long hours in darkened rooms.
  (A) venality
  (B) remuneration
  (C) pallor
  (D) gambol
  (E) festoon

26. Such moving descriptions were not too sentimental or _____ to bring about change. Readers paid attention, and for his labors Dickens was _____ with the payment of better working conditions for the poor.
  (A) evanescent . . . festooned
  (B) commiserative . . . gamboled
  (C) maudlin . . . remunerated
  (D) venal . . . caricatured
  (E) maudlin . . . commiserated

27. But social conditions were not _____; they did not vanish. Sympathy, or _____, with the plight of working people was not enough.
  (A) maudlin . . . remuneration
  (B) ingenuous . . . caricature
  (C) venal . . . festoon
  (D) evanescent . . . gambol
  (E) evanescent . . . commiseration

28. Dickens realized that the days of the _____, gaily adorned carriages had passed. A sophisticated person, he was not _____ enough to believe he could stop change.
  (A) maudlin . . . evanescent
  (B) festooned . . . ingenuous
  (C) ingenuous . . . venal
  (D) commiserative . . . evanescent
  (E) festooned . . . maudlin

29. Dickens wanted to see playfully _____ horses bearing ruddy-cheeked riders on their backs rather than the _____ of pale passengers riding the trains.
  (A) gamboling . . . maudlin
  (B) ingenuous . . . evanescence
  (C) venal . . . remuneration
  (D) evanescent . . . caricature
  (E) gamboling . . . pallor

30. Today, Dickens is remembered as both a novelist and a satirist, whose _____ remind us that adjustment to change is a permanent rather than _____ fact of life.
  (A) pallors . . . a venal
  (B) evanescence . . . an ingenuous
  (C) caricatures . . . an evanescent
  (D) festoons . . . a remunerative
  (E) caricatures . . . a maudlin

MAKING NEW WORDS YOUR OWN

Lesson 28 | CONTEXT: Science and Technology

Artists' Eyes on Health and Housing in Industrial England

How's this for an art exhibition title: "Public Health and Housing in Industrial England"? The title was a bit dry, but the artwork was lively and varied. As a summer intern at our local newspaper, I was given the assignment of reviewing the exhibition at our local Museum of Modern Art. The show was the idea of the museum director, who is from London. He gave local artists information about the unsanitary living conditions in England during the 1800s, and then asked the artists to interpret those conditions in art. Following are some of my comments on the exhibit.

In the following exercises, you will have the opportunity to expand your vocabulary by reading about an art exhibit depicting public health and housing in Victorian England. Below are ten vocabulary words that will be used in these exercises.

abstruse	bauble	fresco	iridescent	promontory
apostasy	bullion	frugal	opulence	usury

EXERCISE 1 | Mapping

Directions. In the item below, a vocabulary word is provided and used in a sentence. Take a guess at the word's meaning and write it in the box labeled **Your Guess**. Then look the word up in your dictionary and write the definition in the box labeled **Definition**. In the **Other Forms** box, write as many other forms of the word, such as adjective and noun forms, as you can think of or find in your dictionary.

Then, following the same procedure, draw your own map for each of the nine remaining vocabulary words. Use a separate sheet of paper.

1.

```
abstruse  →  The background information on health and housing conditions in England
             in the nineteenth century was abstruse. Especially hard to understand was
             the excerpt from the 1842 Report on the Sanitary Conditions of the Labouring
             Population of Great Britain.
```

Your Guess:

Other Forms:

Definition:

2.

apostasy →

My first impression of the exhibit was not favorable because I had always believed that art should show happy, positive views of life. However, my exposure to the exhibit resulted in an **apostasy** of my belief; the works made me realize that art should also show life's unhappiness.

3.

bauble →

One of the first paintings that caught my attention shows a sick child sadly playing with some useless toy, a **bauble**. She is sitting between two houses built so close to each other that little light or air reaches her.

4.

bullion →

Another painting shows the Parliament building made of **bullion**. The brick-shaped gold bars shine like the sun. Around the building, protesting workers carry signs bearing such slogans as "Needed: Clean Water" and "Give Us Sanitary Streets."

5.

fresco →

I know that the **fresco** is Larry Sawyer's preferred artistic medium, but there was no way to exhibit his work with watercolors on wet plaster at the museum. Instead, he did a disturbing oil painting of hospital patients with tuberculosis.

6.

frugal →

Sawyer was extremely **frugal** with his paint, using only thin, spare lines to suggest the patients' forms, their beds, and the walls. Black is the dominant color, as befits tuberculosis, a prominent killer during the industrial era.

7.

iridescent →

On the wall in Sawyer's painting is a small, **iridescent** pattern. These rainbow colors, perhaps symbols of faint hope, are projected from a prism hanging in a window.

8.

opulence →

Several paintings effectively contrast the wealth and **opulence** of the houses of royalty and upper-class citizens with the poverty and miserable living conditions of the poor and working classes.

9.

promontory →

I particularly like the painting showing Edwin Chadwick of London, who began reforms for health and living and working conditions in the mid-nineteenth century. This painting shows Chadwick standing on a rocky **promontory** overlooking the North Sea, welcoming fresh air to English cities.

10.

usury →

An interesting black-and-white drawing portrays moneylenders found guilty of **usury**, the practice of charging a high or unlawful rate of interest on a loan.

EXERCISE 2   *Context Clues* ✍

Directions. Scan the definitions in Column A. Then think about how the boldface words are used in the sentences in Column B. To complete the exercise, match each definition in Column A with the correct vocabulary word from Column B. Write the letter of your choice on the line provided; then write the vocabulary word on the line preceding the definition.

COLUMN A	COLUMN B

COLUMN A

_____ **11.** word: _____
n. a high point of land extending into a body of water

_____ **12.** word: _____
n. wealth or riches; luxuriousness; abundance

_____ **13.** word: _____
adj. hard to understand

_____ **14.** word: _____
adj. avoiding waste; thrifty; economical

_____ **15.** word: _____
n. the practice of charging a very high or an unlawful rate of interest on a loan

_____ **16.** word: _____
n. a complete forsaking of what one has believed in

_____ **17.** word: _____
n. the art of painting with watercolors on wet plaster; a picture so painted

_____ **18.** word: _____
n. a showy trifle of little value; a useless toy or trinket

_____ **19.** word: _____
adj. showing the colors of the rainbow in a changing pattern

_____ **20.** word: _____
n. ingots, bars, or plates of gold or silver

COLUMN B

(A) An artist who signs his work Z, reportedly a former loan officer accused of **usury**, entered one of my favorite paintings in the exhibit.

(B) Biographical information about Z is vague. "I no longer believe in money, and my **apostasy** shocks many," he is quoted as saying.

(C) "I consider my paintings **baubles**," the biographical note continues, "but if anyone finds value in these trifles, that's okay with me."

(D) Z ends his biographical note with this statement: "You'll seldom find me in a studio. Instead, you'll find me, paintbrush in hand, standing on a rocky **promontory**, looking out to sea."

(E) Z's work in the exhibit is a painting within a painting. It portrays an artist working on a **fresco** on a plaster-covered ceiling. The **fresco** within the painting shows the same image: an artist painting on wet plaster.

(F) The connection of Z's painting to the exhibit's theme is **abstruse**, but however difficult the connection is to understand, the painting is extremely colorful.

(G) The **iridescent** windowpanes in Z's painting are beautiful. They throw spots of rainbow colors on the painter and the ceiling.

(H) I wish I could buy the painting. I would guard it as carefully as the government guards the **bullion** in the U.S. Gold Depository at Fort Knox.

(I) Some art collectors aren't exactly **frugal** with their money. As a result, they would probably pay a high price for Z's painting.

(J) The painting seems to belong amid **opulence** because its rich colors and jewellike tones suggest wealth and luxuriousness.

EXERCISE 3 *Sentence Completion* ✒

Directions. For each of the following items, circle the letter of the choice that best completes the meaning of the sentence or sentences.

21. Since you haven't seen the exhibit, I hope my comments are not too _____ and that you can make some sense out of them.

(A) frugal
(B) abstruse
(C) opulent
(D) iridescent
(E) biennial

22. Many subjects were depicted, from urban poverty and tuberculosis to interest rates, loans, and even the crime of _____.

(A) bauble
(B) bullion
(C) abstruseness
(D) usury
(E) iridescence

23. The artistic media are varied, too. Of course, much to artist Larry Sawyer's disappointment, there are no _____, as painted plaster walls would be almost impossible to exhibit.

(A) apostasies
(B) promontories
(C) frescoes
(D) bullion
(E) baubles

24. The 1800s clearly were not a time for _____ in government financing for housing and health; on the contrary, it was a time that called for massive spending.

(A) bauble
(B) apostasy
(C) promontory
(D) opulence
(E) frugality

25. An impressive painting shows a banker confessing _____: He declares that he no longer believes in the values of his profession and wants to help the poor.

(A) a promontory
(B) a bullion
(C) a bauble
(D) an apostasy
(E) an opulence

26. Some children apparently found the exhibit _____; they did not understand it. But one child reached up to touch a brightly colored painting as though it were a pretty _____, meant to be played with.

(A) abstruse . . . bauble
(B) iridescent . . . promontory
(C) opulent . . . apostasy
(D) frugal . . . fresco
(E) opulent . . . bauble

27. The museum itself is situated on _____ overlooking the river. As you enter the museum, be sure to look up at the beautiful _____ painted on the ceiling.

(A) a fresco . . . baubles
(B) a bauble . . . promontories
(C) a promontory . . . frescoes
(D) a usury . . . apostasies
(E) an apostasy . . . usuries

28. The museum is richly decorated, but the _____ is not overdone. It is obvious that the museum was not _____ when purchasing furnishings: everything looks expensive.

(A) promontory . . . abstruse
(B) bullion . . . iridescent
(C) apostasy . . . opulent
(D) usury . . . abstruse
(E) opulence . . . frugal

29. A stained-glass window in the entry hall throws _____ patterns on the walls. The rainbow colors look beautiful below the rich watercolors of the ceiling _____.

(A) frugal . . . promontory
(B) abstruse . . . usury
(C) frugal . . . bauble
(D) iridescent . . . fresco
(E) opulent . . . bullion

30. An interesting painting near the main entrance depicts a well-dressed man standing between two tall stacks of _____; the gold bars cast a golden glow on his face. The meaning of this painting is _____ to me; I don't understand it.

(A) baubles . . . iridescent
(B) bullion . . . abstruse
(C) promontories . . . abstruse
(D) usuries . . . frugal
(E) apostasies . . . frugal

MAKING NEW WORDS YOUR OWN

Lesson 29 **CONTEXT: Science and Technology**

Watson, Crick, and the Double Helix

Last month, my science class did a project on genetics, a branch of biology that deals with hereditary features in plants and animals. During one of our lab periods, my teacher, Mr. Farley, explained the discovery of deoxyribonucleic acid, or DNA. He told us that the currently accepted structural model of DNA was first discovered in 1953 by American James Watson (b. 1928) and Englishman Francis Crick (b. 1916). Watson and Crick were biologists who worked together at the Cavendish Laboratory at Cambridge University in England.

In the following exercises, you will have the opportunity to expand your vocabulary by reading about the discovery of DNA. Below are ten vocabulary words that will be used in these exercises.

abscond	aspersion	ethereal	malign	prognosis
adjure	circumvent	ignominy	malinger	remonstrate

EXERCISE 1 *Mapping*

Directions. In the item below, a vocabulary word is provided and used in a sentence. Take a guess at the word's meaning and write it in the box labeled **Your Guess**. Then look the word up in your dictionary and write the definition in the box labeled **Definition**. In the **Other Forms** box, write as many other forms of the word, such as adjective and noun forms, as you can think of or find in your dictionary.

Then, following the same procedure, draw your own map for each of the nine remaining vocabulary words. Use a separate sheet of paper.

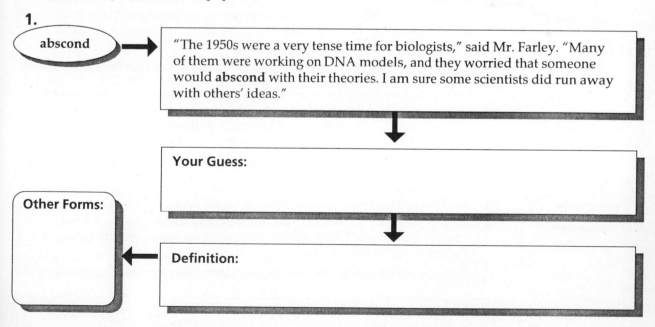

1.

abscond → "The 1950s were a very tense time for biologists," said Mr. Farley. "Many of them were working on DNA models, and they worried that someone would **abscond** with their theories. I am sure some scientists did run away with others' ideas."

Your Guess:

Other Forms:

Definition:

2.

adjure → "Watson and Crick had to **adjure** the other scientists at Cambridge not to reveal their theories," Mr. Farley continued. "They asked their colleagues to swear an oath of secrecy."

3.

aspersion → "At the risk of spreading **aspersion**, I must tell you that Watson and Crick saw some other scientists' models before announcing their discovery. I don't want to slander them, but some people charge that Watson and Crick stole the work of molecular biologist Rosalind Franklin."

4.

circumvent → "I'm sure," stated Mr. Farley, "it would be tempting to try to **circumvent**, or go around, the rules during a race for the Nobel Prize. Besides Crick and Watson, there were many others working on DNA models."

5.

ethereal → "DNA is the basic substance of life, but at the same time it is almost **ethereal**, or unearthly, because of its minute size."

6.

ignominy → "Did any of the scientists ever experience **ignominy**?" asked Cora. "Were they ever publicly disgraced for stealing each other's work?"
"No, for such charges are difficult to prove," said Mr. Farley. "It is natural that they would build somewhat on one another's work."

7.

malign → "As I said before, I do not want to **malign** anyone. I refuse to defame scientists who made such an important contribution to humanity. Along with the splitting of the atom, the discovery of the DNA helix is seen as one of the most important findings of our century."

8.

malinger → "By the way, while I'm thinking of it, we're going to be dissecting frogs next week, and I don't want any of you **malingering** to get out of it. We've had enough fake sicknesses already this term," said Mr. Farley.

9.

prognosis → "Mr. Farley, does knowledge of DNA structure help a doctor make a clearer **prognosis** of a patient?" asked Ira, getting us back on the subject. "It seems that it would help doctors make more accurate predictions about a patient's chance of recovery."

10.

remonstrate → Mr. Farley was just about to answer when Cora spoke up. "I **remonstrate** against dissecting frogs next week. I am an animal rights activist, and I object to your use of frogs for lab experiments."

EXERCISE 2   *Context Clues* ✍

Directions. Scan the definitions in Column A. Then think about how the boldface words are used in the sentences in Column B. To complete the exercise, match each definition in Column A with the correct vocabulary word from Column B. Write the letter of your choice on the line provided; then write the vocabulary word on the line preceding the definition.

COLUMN A

_____ **11.** word: _____
n. public disgrace; public dishonor; disgraceful, shameful behavior

_____ **12.** word: _____
v. to surround and trap by cleverness; to avoid or go around

_____ **13.** word: _____
v. to pretend to be sick to escape work or duty; to shirk

_____ **14.** word: _____
n. a damaging, false remark; slander; a slur; the act of slandering or defaming someone

_____ **15.** word: _____
v. to object; to protest; to argue against some action

_____ **16.** word: _____
n. a forecast; a prediction about the course of a disease and the chance of recovery

_____ **17.** word: _____
v. to command or charge someone, often under oath or penalty, to do something; to ask or to entreat earnestly

_____ **18.** word: _____
v. to run away; to leave suddenly and secretly and hide, especially to escape the law

_____ **19.** word: _____
adj. evil; malicious; *v.* to speak evil of; to defame or slander

_____ **20.** word: _____
adj. very light and airy; delicate; unearthly; celestial

COLUMN B

(A) "We should really get back to DNA," Mr. Farley **adjured,** earnestly entreating us to pay attention.

(B) "You certainly have the right to **remonstrate,** but it would be best to save your protestations for later so that we can continue discussing DNA structure."

(C) "In the 1950s, some scientists hypothesized that DNA might be a helix so **ethereal** and delicate that it could not be seen by a microscope."

(D) "But no one was able to **circumvent** the exact structure, despite attempts to surround and cleverly trap the solution," Mr. Farley said.

(E) "Several scientists suffered **ignominy** when they were publicly disgraced for drawing obviously incorrect conclusions."

(F) "Although other scientists cast **aspersions** on these errors, the theories, though incorrect, did not deserve these slurs."

(G) "The scientists did not deserve malicious comments about their work," Mr. Farley said. "They should not have been **maligned**. They were, after all, able to rule out some faulty theories and come up with new ones."

(H) "The **prognosis** for DNA was good," he continued, "because forecasts in a field are always best when there is both competition and cooperation."

(I) "The scientists helped each other. They didn't just **abscond** or run away with each others' theories.

(J) "But the race was far too tight for **malingering,**" said Mr. Farley. "No one shirked his or her research for even a few minutes."

EXERCISE 3 *Sentence Completion* 🖎

Directions. For each of the following items, circle the letter of the choice that best completes the meaning of the sentence or sentences.

21. "Watson and Crick often thought that someone else would ____ with the Nobel Prize and run away with the fame," Mr. Farley said.
(A) adjure
(B) abscond
(C) circumvent
(D) malign
(E) malinger

22. "But Watson and Crick were destined for public honor and fame, rather than ____ and shame."
(A) aspersion
(B) prognosis
(C) ignominy
(D) remonstration
(E) adjuration

23. "In 1953," he continued, "they published their discovery in *Nature* magazine. No one ____, or protested, the authenticity of their finding."
(A) absconded
(B) adjured
(C) circumvented
(D) remonstrated
(E) malingered

24. "At last, someone had made substance of the unearthly, ____ DNA," said Mr. Farley. "Crick and Watson had pinpointed it as a helical acid."
(A) ethereal
(B) maligned
(C) ignominable
(D) prognostic
(E) adjuratory

25. "Their model was unlike any previously proposed, but it did not ____ scientific evidence," he continued. "It dealt directly with the facts."
(A) adjure
(B) circumvent
(C) abscond
(D) malign
(E) remonstrate

26. "Watson and Crick were not ____; they had worked tirelessly. It was difficult to ____, or protest, when they won the Nobel Prize."
(A) aspersions . . . malinger
(B) ignominies . . . circumvent
(C) prognoses . . . adjure
(D) malingerers . . . remonstrate
(E) aspersions . . . abscond

27. "Still," he said, "some critics cast ____ on Watson and Crick. These damaging reports stated that Watson and Crick had ____ ethics by going around the usual acknowledgment rules."
(A) aspersions . . . remonstrated
(B) prognoses . . . adjured
(C) ignominies . . . maligned
(D) remonstrations . . . malingered
(E) aspersions . . . circumvented

28. "They ____ other scientists to enforce these rules, entreating them to protect female researchers. They wanted to prevent male scientists from ____, or running away, with their female colleagues' work."
(A) adjured . . . circumventing
(B) remonstrated . . . malingering
(C) adjured . . . absconding
(D) absconded . . . maligning
(E) remonstrated . . . maligning

29. "The truth of these statements is a matter of opinion," said Mr. Farley. "The ____ who defame these scientists may be justified, or they may simply be casting slanderous ____."
(A) aspersions . . . prognoses
(B) maligners . . . aspersions
(C) ignominies . . . circumvention
(D) etherealness . . . adjuration
(E) maligners . . . prognoses

30. "The discovery of DNA structure, bringing it from the ____, theoretical sphere to a material level, provided a positive ____ for the future of genetics."
(A) ethereal . . . prognosis
(B) malign . . . remonstration
(C) ignominious . . . aspersion
(D) prognostic . . . adjuration
(E) ethereal . . . ignominy

MAKING NEW WORDS YOUR OWN

Lesson 30 | CONTEXT: Science and Technology
Making a BBC Documentary

Reading the book *Framing Science—The Making of a BBC Documentary* by Roger Silverstone gave me the idea for a short story recently assigned by my creative writing teacher. The author of the book details the production of a program for the British Broadcasting Corporation's *Horizon* science series. My idea was to write a story about a recent high school graduate, Len, who wins a prize to make a BBC documentary of his own. Would you like to read some excerpts from my story? Afterward, you may want to read *Framing Science* for a close look at documentary filmmaking.

In the following exercises, you will have the opportunity to expand your vocabulary by reading excerpts from the fictional account of a young man's experiences in making a BBC documentary. Below are ten vocabulary words that will be used in these exercises.

biennial	elicit	equivocal	fiasco	reprisal
capricious	emaciate	extort	longevity	taciturn

EXERCISE 1 *Mapping*

Directions. In the item below, a vocabulary word is provided and used in a sentence. Take a guess at the word's meaning and write it in the box labeled **Your Guess**. Then look the word up in your dictionary and write the definition in the box labeled **Definition**. In the **Other Forms** box, write as many other forms of the word, such as adjective and noun forms, as you can think of or find in your dictionary.

Then, following the same procedure, draw your own map for each of the nine remaining vocabulary words. Use a separate sheet of paper.

1.

biennial → "This isn't a **biennial** series, you know. We'd all have more time if it were, but a new *SciSense* season starts every year, not every two years," said Mr. Russell, the producer.

Your Guess:

Other Forms:

Definition:

2.

(capricious) ➔ "We need to get busy and come up with an idea for the show right now," Len said to the production crew. Then he quickly changed his mind and said, "No, let's take as much time as we need," displaying his **capricious** nature.

3.

(elicit) ➔ "Actually," he said, "you should stay because I need to **elicit** from you some ideas about the subject for our program, which we need to start filming in two weeks. Does anybody have any ideas I can draw out?"

4.

(emaciate) ➔ Mr. Berry, the program's longtime scriptwriter, said, "How about a program showing what people can do to protect their cats from distemper and other diseases? Distemper can **emaciate** ailing cats by robbing them of their appetite. You should see how gaunt and skinny they can get."

5.

(equivocal) ➔ "The last time we did a program like that," said Ms. Lofler, the program's assistant director, "the public response was **equivocal**. We weren't sure whether the public liked it or not."

6.

(extort) ➔ "I don't think anyone would let us film his or her sick cat," said the camera operator. "Of course," he continued with a wicked grin, "we could always **extort** permission by threatening to film the cats with hidden cameras."

7.

(fiasco) ➔ "You have a weird sense of humor," Len said. "But anyway, a show about sick cats would be a complete failure. I don't want a **fiasco**, so we need to get serious and think of a good science subject that would interest the whole family."

8.

(longevity) ➔ "A subject such as **longevity** would be good," Ms. Lofler said. "We could find out who the oldest people in England are, interview them and their families, and show photographs from their lives."

9.

(reprisal) ➔ "Another good subject is the environmental impact of war on a country," Len said, "and the damages done when one nation starts a fight and another nation begins a **reprisal** in order to retaliate."

10.

(taciturn) ➔ One of the show's writers, Mr. Edwards, who is known for being **taciturn**, startled everyone by speaking up: "I don't want to write about sick cats or war, so let's talk to the elderly Brits."

EXERCISE 2   Context Clues ✍

Directions. Scan the definitions in Column A. Then think about how the boldface words are used in the sentences in Column B. To complete the exercise, match each definition in Column A with the correct vocabulary word from Column B. Write the letter of your choice on the line provided; then write the vocabulary word on the line preceding the definition.

COLUMN A

_____ **11.** word: _____

v. to obtain by threats or force

_____ **12.** word: _____

n. injury done for injury received, especially by one nation to another; the act of returning an injury for an injury received; retaliation

_____ **13.** word: _____

v. to draw out; to bring forth; to evoke

_____ **14.** word: _____

adj. not fond of speaking; quiet; reserved

_____ **15.** word: _____

n. a complete or ridiculous failure

_____ **16.** word: _____

adj. occurring every two years; living or lasting for two years

_____ **17.** word: _____

v. to make unnaturally thin; to waste away from hunger or disease

_____ **18.** word: _____

n. long life; length of life

_____ **19.** word: _____

adj. tending to change quickly without apparent reason; erratic; impulsive

_____ **20.** word: _____

adj. having two or more meanings; ambiguous; evasive; of uncertain value or outcome; undecided; doubtful; obscure

COLUMN B

(A) I read part of *Framing Science*, Len thought, and I certainly don't recall reading about any **fiascoes** like this—not even any minor failures.

(B) I'm still young, but at this rate my **longevity** is questionable. Do all directors burn out early?

(C) One of the writers called me **capricious**, but I don't think I'm an impulsive or erratic person.

(D) Working almost around the clock and forgetting to eat may **emaciate** me. My mother says I'm already too thin.

(E) I'm really glad that my director's prize is just for one year and not a **biennial** job that I have to do every two years.

(F) The hardest part of directing is getting straight answers from people who talk out of both sides of their mouths. Some of them actually seem to enjoy being **equivocal**.

(G) For **taciturn** people like Mr. Edwards or myself, having to speak loudly to get people's attention can be very uncomfortable.

(H) Sometimes I try to **elicit** responses from people, but it's hard to get them to answer me, probably because I'm young and inexperienced.

(I) Then I start thinking of things I could do to get even with the people who ignored me, but so far any **reprisals** are just in my head.

(J) As the director, I guess I could **extort** responses from them, but threats and the use of force usually backfire.

EXERCISE 3 Sentence Completion ✍

Directions. For each of the following items, circle the letter of the choice that best completes the meaning of the sentence or sentences.

21. Len worried that shooting on location at a retirement home would be _____, but the filming was a great success.
(A) a reprisal
(B) a longevity
(C) an elicitation
(D) a fiasco
(E) an extortion

22. One woman, who was 103, was especially willing to share her secrets of _____ with television audiences.
(A) extortion
(B) fiasco
(C) longevity
(D) equivocalness
(E) reprisal

23. "Always be gentle and nonthreatening," she said. "Don't ever _____ anyone to do or say anything. It will always backfire on you."
(A) elicit
(B) extort
(C) gambol
(D) emaciate
(E) festoon

24. "It seems to be human nature to return an injury for an injury," she said, "but you will live longer if you avoid _____."
(A) longevity
(B) equivocalness
(C) benniums
(D) taciturnity
(E) reprisals

25. Len thought that the senior citizens would be reserved and _____, but instead they were very outgoing and talkative.
(A) taciturn
(B) biennial
(C) equivocal
(D) capricious
(E) emaciated

26. Len hired a famous actor to _____ responses from residents. The actor skillfully drew forth the secrets of the elderly residents' _____.
(A) elicit . . . reprisal
(B) emaciate . . . biennium
(C) elicit . . . longevity
(D) emaciate . . . extortion
(E) extort . . . fiasco

27. One _____ woman, who weighed about eighty pounds, was so _____ that when she spoke her voice was barely audible.
(A) biennial . . . taciturn
(B) equivocal . . . capricious
(C) capricious . . . biennial
(D) emaciated . . . taciturn
(E) biennial . . . capricious

28. Len _____ from one man the secret of his long life: _____ hike in the mountains. "Every other year is my limit," he said.
(A) emaciated . . . a taciturn
(B) extorted . . . an elicitable
(C) elicited . . . an emaciated
(D) emaciated . . . a capricious
(E) elicited . . . a biennial

29. A 101-year-old woman was _____; she changed her answer fives times. Len pretended to be _____ the truth from her, and after several joking "threats," she laughingly shouted, "Radishes!"
(A) emaciated . . . eliciting
(B) biennial . . . emaciating
(C) capricious . . . extorting
(D) extortive . . . emaciating
(E) elicited . . . extorting

30. The interview results may seem _____ to some viewers, but the overall impression was not at all ambiguous. Len hoped the program would _____ favorable reviews and draw out a positive viewer response.
(A) taciturn . . . extort
(B) equivocal . . . elicit
(C) biennial . . . elicit
(D) capricious . . . emaciate
(E) emaciated . . . extort

CONNECTING NEW WORDS AND PATTERNS

Why We Practice Analogies

Practice with analogies develops proficiency in logic. To answer analogy questions correctly, you analyze two words and identify the relationship between them; then you identify another pair of words that has the same relationship. In addition, when you study analogies, you think about the precise meanings of words and fix these definitions in your memory. Finally, studying word analogies will help you to gain higher scores on national tests that include multiple-choice analogy questions. The new Scholastic Aptitude Test-I Verbal Reasoning Test, for example, includes analogy questions.

Understanding Word Analogies

A word analogy is a comparison between two pairs of words. Here's how word analogies are written:

EXAMPLE 1   FIND : LOCATE :: lose : misplace

The colon (:) stands for the phrase "is related to." Here's how to read the relationships in Example 1:

> FIND [is related to] LOCATE
> lose [is related to] misplace

The double colon [::] between the two pairs of words stands for the phrase "in the same way that." Here's how to read the complete analogy:

> FIND [is related to] LOCATE
> [in the same way that]
> lose [is related to] misplace

Here's another way:

> FIND is to LOCATE as lose is to misplace.

A properly constructed analogy, then, tells us that the relationship between the first pair of words is the same as the relationship between the second pair of words. In Example 1, *find* and *locate* are synonyms, just as *lose* and *misplace* are synonyms.

Let's look at another example:

EXAMPLE 2   GIFT : JOY :: grief : tears

What's the relationship here? A *gift* causes *joy*, just as *grief* causes *tears*. A cause-and-effect relationship links the two pairs of words in Example 2. To help you identify the relationships expressed in analogies, we have designed the chart on page 124. No chart, of course, could include all possible relationships between words, but these twelve relationships are frequently presented. You should familiarize yourself with these relationships.

TYPES OF ANALOGIES		
RELATIONSHIP	**EXAMPLE**	**EXPLANATION**
Synonym	DRY : ARID :: lost : mislaid	*Dry* is similar in meaning to *arid,* just as *lost* is similar in meaning to *mislaid.*
Antonym	KIND : CRUEL :: happy : sad	*Kind* is the opposite of *cruel,* just as *happy* is the opposite of *sad.*
Part and Whole	CHAPTER : BOOK :: fender : automobile	A *chapter* is a part of a *book,* just as a *fender* is a part of an *automobile.*
	POEM : STANZAS :: play : acts	A *poem* is composed of *stanzas,* just as a *play* is composed of *acts.*
Characteristic Quality	MIRROR : SMOOTH :: sandpaper : rough	*Mirrors* are characteristically *smooth,* just as *sandpaper* is characteristically *rough.*
Classification	POLKA : DANCE :: frog : amphibian	A *polka* may be classified as a *dance,* just as a *frog* may be classified as an *amphibian.*
	BIRD : CARDINAL :: house : igloo	A *cardinal* is classified as a *bird,* just as an *igloo* is classified as a *house.*
Cause and Effect	GIFT : JOY :: rain : flood	A *gift* can cause *joy,* just as *rain* can cause a *flood.*
	TEARS : SADNESS :: smiles : joy	*Tears* are an effect of *sadness,* just as *smiles* are an effect of *joy.*
Function	KNIFE : CUT :: shovel : dig	The function of a *knife* is to *cut,* just as the function of a *shovel* is to *dig.*
Location	FISH : SEA :: moose : forest	A *fish* can be found in the *sea,* just as a *moose* can be found in a *forest.*
Degree	CHUCKLE : LAUGH :: whimper : cry	*Chuckle* and *laugh* have similar meanings, but differ in degree in the same way that *whimper* and *cry* have similar meanings but differ in degree.
Performer and Related Object	CASHIER : CASH :: plumber : pipe	A *cashier* works with *cash,* just as a *plumber* works with *pipe.*
Performer and Related Action	AUTHOR : WRITE :: chef : cook	You expect an *author* to *write,* just as you expect a *chef* to *cook.*
Action and Related Object	BOIL : EGG :: throw : ball	You *boil* an *egg,* just as you *throw* a *ball.* (In these items, the object always receives the action.)

A Process for Solving Analogies

Your job in solving multiple-choice analogy questions is to identify the relationship between the first two words and then to find the pair of words that has the most similar relationship. Here are four hints to help you:

Hint #1.   Eliminate choices that represent relationships that do not match the relationship between the capitalized words.

Hint #2.   Eliminate choices that have vague relationships. Remember, the original relationship will always be clear. So, too, will the answer's relationship.

Hint #3.   Eliminate word pairs that express the same relationship as the capitalized pair, but appear in the opposite word order.

Hint #4.   If you can't determine the relationship between two words, try reading them backward. Remember that a cause-and-effect relationship, for example, exists whether the pair is written *Cause : Effect* or *Effect : Cause*.

Here's a process that will help you with analogy questions:

Answering Analogy Questions: A 3-Step Method

1.   Identify the relationship between the capitalized pair of words.
2.   Look for that relationship in the pairs of words in the answer choices. Eliminate those that do not have that relationship.
3.   Choose the pair of words whose relationship and word order match those of the capitalized pair.

Let's apply this pattern to a sample question in Example 3.

EXAMPLE 3   FISH : SEA ::

      (A)   sun : star
      (B)   hero : villain
      (C)   moose : forest
      (D)   spacesuit : astronaut
      (E)   garage : car

1.   *Identify the relationship.* It's location; a *fish* can be found in the *sea.*
2.   *Eliminate choices.* Choice A has a relationship of classification; the *sun* is a *star.* Choice B has two opposites; *hero* is an antonym for *villain.* Choice D consists of a performer (*astronaut*) and a related object (*spacesuit*). None of these choices match.
3.   *Choose the correct answer.* Choices C and E both have location relationships: A *moose* can be found in a *forest,* and a *car* can be found in a *garage.* But Choice E could only be correct if the words appeared in the opposite order— *car : garage.* So Choice C must be correct.

A Final Word

Analogies are easier to tackle if you approach them with flexibility. Allow yourself to discover the relationship between the first pair of words and to explore the relationships between the words in the answer choices. Keep in mind that some words can represent more than one part of speech and that most words have multiple meanings. Remember, these little verbal puzzles are a test of your ability to demonstrate flexibility as well as logic.

CONNECTING NEW WORDS AND PATTERNS

Lesson 1 | ANALOGIES

Directions. For each of the following items, choose the lettered pair of words that expresses a relationship that is most similar to the relationship between the pair of capitalized words. Write the letter of your answer on the line provided before the number of the item. (*1 point each*)

____ **1.** ADMONISH : CONDEMN ::
  (A) change : alter
  (B) acknowledge : ignore
  (C) glance : stare
  (D) advise : suggest
  (E) admit : deny

____ **2.** BANAL : COMMONPLACE ::
  (A) extraordinary : average
  (B) forbidden : acceptable
  (C) nosy : respectful
  (D) famous : familiar
  (E) strange : unusual

____ **3.** LUGUBRIOUS : SAD ::
  (A) luxurious : shabby
  (B) dismayed : happy
  (C) awkward : silly
  (D) cluttered : tidy
  (E) jubilant : pleased

____ **4.** NEBULOUS : FOG ::
  (A) dry : shower
  (B) hazy : mirror
  (C) soft : blanket
  (D) hoarse : whisper
  (E) cold : sun

____ **5.** NEFARIOUS : VILLAIN ::
  (A) cowardly : hero
  (B) neat : chaos
  (C) vicious : rabbit
  (D) amusing : clown
  (E) grievous : merriment

____ **6.** NEMESIS : PUNISH ::
  (A) savior : save
  (B) crane : hoist
  (C) stranger : avoid
  (D) masterpiece : imitate
  (E) pillow : sleep

____ **7.** PHLEGMATIC : LOAFER ::
  (A) congested : vacuum
  (B) creative : artist
  (C) plentiful : void
  (D) cloudy : clarity
  (E) unusual : system

____ **8.** PROSAIC : EXCEPTIONAL ::
  (A) mistaken : erased
  (B) written : composed
  (C) poetic : theatrical
  (D) promoted : elevated
  (E) fancy : plain

____ **9.** PSEUDONYM : NAME ::
  (A) actor : performer
  (B) preface : novel
  (C) classroom : textbook
  (D) artist : musician
  (E) staff : writer

____ **10.** PURLOIN : THIEF ::
  (A) protect : vault
  (B) rob : bank
  (C) hide : disguise
  (D) counterfeit : money
  (E) measure : surveyor

CONNECTING NEW WORDS AND PATTERNS

Lesson 2 | ANALOGIES

Directions. For each of the following items, choose the lettered pair of words that expresses a relationship that is most similar to the relationship between the pair of capitalized words. Write the letter of your answer on the line provided before the number of the item. *(1 point each)*

_____ **1.** ASSIMILATE : FOOD ::
   (A) serve : waiter
   (B) water : hose
   (C) build : carpenter
   (D) join : organization
   (E) bolt : horse

_____ **2.** BLAZON : KNIGHT ::
   (A) helmet : safety
   (B) badge : police officer
   (C) professional : lawyer
   (D) border : carpet
   (E) musician : performance

_____ **3.** CHOLERIC : HOTHEAD ::
   (A) brilliant : genius
   (B) intolerant : baby sitter
   (C) weak : gorilla
   (D) aggressive : butterfly
   (E) patriotic : traitor

_____ **4.** COLLOQUY : CHAT ::
   (A) bridge : river
   (B) field : grain
   (C) conclusion : argument
   (D) opinion : disagreement
   (E) festival : gathering

_____ **5.** CONFER : GIVE ::
   (A) destroy : invent
   (B) discover : find
   (C) expect : wish
   (D) erase : add
   (E) ridicule : advise

_____ **6.** DIRGE : FUNERAL ::
   (A) cousin : relative
   (B) death : sorrow
   (C) hymn : music
   (D) intermission : play
   (E) instrument : composition

_____ **7.** ENNUI : INACTIVITY ::
   (A) route : map
   (B) placement : location
   (C) number : graph
   (D) energy : power
   (E) fatigue : labor

_____ **8.** FARCICAL : HILARIOUS ::
   (A) sincere : charitable
   (B) foolish : intense
   (C) good : excellent
   (D) violent : valiant
   (E) foreign : familiar

_____ **9.** FEIGN : PRETENDER::
   (A) operate : surgeon
   (B) nourish : food
   (C) falsify : document
   (D) gain : loser
   (E) write : proposal

_____ **10.** FORTUITOUS : PLANNED ::
   (A) forfeited : given up
   (B) punished : blamed
   (C) functional : practical
   (D) wealthy : prosperous
   (E) unfortunate : lucky

CONNECTING NEW WORDS AND PATTERNS

Lesson 3 **ANALOGIES**

Directions. For each of the following items, choose the lettered pair of words that expresses a relationship that is most similar to the relationship between the pair of capitalized words. Write the letter of your answer on the line provided before the number of the item. *(1 point each)*

_____ **1.** ASCETIC : SELF-DENYING ::
  (A) supporter : condemning
  (B) avenue : directionless
  (C) visitor : unwelcoming
  (D) concrete : rubbery
  (E) athlete : active

_____ **2.** DOGGEREL : VERSE ::
  (A) sonnet : poem
  (B) kennel : puppy
  (C) leash : trainer
  (D) list : item
  (E) book : literature

_____ **3.** DOGMA : PREACH ::
  (A) opinion : shout
  (B) lesson : teach
  (C) memo : remind
  (D) shepherd : watch
  (E) bridle : restrain

_____ **4.** EXHORT : ADVISOR ::
  (A) inspire : poem
  (B) ignore : counselor
  (C) correct : mistake
  (D) exhale : oxygen
  (E) testify : witness

_____ **5.** FACILE : SINCERE ::
  (A) remorseful : regretful
  (B) guilty : innocent
  (C) fatal : fanciful
  (D) honest : frank
  (E) sorrowful : unhappy

_____ **6.** INVEIGLE : DECEIVER ::
  (A) befriend : enemy
  (B) investigate : detective
  (C) follow : leader
  (D) celebrate : deputy
  (E) ring : receiver

_____ **7.** PROFFER : OFFER ::
  (A) certificate : gift
  (B) package : wrapping
  (C) thought : dilemma
  (D) trade : exchange
  (E) offense : defense

_____ **8.** SANGUINE : OPTIMIST ::
  (A) joyful : day
  (B) defenseless : warrior
  (C) sorrowful : mourner
  (D) genuine : hypocrisy
  (E) bright : shadow

_____ **9.** SCURRILOUS : REFINED ::
  (A) horrible : unpleasant
  (B) favorable : fortunate
  (C) scattered : distributed
  (D) flexible : rigid
  (E) hurried : frenzied

_____ **10.** SERAPHIC : ANGELIC ::
  (A) earnest : superficial
  (B) impatient : stubborn
  (C) spiritual : worldly
  (D) wicked : kindly
  (E) anxious : worried

CONNECTING NEW WORDS AND PATTERNS

Lesson 4 ANALOGIES

Directions. For each of the following items, choose the lettered pair of words that expresses a relationship that is most similar to the relationship between the pair of capitalized words. Write the letter of your answer on the line provided before the number of the item. *(1 point each)*

_____ **1.** ABSOLVE : JURY ::
  (A) lead : baton
  (B) conduct : orchestra
  (C) absorb : plastic
  (D) harmonize : choir
  (E) reach : solution

_____ **2.** ANTIPATHY : AVOIDANCE ::
  (A) success : confidence
  (B) emotion : happiness
  (C) remorse : victory
  (D) felony : crime
  (E) withdrawal : embrace

_____ **3.** ANTIPODES : OPPOSITES ::
  (A) circles : squares
  (B) electrons : atoms
  (C) friends : comrades
  (D) antagonists : conflicts
  (E) petals : flowers

_____ **4.** CHARLATAN : DECEIVE ::
  (A) banner : advertise
  (B) chivalry : rescue
  (C) campaign : organize
  (D) pedestrian : swim
  (E) impostor : trick

_____ **5.** ERUDITE : SCHOLAR ::
  (A) faithless : dog
  (B) strong : wrestler
  (C) freezing : sunshine
  (D) shy : leader
  (E) responsible : winner

_____ **6.** IMMUTABLE : CHANGEABLE ::
  (A) copied : imitated
  (B) sound : solid
  (C) allowable : permissible
  (D) steadfast : fickle
  (E) magnetic : powerful

_____ **7.** INDIGENT : WEALTHY ::
  (A) desperate : frantic
  (B) impoverished : poor
  (C) dignified : conservative
  (D) accurate : precise
  (E) solemn : silly

_____ **8.** INFRINGE : VIOLATOR ::
  (A) predict : outcome
  (B) cooperate : team
  (C) arrange : meeting
  (D) protect : awning
  (E) substitute : original

_____ **9.** NETTLE : PLANT ::
  (A) herd : cattle
  (B) cactus : desert
  (C) quarter : coin
  (D) kettle : whistle
  (E) crystal : gold

_____ **10.** OSTENSIBLE : APPARENT ::
  (A) fragile : delicate
  (B) clever : foolish
  (C) obvious : hidden
  (D) radiant : radical
  (E) sensible : sensitive

CONNECTING NEW WORDS AND PATTERNS

Lesson 5 | ANALOGIES

Directions. For each of the following items, choose the lettered pair of words that expresses a relationship that is most similar to the relationship between the pair of capitalized words. Write the letter of your answer on the line provided before the number of the item. *(1 point each)*

_____ **1.** ELEGY : POEM ::
    (A) stanza : line
    (B) preface : novel
    (C) fabric : linen
    (D) jet : airplane
    (E) forest : fern

_____ **2.** EULOGY : PRAISE ::
    (A) apology : demand
    (B) cartoon : amuse
    (C) fire : ignite
    (D) gymnast : exercise
    (E) masterpiece : create

_____ **3.** EUPHONY : PLEASANT ::
    (A) lightning : bright
    (B) whale : miniature
    (C) thunder : silent
    (D) miracle : understandable
    (E) mirror : dull

_____ **4.** EXTRANEOUS : ESSENTIAL ::
    (A) outrageous : enraged
    (B) excessive : limitless
    (C) assured : confident
    (D) desirable : worthwhile
    (E) cautious : careless

_____ **5.** HOMILY : MINISTER ::
    (A) greenhouse : orchid
    (B) tropics : parrot
    (C) steeple : church
    (D) examination : doctor
    (E) politician : senator

_____ **6.** INTROVERT : WITHDRAW ::
    (A) proposal : present
    (B) destination : arrive
    (C) entertainer : perform
    (D) announcement : permit
    (E) change : suggest

_____ **7.** MUNDANE : EXCEPTIONAL ::
    (A) meaningful : kindly
    (B) simple : complex
    (C) acceptable : appropriate
    (D) insufferable : unbearable
    (E) matted : woven

_____ **8.** PARAGON : MODEL ::
    (A) football : goal
    (B) teenager : high school
    (C) column : base
    (D) narrative : story
    (E) thoughtfulness : appreciation

_____ **9.** PROGENY : DESCENDANTS ::
    (A) retina : eye
    (B) granite : rock
    (C) projector : film
    (D) test : problem
    (E) kin : relatives

_____ **10.** SONOROUS : CELLO ::
    (A) destructive : bomb
    (B) silver : jewelry
    (C) functional : decoration
    (D) electrical : field
    (E) public : elopement

CONNECTING NEW WORDS AND PATTERNS

Lesson 6 | ANALOGIES

Directions. For each of the following items, choose the lettered pair of words that expresses a relationship that is most similar to the relationship between the pair of capitalized words. Write the letter of your answer on the line provided before the number of the item. *(1 point each)*

_____ **1.** CANDOR : DECEITFULNESS ::
 (A) frankness : openness
 (B) growth : decline
 (C) concern : consideration
 (D) respect : honor
 (E) art : creativity

_____ **2.** CONFIGURATION : SHAPE ::
 (A) science : chemistry
 (B) alteration : change
 (C) element : formula
 (D) constellation : star
 (E) museum : collection

_____ **3.** CORROBORATE : EVIDENCE ::
 (A) confirm : fact
 (B) meet : convention
 (C) cooperate : team
 (D) assist : copilot
 (E) hold : anchor

_____ **4.** DEARTH : SCARCITY ::
 (A) planet : galaxy
 (B) pleasure : anxiety
 (C) starvation : appetite
 (D) exaggeration : overstatement
 (E) wedding : ceremony

_____ **5.** DEDUCE : THINKER ::
 (A) reduce : taxes
 (B) give : contributor
 (C) produce : evidence
 (D) sing : orator
 (E) dedicate : monument

_____ **6.** DIURNAL : NOCTURNAL ::
 (A) urban : rural
 (B) advanced : sophisticated
 (C) argumentative : quarrelsome
 (D) fragile : breakable
 (E) vocational : occupational

_____ **7.** EXTANT : EXTINCT ::
 (A) swollen : enlarged
 (B) sheltered : exposed
 (C) tolerable : bearable
 (D) delightful : divine
 (E) exact : precise

_____ **8.** HERCULEAN : DIFFICULT ::
 (A) noble : mean
 (B) debatable : agreeable
 (C) exceptional : commonplace
 (D) challenging : easy
 (E) fascinating : interesting

_____ **9.** LUDICROUS : FOOL ::
 (A) remorseful : guilt
 (B) punctual : arrival
 (C) offensive : joke
 (D) funny : comedian
 (E) cloudy : day

_____ **10.** PROPONENT : SUPPORT ::
 (A) volcano : extinct
 (B) wool : spin
 (C) expenses : report
 (D) column : rise
 (E) forerunner : precede

CONNECTING NEW WORDS AND PATTERNS

Lesson 7 | ANALOGIES

Directions. For each of the following items, choose the lettered pair of words that expresses a relationship that is most similar to the relationship between the pair of capitalized words. Write the letter of your answer on the line provided before the number of the item. *(1 point each)*

____ 1. BUFFOON : AMUSE ::
    (A) proofreader : check
    (B) newspaper : print
    (C) balloon : inflate
    (D) narrator : narrow
    (E) editor : calculate

____ 2. CAPITULATE : LOSER ::
    (A) invest : money
    (B) complete : assignment
    (C) cook : chef
    (D) tune : instrument
    (E) reason : fanatic

____ 3. CIVILITY : RUDENESS ::
    (A) receiver : telephone
    (B) civilization : behavior
    (C) decency : courtesy
    (D) disobedience : anger
    (E) acceptance : rejection

____ 4. CONNOISSEUR : APPRECIATE ::
    (A) loner : join
    (B) scholar : study
    (C) conversationalist : convert
    (D) warrant : issue
    (E) initiator : follow

____ 5. FOIBLE : WEAKNESS ::
    (A) step : procedure
    (B) edge : disadvantage
    (C) oil : engine
    (D) failure : discouragement
    (E) division : separation

____ 6. GUFFAW : JOKE ::
    (A) expression : face
    (B) drawer : bureau
    (C) giggle : laugh
    (D) error : carelessness
    (E) inch : measurement

____ 7. INDULGENT : LENIENT ::
    (A) melodious : mellow
    (B) legitimate : illegal
    (C) fortified : strengthened
    (D) intense : evidence
    (E) diligent : lazy

____ 8. MAGNANIMOUS : SELFISH ::
    (A) divided : united
    (B) despised : hated
    (C) magnetic : attractive
    (D) selected : chosen
    (E) insistent : instant

____ 9. OBSEQUIOUS : OBEDIENT ::
    (A) impolite : impatient
    (B) gigantic : large
    (C) inspirational : boring
    (D) sequential : disorganized
    (E) obliging : harmful

____ 10. PUNCTILIOUS : CAREFUL ::
    (A) valuable : worthless
    (B) hostile : unfriendly
    (C) prompt : tardy
    (D) careless : thorough
    (E) superficial : artificial

CONNECTING NEW WORDS AND PATTERNS

Lesson 8   ANALOGIES

Directions. For each of the following items, choose the lettered pair of words that expresses a relationship that is most similar to the relationship between the pair of capitalized words. Write the letter of your answer on the line provided before the number of the item. *(1 point each)*

_____ **1.** CHASTISE : DISCIPLINARIAN ::
   (A) limit : regulation
   (B) study : student
   (C) pose : solution
   (D) enclose : wall
   (E) arise : question

_____ **2.** DEMAGOGUE : LEADER ::
   (A) democracy : equality
   (B) government : dictatorship
   (C) flavoring : vanilla
   (D) banana : fruit
   (E) vessel : ocean

_____ **3.** DETRIMENT : HARM ::
   (A) secretary : schedule
   (B) scheme : plot
   (C) garden : lettuce
   (D) retirement : relaxation
   (E) error : correction

_____ **4.** DISCREPANCY : INCONSISTENCY ::
   (A) failure : achievement
   (B) grief : jubilation
   (C) constancy : irregularity
   (D) harassment : prejudice
   (E) resolution : determination

_____ **5.** ILLICIT : BRIBERY ::
   (A) absent : presence
   (B) forgotten : remembrance
   (C) rough : silkiness
   (D) tall : skyscraper
   (E) strenuous : ease

_____ **6.** INSCRUTABLE : MYSTERIOUS ::
   (A) scholarly : learned
   (B) immeasurable : sufficient
   (C) worthless : valuable
   (D) exquisite : coarse
   (E) suitable : inappropriate

_____ **7.** INTERCEDE : PEACEMAKER ::
   (A) interfere : loner
   (B) interject : opinion
   (C) advertise : commercial
   (D) climb : ladder
   (E) oppose : antagonist

_____ **8.** OBNOXIOUS : PLEASANT ::
   (A) opinionated : inflexible
   (B) nozzle : hose
   (C) retiring : modest
   (D) ornery : agreeable
   (E) decent : respectable

_____ **9.** PERFIDIOUS : FAITHFUL ::
   (A) cordial : unfriendly
   (B) accommodating : helpful
   (C) strained : awkward
   (D) elevated : raised
   (E) stern : serious

_____ **10.** SUMPTUOUS : PALACE ::
   (A) crooked : highway
   (B) delicious : scenery
   (C) strenuous : relaxation
   (D) humble : mansion
   (E) skeptical : doubter

CONNECTING NEW WORDS AND PATTERNS

Lesson 9 | ANALOGIES

Directions. For each of the following items, choose the lettered pair of words that expresses a relationship that is most similar to the relationship between the pair of capitalized words. Write the letter of your answer on the line provided before the number of the item. *(1 point each)*

_____ **1.** ANARCHY : CHAOS ::
   (A) gorge : mountain
   (B) treaty : diplomat
   (C) order : court
   (D) diploma : graduate
   (E) virus : illness

_____ **2.** CAJOLE : COAX ::
   (A) hinder : encourage
   (B) advance : retreat
   (C) coach : play
   (D) start : begin
   (E) joke : insult

_____ **3.** COMMODIOUS : CRAMPED ::
   (A) melodious : harmonic
   (B) packed : concentrated
   (C) confident : assured
   (D) defensible : attached
   (E) boundless : limited

_____ **4.** ETHNOLOGY : ANTHROPOLOGY ::
   (A) technology : artistry
   (B) pediatrics : medicine
   (C) obstetrician : delivery
   (D) botany : plants
   (E) talent : culture

_____ **5.** IMPAIR : DESTROY ::
   (A) group : gather
   (B) decrease : build
   (C) create : finish
   (D) nibble : devour
   (E) persuade : discourage

_____ **6.** NADIR : HIGH POINT ::
   (A) galaxy : Milky Way
   (B) ocean : valley
   (C) failure : success
   (D) nation : country
   (E) tropics : heat

_____ **7.** PESTILENCE : DESTRUCTIVE ::
   (A) misconduct : acceptable
   (B) benefactor : charitable
   (C) violence : creative
   (D) complexion : pale
   (E) revolution : peaceful

_____ **8.** RESTITUTION : COMPENSATION ::
   (A) evaluation : recommendation
   (B) cowardice : intimidation
   (C) disintegration : composition
   (D) consideration : thoughtfulness
   (E) intrusion : invitation

_____ **9.** SUBVERSION : ESTABLISHMENT ::
   (A) conclusion : ending
   (B) initiation : acceptance
   (C) reduction : increase
   (D) substitution : replacement
   (E) division : subtraction

_____ **10.** VIRULENT : DEADLY ::
   (A) courageous : brave
   (B) tiny : immense
   (C) polluted : purified
   (D) healthful : alive
   (E) aggressive : meek

CONNECTING NEW WORDS AND PATTERNS

Lesson 10 | ANALOGIES

Directions. For each of the following items, choose the lettered pair of words that expresses a relationship that is most similar to the relationship between the pair of capitalized words. Write the letter of your answer on the line provided before the number of the item. *(1 point each)*

____ **1.** AUSTERITY : SIMPLICITY ::
(A) complexity : comprehension
(B) imagination : facts
(C) contract : lease
(D) starvation : hunger
(E) constitution : law

____ **2.** CALUMNY : SLANDER ::
(A) shock : ease
(B) thrill : excitement
(C) bribery : crime
(D) remorse : wrongdoing
(E) barbarity : civility

____ **3.** FOMENT : INSTIGATOR ::
(A) torment : tournament
(B) sleep : insomniac
(C) instruct : teacher
(D) conduct : investigation
(E) invent : computer

____ **4.** IMPASSIVE : EMOTIONAL ::
(A) refined : wealthy
(B) nervous : frantic
(C) violated : abused
(D) maintained : neglected
(E) quiet : shy

____ **5.** LITIGATION : LAWYER ::
(A) negotiation : diplomat
(B) publication : president
(C) calculator : computer
(D) curriculum : course
(E) university : library

____ **6.** MOLLIFY : SOOTHE ::
(A) welcome : thank
(B) moisten : saturate
(C) glorify : degrade
(D) offend : protect
(E) scramble : mix

____ **7.** OBESE : SKINNY ::
(A) dashing : attractive
(B) exhausted : empty
(C) agitated : calm
(D) obstructive : obstinate
(E) devoted : incompetent

____ **8.** SALINE : SALTY ::
(A) forbidding : crude
(B) shallow : deep
(C) excessive : sufficient
(D) occasional : regular
(E) coarse : rough

____ **9.** SEDENTARY : TYPIST ::
(A) willing : hostage
(B) passive : aggressor
(C) retiring : celebrity
(D) conceited : snob
(E) sincere : deceiver

____ **10.** TEMERITY : NERVE ::
(A) absurdity : silliness
(B) agility : awkwardness
(C) convenience : suitability
(D) timidity : braveness
(E) grace : skill

CONNECTING NEW WORDS AND PATTERNS

Lesson 11   ANALOGIES

Directions. For each of the following items, choose the lettered pair of words that expresses a relationship that is most similar to the relationship between the pair of capitalized words. Write the letter of your answer on the line provided before the number of the item. *(1 point each)*

_____ **1.** CHAUVINISM : DEVOTION ::
  (A) criticism : insecurity
  (B) foreigner : nationality
  (C) cavalry : soldier
  (D) reverence : respect
  (E) nationalism : anthem

_____ **2.** FACETIOUS : SERIOUS ::
  (A) sane : reasonable
  (B) comic : ridiculous
  (C) uplifting : inspiring
  (D) ashamed : hopeful
  (E) caring : indifferent

_____ **3.** INEXORABLE : UNRELENTING ::
  (A) variable : constant
  (B) intricate : complex
  (C) competitive : cooperative
  (D) delicate : robust
  (E) creative : unoriginal

_____ **4.** MOOT : CONTROVERSY ::
  (A) flimsy : vault
  (B) strange : familiarity
  (C) moist : desert
  (D) gritty : velvet
  (E) illegal : crime

_____ **5.** OFFICIOUS : MEDDLER ::
  (A) graceless : ballerina
  (B) urban : farmer
  (C) innocent : flatterer
  (D) inhospitable : host
  (E) photogenic : model

_____ **6.** QUIESCENT : INACTIVE ::
  (A) quiet : absent
  (B) skeptical : doubting
  (C) extinguished : kindled
  (D) secretive : public
  (E) uncertain : confident

_____ **7.** REGIMEN : SOLDIER ::
  (A) barracks : sailor
  (B) region : country
  (C) coast : harbor
  (D) base : military
  (E) curriculum : student

_____ **8.** RENOUNCE : ADOPT ::
  (A) reinforce : strengthen
  (B) withhold : give
  (C) assume : guess
  (D) allow : permit
  (E) announce : whisper

_____ **9.** REPOSITORY : CONTAIN ::
  (A) sieve : strain
  (B) method : devise
  (C) scoop : drill
  (D) dialogue : establish
  (E) paratrooper : jump

_____ **10.** TREATISE : SCHOLAR ::
  (A) contract : document
  (B) lobby : hotel
  (C) treaty : peace
  (D) novel : scientist
  (E) memorandum : administrator

CONNECTING NEW WORDS AND PATTERNS

Lesson 12 | ANALOGIES

Directions. For each of the following items, choose the lettered pair of words that expresses a relationship that is most similar to the relationship between the pair of capitalized words. Write the letter of your answer on the line provided before the number of the item. *(1 point each)*

_____ 1. ACRIMONIOUS : BITTER ::
    (A) recognized : introduced
    (B) pale : colorful
    (C) dutiful : disobedient
    (D) shocked : enraged
    (E) perpetual : continual

_____ 2. BENEVOLENCE : GRATITUDE ::
    (A) balcony : theater
    (B) study : learning
    (C) donation : charity
    (D) production : auditorium
    (E) overweight : gluttony

_____ 3. COERCE : TYRANT ::
    (A) sculpt : model
    (B) transport : freighter
    (C) grieve : mourner
    (D) solve : problem
    (E) pierce : needle

_____ 4. CONSTERNATION : TRAGEDY ::
    (A) celebration : victory
    (B) scandal : embarrassment
    (C) miracle : amazement
    (D) academy : institution
    (E) celebrity : autograph

_____ 5. DESIST : PERSIST ::
    (A) detach : separate
    (B) affirm : confirm
    (C) occupy : vacate
    (D) inspire : conspire
    (E) determine : decide

_____ 6. ENIGMA : MYSTERIOUS ::
    (A) enthusiasm : deadly
    (B) satin : bumpy
    (C) neatness : tidiness
    (D) honey : sweet
    (E) elastic : rigid

_____ 7. FIRMAMENT : STARS ::
    (A) recited : number
    (B) ocean : whales
    (C) moon : planets
    (D) veranda : porches
    (E) rocket : spacecraft

_____ 8. GAUNTLET : ARMOR ::
    (A) museum : gallery
    (B) knight : horse
    (C) infirmary : patient
    (D) bristle : brush
    (E) chivalry : death

_____ 9. LOQUACIOUS : TALKATIVE ::
    (A) abrupt : dull
    (B) venomous : poisonous
    (C) slippery : shiny
    (D) horizontal : vertical
    (E) gratifying : frustrating

_____ 10. MISNOMER : ERROR ::
    (A) name : passport
    (B) editor : review
    (C) word : speech
    (D) distraction : mistake
    (E) nickel : coin

CONNECTING NEW WORDS AND PATTERNS

Lesson 13 ANALOGIES

Directions. For each of the following items, choose the lettered pair of words that expresses a relationship that is most similar to the relationship between the pair of capitalized words. Write the letter of your answer on the line provided before the number of the item. *(1 point each)*

_____ 1. ASSIDUOUS : CARELESS ::
  (A) meaningful : significant
  (B) prompt : tardy
  (C) important : critical
  (D) abrupt : sudden
  (E) careful : precise

_____ 2. AVARICE : GREED ::
  (A) tray : waiter
  (B) monotony : variety
  (C) hill : depression
  (D) vice : fault
  (E) selfishness : solitude

_____ 3. CONCILIATE : NEGOTIATOR ::
  (A) converse : conservationist
  (B) push : lever
  (C) arrive : deserter
  (D) measure : fabric
  (E) inherit : heir

_____ 4. DENIZEN : INHABIT ::
  (A) ornament : decorate
  (B) occupant : dwell
  (C) ruler : measure
  (D) tape : rewind
  (E) rent : collect

_____ 5. DURESS : FORCE ::
  (A) perfection : flawlessness
  (B) convenience : necessity
  (C) entrance : exit
  (D) communication : understanding
  (E) punishment : reward

_____ 6. EQUANIMITY : EXCITABILITY ::
  (A) arrangement : schedule
  (B) oversight : accident
  (C) enforcement : obedience
  (D) order : chaos
  (E) equality : democracy

_____ 7. INCARCERATE : JAILER ::
  (A) control : traffic
  (B) ignite : carburetor
  (C) lose : victor
  (D) fly : pilot
  (E) circulate : news

_____ 8. INIQUITY : PUNISHMENT ::
  (A) monarchy : government
  (B) physician : surgery
  (C) experimentation : discovery
  (D) money : poverty
  (E) hospital : institution

_____ 9. INORDINATE : EXCESSIVE ::
  (A) intellectual : physical
  (B) foolhardy : reckless
  (C) ordinary : exceptional
  (D) experimental : traditional
  (E) insubstantial : solid

_____ 10. MERCURIAL : CONSTANT ::
  (A) mischievous : harmful
  (B) virtuous : evil
  (C) villainous : wicked
  (D) consistent : habitual
  (E) parched : dry

CONNECTING NEW WORDS AND PATTERNS

Lesson 14 | ANALOGIES

Directions. For each of the following items, choose the lettered pair of words that expresses a relationship that is most similar to the relationship between the pair of capitalized words. Write the letter of your answer on the line provided before the number of the item. *(1 point each)*

_____ **1.** BAUBLE : SHOWY ::
(A) attic : underground
(B) marionette : alive
(C) cellar : elevated
(D) fish : feathered
(E) lace : delicate

_____ **2.** COMMISERATE : SYMPATHIZER ::
(A) memorize : motto
(B) investigate : investor
(C) penalize : penalty
(D) argue : debater
(E) protect : shield

_____ **3.** FESTOON : DECORATIVE ::
(A) repellent : pleasant
(B) ring : round
(C) festival : mournful
(D) vegetable : plastic
(E) peacock : plain

_____ **4.** FRESCO : PAINTER ::
(A) blueprint : architect
(B) monastery : church
(C) painting : frame
(D) stanza : poem
(E) bishop : cathedral

_____ **5.** FRUGAL : THRIFTY ::
(A) momentary : eternal
(B) frigid : cool
(C) new : antique
(D) frustrated : satisfied
(E) evident : obvious

_____ **6.** MAUDLIN : SENTIMENTAL ::
(A) modern : antique
(B) priceless : valuable
(C) crude : refined
(D) indestructible : fragile
(E) insufficient : enough

_____ **7.** OPULENCE : POVERTY ::
(A) privacy : solitude
(B) insurance : protection
(C) simplicity : complexity
(D) interruption : disturbance
(E) luxury : comfort

_____ **8.** PALLOR : ILLNESS ::
(A) cancer : disease
(B) patient : medicine
(C) tiredness : insomnia
(D) hospital : lobby
(E) isolation : loneliness

_____ **9.** PROMONTORY : SEACOAST ::
(A) height : ladder
(B) alligator : swamp
(C) state : county
(D) theater : projector
(E) island : beach

_____ **10.** REMUNERATION : COMPENSATION ::
(A) calculation : retaliation
(B) expectation : disappointment
(C) analysis : economics
(D) comprehension : understanding
(E) detonation : bomb

CONNECTING NEW WORDS AND PATTERNS

Lesson 15 | ANALOGIES

Directions. For each of the following items, choose the lettered pair of words that expresses a relationship that is most similar to the relationship between the pair of capitalized words. Write the letter of your answer on the line provided before the number of the item. *(1 point each)*

_____ **1.** ABSCOND : CRIMINAL ::
  (A) exchange : money
  (B) hoard : miser
  (C) whisper : secret
  (D) arrest : prisoner
  (E) write : report

_____ **2.** ADJURE : COMMAND ::
  (A) acquire : lose
  (B) require : suggest
  (C) acknowledge : deny
  (D) plead : beg
  (E) allow : forbid

_____ **3.** CAPRICIOUS : FICKLE ::
  (A) conditional : absolute
  (B) friendly : hostile
  (C) nonsensical : silly
  (D) sensible : sensitive
  (E) stylish : functional

_____ **4.** EMACIATE : BODY ::
  (A) carve : knife
  (B) sharpen : blade
  (C) nourish : food
  (D) build : carpenter
  (E) eat : dieter

_____ **5.** ETHEREAL : WORLDLY ::
  (A) required : optional
  (B) similar : identical
  (C) striped : marked
  (D) popular : common
  (E) elegant : luxurious

_____ **6.** FIASCO : UNSUCCESSFUL ::
  (A) scheme : unplanned
  (B) insult : kind
  (C) obligation : optional
  (D) outburst : calm
  (E) disagreement : unpleasant

_____ **7.** IGNOMINY : WRONGDOING ::
  (A) magazine : publication
  (B) manuscript : writer
  (C) persistence : success
  (D) virtue : reward
  (E) skill : training

_____ **8.** LONGEVITY : HEALTHFULNESS ::
  (A) distance : perspective
  (B) personality : humor
  (C) teaching : vocation
  (D) fitness : exercise
  (E) vandalism : destruction

_____ **9.** MALIGN : SLANDERER ::
  (A) play : umpire
  (B) govern : mayor
  (C) regulate : law
  (D) spread : rumor
  (E) designate : designer

_____ **10.** PROGNOSIS : PHYSICIAN ::
  (A) tradesman : butcher
  (B) sentencing : judge
  (C) athlete : gymnasium
  (D) education : course
  (E) vacation : camera

READING NEW WORDS IN CONTEXT

Why We Read Strategically

Reading is active. As you read, you step into the writer's world. When you come across a new idea, you usually look for a clue to help you determine the writer's meaning. You move ahead to see if the idea is explained, or you retrace your steps to look for any signs you missed.

You can use these same strategies to build your vocabulary. If you don't know the meaning of a word, you should look in the passage surrounding the word for hints. These hints are called context clues. The more you practice hunting for context clues, the better you can teach yourself new words, and the greater your vocabulary will grow. And strengthening your vocabulary skills will help you to score higher on standardized vocabulary tests.

The following example shows the kinds of context clues you will find in Reading New Words in Context lessons.

Strategic Reading: An Example

The state of Oklahoma is a state of nations. Although many people are aware that large numbers of Native Americans such as the Choctaw and the Chickasaw live in Oklahoma, they are not aware that the Indian nations of Oklahoma are **sovereign** peoples with their own constitutional governments. *In other words, like any other nation, they have the right to manage their own affairs.* However, because the tribes are nations within a nation, the United States government does have some **jurisdiction** over them. *For example, the federal government has the authority to govern its own activities when they take place on Native American land.* Even in these cases, though, the federal government's authority is limited.

The ancestors of large numbers of Native Americans living in Oklahoma today came to Oklahoma on the **infamous** Trail of Tears. *In the 1830s, the United States government began to remove tribes of the Southeastern United States from their homelands. The government pushed these tribes on a forced march to the west that resulted in the death of up to one half of the members of some nations.* At the time, many Americans did not seem to recognize the inhumanity of this action. Today, *however,* almost everyone **acknowledges** the tragedy of the Indian Removal. It remains a *barbaric,* **hideous,** *and shameful* blot on the pages of United States history.

In this case, the writer uses *restatement* to provide a clue to the meaning of the word **sovereign**.

Here, an *example* is used to provide a clue to the meaning of **jurisdiction**.

A *summary* of the events concerning the Trail of Tears provides a clue to the meaning of **infamous**.

Here, the writer makes the meaning of **acknowledges** clear though *contrast*. The use of *items in a series* clarifies the meaning of **hideous**.

Many people who live in states without large American Indian populations mistakenly believe that the tribes in Oklahoma live on large federal reservations. *This* **fallacy** may result from the assumption that American Indians have been unable *either* to accommodate modern society *or* to **reconcile** ancient ways with the modern world. The fact is that Native Americans in Oklahoma own their own tribal lands and are not tenants on government-owned property.

A *pronoun reference* is used here to provide a clue to the meaning of **fallacy**.

Note that a *coordinate conjunction* helps clarify the meaning of **reconcile**.

Today, the Choctaw, the Chickasaw, the Creek, the Seminole, and the Cherokee—as well as the other tribes in Oklahoma—are involved in modern occupations. Native Americans are employed in the fields of education, civil service, law, medicine, computer technology, and so on. But maintaining the traditional cultures remains a **priority**, *the number-one concern,* of many tribal elders.

An *appositive* provides a clue to the meaning of **priority**.

In many cases, the younger tribal members in Oklahoma are most **reluctant** to abandon the values of their traditional culture *because they find those values important in their own lives.* They are also learning the old arts and crafts. A young Choctaw might learn to create the jewelry, headpieces, shawls, or leggings that *are* the traditional **garb** of the tribe. Others concentrate on preserving the stories and the language. Some research and write about the history of their people so that the events of the past will not be **irretrievably** lost.

The writer indicates the meaning of **reluctant** through a *cause-and-effect relationship*.

Note that a form of the verb *to be (are)* provides a clue to the meaning of **garb**.

As a poet who writes a verse in the sand watches the tide erase it forever, Native Americans have watched the dreams and traditions of their grandparents fade into distant memories. Today, however, the Indian nations of Oklahoma struggle to regain their traditions and to make them meaningful in the present.

Figurative language is the key to understanding the meaning of **irretrievably**.

A Final Note

How can you learn strategic reading? Practice is a great way to improve your ability. The following lessons will help you recognize the different context clues a writer uses. As you complete each lesson, you will become a more effective reader.

READING NEW WORDS IN CONTEXT

Lesson 1 CONTEXT: Literary Figures

The passage gives you an opportunity to expand your vocabulary. Below are twenty vocabulary words that are used in the passage and in the exercises that follow it.

abject	distraught	lugubrious	propriety
admonish	euphemism	nebulous	prosaic
banal	finesse	nefarious	pseudonym
bellicose	glib	nemesis	purloin
commensurate	lampoon	phlegmatic	revile

Mary Shelley's Monster

Mr. Conlee said, "We've spent a few weeks studying the Gothic novel. By now, you probably have a good idea of the techniques that Gothic writers used. Can anyone give me some examples of Gothic conventions?"

Adam grinned and raised his hand. "Most of the stories have creepy settings—you know, like old castles full of cobwebs or dungeons with torture chambers."

"That's right. Writers of Gothic novels wanted to create an atmosphere of gloom or horror, and eerie settings helped establish the mood. Of course, the image of a dark, cobwebby castle or a chattering skeleton seems **banal** (1) to most readers today. But in the eighteenth and nineteenth centuries, such descriptions weren't yet stale from overuse; they were still quite effective. Yes, Dolores?"

"I notice that a lot of movies **lampoon** (2) those old Gothic novels—for example, I just saw one movie, *Young Frankenstein*, that satirized the original *Frankenstein*."

"Yes—Gothic tales are popular subjects for movie spoofs. Watching old film versions of the Frankenstein story, you may have difficulty appreciating how strange and horrifying the original novel was to nineteenth-century readers.

"And speaking of *Frankenstein*, I hope you all finished the book last night, because it's our next novel for discussion. Here's a tricky question: For two extra credit points, can anyone tell me whether Mary Shelley published *Frankenstein* under a **pseudonym** (3) or under her real name?"

One student piped up, "She didn't use any name! She published it anonymously in 1818."

"Emma is correct! Here's another question. What prompted Mary Shelley to write *Frankenstein*? I'm looking for a very specific reason, not a **nebulous** (4), or vague one."

Malcolm raised his hand. "Shelley and her husband, the poet Percy Bysshe Shelley, along with the poet Lord Byron and Mary's stepsister Claire, were staying in some villas in Switzerland. One night Byron suggested that they all write ghost stories, and Mary came up with the idea for *Frankenstein*."

Mr. Conlee nodded and picked up the story from there.

"Mary Shelley's thoughts turned to recent scientific discussions about the possibility of creating life. Such radical thoughts were not uncommon for Mary Shelley. She frequently disregarded conventional standards of acceptable behavior, what we call **propriety**

(5). And there was nothing **prosaic** (6), or dull and ordinary, about her intellect and imagination."

The Creation of the Monster

"Can anyone explain how the young Dr. Frankenstein created his monster?" Mr. Conlee asked.

"He **purloined** (7), uh, remains from graveyards, and he also stole remains from dissecting rooms," Emma responded.

"That's right. But I think you're being rather careful in your choice of words, Emma. Can you be more direct?"

"You're right. I used the **euphemism** (8) remains because I thought the word corpses was too gross."

"Well, it's true that Dr. Frankenstein used rather gruesome materials. And, as a result of using parts of dead bodies, he produced a creature that was not too pleasing to look at. Shelley notes that he has yellow skin and a 'shrivelled complexion.'

Good, Bad, or Unlucky?

"Now we must talk about the character of the creation," Mr. Conlee continued. "We usually think of Frankenstein's monster as a **nefarious** (9) character—a wicked villain, right? And we also tend to think of him as **bellicose** (10). He did, after all, wage war against his community, committing hostile acts such as killing innocent people. He even killed a child—Dr. Frankenstein's younger brother. The monster was so dangerous, in fact, that he became the **nemesis** (11) of his creator, inflicting punishment for what he saw as wrongs committed against him, like a Gothic Darth Vader. But is this the only impression the reader gets of the monster? Is he truly all evil?"

Dolores replied, "No. There actually is much sadness in his character. He wasn't bad to begin with."

"Yes, he is a **lugubrious** (12) character," Mr. Conlee agreed. "That he is deeply sad is evident in his question, 'Am I not alone, miserably alone?' He wants love but becomes **distraught** (13) when people flee from him in horror. Similarly, he wants acceptance but becomes agitated when he cannot find it.

"The creature tries to **admonish** (14) Dr. Frankenstein to let him know what he is becoming," Mr. Conlee continued, "but the doctor ignores the warning. In fact, the good doctor, unable to face his hideous creation, flees from it. He refuses to accept responsibility, and so ends up truly creating a monster, for his creation turns to evil out of bitterness.

"In probing the psychological aspects of both Dr. Frankenstein and his creation, Mary Shelley shows quite a bit of **finesse** (15)—that is, delicate skill and subtlety. She presents a haunting, heartbreaking story of an **abject** (16) creature. And his miserable condition is through no fault of his own; he didn't ask to be created and then abandoned. Throughout the novel, the tormented creature **reviles** (17) himself, cruelly attacking himself with such descriptions as 'deformed and horrible.'

"Mr. Conlee, do you think we are supposed to feel sorry for the monster?" Dolores asked.

"Yes, Dolores, I do. It certainly is difficult for a reader to have a **phlegmatic** (18) or indifferent response toward him. And I think Mary Shelley wanted us to feel the creature's misery."

Mr. Conlee concluded his introduction to *Frankenstein*. "Mary Shelley said she wanted to write a tale 'which would speak to the mysterious fears of our nature and awaken thrilling horror.' I think she was speaking sincerely, not **glibly** (19), because her *Frankenstein* is just such a tale. Her writing talent was **commensurate** (20) with her imagination—totally equal to it. I hope you'll see that as we discuss the novel."

EXERCISE 1   *Finding Synonyms* ✍

Directions. Reread the preceding passage. Then write on the line provided a synonym for each of the words in boldface. If you cannot think of an exact synonym, you may write a brief definition of the word.

1. banal _____

2. lampoon _____

3. pseudonym _____

4. nebulous _____

5. propriety _____

6. prosaic _____

7. purloined _____

8. euphemism _____

9. nefarious _____

10. bellicose _____

11. nemesis _____

12. lugubrious _____

13. distraught _____

14. admonish _____

15. finesse _____

16. abject _____

17. reviles _____

18. phlegmatic _____

19. glibly _____

20. commensurate _____

EXERCISE 2 *Reading Strategically* 👉

Directions. Now that you have read the passage and thought about the words in boldface, circle the letter of the correct answer to each of the following items. The numbers of the items are the same as the numbers of the boldface vocabulary words in the passage.

1. According to the passage, when does a word, phrase, or image become **banal**?
   - (A) It becomes **banal** when it is no longer used.
   - (B) It becomes **banal** when it becomes a useful part of our language.
   - (C) It becomes **banal** when it is used in a book about a monster.
   - (D) It becomes **banal** when it is overused and becomes stale.
   - (E) It becomes **banal** when it is used only in special situations.

2. In the passage, the word _____ provides a clue to the meaning of **lampoon**.
   - (A) serialized
   - (B) specialized
   - (C) satirized
   - (D) copied
   - (E) immortalized

3. How does the writer provide a clue to the meaning of **pseudonym**?
   - (A) The writer defines **pseudonym**.
   - (B) The writer contrasts **pseudonym** with the words real name.
   - (C) The writer uses an example of a **pseudonym**.
   - (D) The writer gives a list of **pseudonyms**.
   - (E) The writer contrasts **pseudonym** with the word anonymously.

4. In the passage, **nebulous** means
   - (A) specific
   - (B) Romantic
   - (C) lucky
   - (D) vague
   - (E) satirical

5. If Mary Shelley disregarded **propriety**, as the writer of the passage suggests, she
   - (A) cared little about what others thought of her
   - (B) was very concerned about proper behavior
   - (C) conformed to the conventional standards
   - (D) wrote stories everyone enjoys reading
   - (E) depended on society for acceptance and approval

6. In the passage, why is there nothing **prosaic** about Mary Shelley's intellect and imagination?
   - (A) Her intellect and imagination were extraordinary, not dull and ordinary.
   - (B) She never used her intellect and imagination to write prose.
   - (C) She was actually a rather dull person with an average intellect and imagination.
   - (D) She used her intellect and imagination rarely.
   - (E) Her intellect and imagination were used only in the pursuit of writing poetry.

7. We can infer from the passage that when Dr. Frankenstein **purloined** remains, he
   (A) stole them
   (B) destroyed them
   (C) made them
   (D) traded them
   (E) purchased them

8. In the passage, Emma uses the word _____ as a **euphemism** for the word corpses.
   (A) materials
   (B) monsters
   (C) bodies
   (D) people
   (E) remains

9. According to the passage, what does it mean to be **nefarious**?
   (A) It means to be agreeable.
   (B) It means to be kind and good.
   (C) It means to be misunderstood.
   (D) It means to be villainous.
   (E) It means to be inexperienced.

10. What strategy does the writer use to tell us that **bellicose** is defined as warlike and hostile?
   (A) The writer contrasts **bellicose** with an antonym.
   (B) The writer uses **bellicose** in a simile.
   (C) The writer says the monster was **bellicose** because he committed hostile acts.
   (D) The writer uses a metaphor as an example.
   (E) The writer uses **bellicose** in a series of words similar in meaning.

11. Because the monster becomes Dr. Frankenstein's **nemesis** after Dr. Frankenstein rejects him, the writer compares the monster by simile to
   (A) a Gothic creator
   (B) a wicked stepsister
   (C) a Gothic Darth Vader
   (D) Boris Karloff
   (E) a Gothic avenging son

12. The word in the passage that provides a clue to the meaning of **lugubrious** is
   (A) alone
   (B) evident
   (C) character
   (D) question
   (E) sad

13. In the passage, if someone becomes **distraught** because of unfair treatment, we may expect the person
   (A) to be happy
   (B) to be hostile
   (C) to be free from pain
   (D) to be agitated
   (E) to be alone

14. In the passage, **admonish** means
   (A) blame
   (B) warn
   (C) destroy
   (D) accept
   (E) show

15. When we read in the passage that Mary Shelley shows **finesse** in probing the psychological aspects of Dr. Frankenstein and the monster, we should realize that she
   (A) shows delicate skill and subtlety
   (B) shows very little sympathy for either character
   (C) views the outcome as disastrous
   (D) does not focus on the thoughts and feelings of the characters
   (E) exaggerates the traits of the characters

16. In the passage, the word _____ provides a clue to the meaning of **abject**.
   (A) haunting
   (B) abandoned
   (C) fault
   (D) condition
   (E) miserable

17. In the passage, **reviles** means
   (A) compliments enthusiastically
   (B) reveals
   (C) attacks with cruel language
   (D) lives in fear of
   (E) shows fondness for

18. According to the passage, why is it difficult to remain **phlegmatic** about the creature?
   (A) It is difficult because we don't understand him.
   (B) It is difficult because we can identify with his pain and sadness.
   (C) It is difficult because he is totally unlikeable.
   (D) It is difficult because we are bored by the story.
   (E) It is difficult because his behavior is unjustified.

19. What strategy does the writer use to let us know that **glibly** is defined as in a way that is too smooth to be sincere?
   (A) The writer uses a synonym for **glibly**.
   (B) The writer contrasts **glibly** with the word sincerely.
   (C) The writer uses **glibly** in a metaphor.
   (D) The writer uses **glibly** in a series of words similar in meaning.
   (E) The writer links **glibly** to the words thrilling horror.

20. We can infer from the passage that **commensurate** means
   (A) sincere
   (B) unrelated
   (C) equal
   (D) talented
   (E) imaginative

READING NEW WORDS IN CONTEXT

Lesson 2 | CONTEXT: Literary Figures

The passage gives you an opportunity to expand your vocabulary. Below are twenty vocabulary words that are used in the passage and in the exercises that follow it.

adroit	choleric	discursive	fortuitous
allay	cognizant	ennui	hyperbole
assimilate	colloquy	expatriate	incognito
blazon	confer	farcical	mesmerism
bravado	dirge	feign	omniscient

A Conference on Shakespeare

"All the world's a stage," William Shakespeare (1564–1616) wrote in *As You Like It*. For Shakespeare, all the world—at least the world of which he was **cognizant** (1)—was also a source of play material. One part of the world Shakespeare was aware of was the New World of the Americas, which was being explored by Europeans in the 1600s. You may be surprised to learn that Shakespeare **assimilated** (2) or absorbed knowledge about the New World and used what he had learned in his final play, *The Tempest* (1611).

My information about Shakespeare's "American" play came during a recent **colloquy** (3) of Shakespearean scholars, who were meeting to **confer** (4) about the sources, characters, and themes of Shakespeare's plays. Since the conference was open to the public, I attended several of the meetings to earn extra credit in my senior English course.

In the program, the discussion about *The Tempest* was called "Shakespeare Discovers America!" I suspected that the title of the discussion was a **hyperbole** (5), an obvious exaggeration made for effect. It was designed to catch people's attention, and it certainly caught mine.

Waiting for the discussion to begin, I was intensely curious: What was Shakespeare's connection to the New World? The speaker was quick to **allay** (6) or lessen the suspense. He explained that *The Tempest* is not set in America and that Shakespeare did not write about New World explorations. However, the speaker said that Shakespeare must have read about the explorations and must have been inspired by them, for *The Tempest* is full of references to Renaissance exploration.

The Bermuda Connection

In particular, it is almost certain that Shake–speare knew about the adventures of a group of English sailors who were stranded on the Bermuda islands in 1609–1610. For nine months, the sailors thrived on these islands and experienced a kind of natural paradise. It is probable, some scholars say, that Shake–speare had read the published narratives of the sailors' adventures, as well as a letter from William Strachey, one of the seafarers. There is a deliberate connection between the Bermuda adventures and *The Tempest*, some scholars maintain. They say it is not just **fortuitous** (7) that *The Tempest* includes some details from the narratives, nor is it accidental that Shakespeare emphasized a sense of wonder connected with an island paradise.

Shakespeare very **adroitly** (8), or skillfully, captures the mystery and wonder of an island paradise in *The Tempest*. In the play, Prospero, the rightful duke of Milan, and his daughter, Miranda, live on an enchanted island with the half-human Caliban and the sprite Ariel. The play includes **mesmerism** (9) in the hypnotic abilities of Prospero, a magician; **farcical** (10) incidents, such as the comical scene of the disappearing banquet; and **choleric** (11) characters whose bad tempers are no match for magic.

Caliban, scholars point out, is almost an anagram of the word cannibal. It is likely that the character Caliban represents the image of primitive people that was held by early New World adventurers. The conference speaker reminded us that today's scholars are not **omniscient** (12). They are not all-knowing, and thus cannot say for sure what source, if any, Shakespeare used for Caliban's character.

Other Shakespearean Topics

Some of the other meetings I attended were interesting; others were not. One meeting featured a **discursive** (13) speaker who rambled on for what seemed like hours about **blazons** (14) or coats of arms used on shields, flags, and pennants in Shakespeare's plays. I'm afraid my **ennui** (15) was obvious during that meeting. I experienced similar boredom

during the lecture and demonstration by a Shakespearean director who incorporates **dirges** (16) into Shakespeare's tragedies. To me, listening to funeral hymns is like watching ice melt. Thank goodness some of the other sessions were more exciting.

I especially liked the talk titled "**Expatriates** (17) in Shakespeare's Plays." Several of Shakespeare's plays, it turns out, deal with a central character who is an **expatriate**—a person who is exiled or who has withdrawn from his or her native land. Another lively meeting was about Shakespearean characters who travel **incognito** (18), their true identities unknown to others. In *Twelfth Night*, for example, Viola disguises herself as a boy and **feigns** (19) being a duke's page. Such characters in Shakespeare's plays usually succeed quite well in pretending to be other people. Such disguises, the speaker said, sometimes give the characters an amusing air of **bravado** (20), like cartoon mice showing false bravery against stalking cats.

I suppose that Shakespeare has been written about and discussed more than any other writer in the English language. The conference I attended was only one of many such conferences held all over the world. It's easy to see why there's such enthusiasm for Shakespeare's works: He offers something for everyone. My only misgiving about the conference was that I missed a session with the most intriguing title of all: "Shakespeare in Outer Space."

EXERCISE 1 *Finding Synonyms*

Directions. Reread the preceding passage. Then write on the line provided a synonym for each of the words in boldface. If you cannot think of an exact synonym, you may write a brief definition of the word.

1. cognizant _____

2. assimilated _____

3. colloquy _____

4. confer _____

5. hyperbole _____

6. allay _____

7. fortuitous _____

8. adroitly _____

9. mesmerism _____

10. farcical _____

11. choleric _____

12. omniscient _____

13. discursive _____

14. blazons _____

15. ennui _____

16. dirges _____

17. expatriates _____

18. incognito _____

19. feigns _____

20. bravado _____

EXERCISE 2 *Reading Strategically*

Directions. Now that you have read the passage and thought about the words in boldface, circle the letter of the correct answer to each of the following items. The numbers of the items are the same as the numbers of the boldface vocabulary words in the passage.

1. In the passage, the word that provides a clue to the meaning of **cognizant** is
   (A) explored
   (B) aware
   (C) world
   (D) stage
   (E) source

2. According to the passage, what does it mean that Shakespeare **assimilated** knowledge?
   (A) It means that he investigated it.
   (B) It means that he absorbed it.
   (C) It means that he explored it.
   (D) It means that he rejected it.
   (E) It means that he ignored it.

3. In the passage, a **colloquy** is a
   (A) university
   (B) play
   (C) scholar
   (D) character
   (E) conference

4. If Shakespearean scholars **confer** about Shakespeare's plays, we may expect them to
   (A) watch the plays
   (B) discuss the plays
   (C) revise the plays
   (D) ridicule the plays
   (E) collect the plays

5. In the passage, a **hyperbole** is an _____ exaggeration.
   (A) exciting
   (B) unintentional
   (C) overused
   (D) obvious
   (E) unpleasant

6. In the passage, **allay** means to
   (A) increase
   (B) activate
   (C) lessen
   (D) understand
   (E) question

7. What strategy does the writer use to let us know that **fortuitous** means accidental?
   (A) The writer defines **fortuitous** as being a sense of wonder.
   (B) The writer links **fortuitous** to the synonym emphasized.
   (C) The writer links **fortuitous** to the synonym accidental.
   (D) The writer uses **fortuitous** in a simile about an island paradise.
   (E) The writer uses **fortuitous** to describe a shipwreck.

8. In the passage, **adroitly** means
   (A) skillfully
   (B) mysteriously
   (C) playfully
   (D) dishonestly
   (E) enchantingly

9. In the passage, the word _____ provides a clue to the meaning of **mesmerism**.
   (A) mystery
   (B) hypnotic
   (C) paradise
   (D) comical
   (E) tempers

10. We can infer from the passage that **farcical** incidents are
   (A) serious
   (B) magical
   (C) comical
   (D) hypnotic
   (E) enchanted

11. According to the passage, why can magic triumph over **choleric** characters?
   (A) Magic can make them more **choleric**.
   (B) Magic can make them feel guilty.
   (C) Magic is strong enough to defeat bad tempers.
   (D) Magic can destroy laughter.
   (E) Magic can make **choleric** characters even more angry.

12. When we read in the passage that today's scholars are not **omniscient,** we should realize that they
   (A) know everything
   (B) question all theories
   (C) understand the sources
   (D) don't know everything
   (E) rely on anagrams

13. If someone is **discursive** about a subject, the writer of the passage suggests we may expect the person to
   (A) keep strictly to the subject at hand
   (B) speak loudly, clearly, and plainly
   (C) read the entire speech rapidly
   (D) present charts and graphs as examples
   (E) talk a lot and not get to the point

14. We can infer from the passage that **blazons** are
   (A) coats of arms
   (B) dull speakers
   (C) jackets
   (D) boring meetings
   (E) lectures

15. The writer provides a clue to the meaning of **ennui** by
   (A) praising a director's lecture
   (B) linking **ennui** to the word boredom
   (C) implying that **ennui** is excitement
   (D) giving an example of **ennui**
   (E) using a simile to explain what **ennui** is

16. The writer finds listening to **dirges** very boring and compares it by simile to
   (A) attending a funeral
   (B) watching a sad play
   (C) reading a dull book
   (D) watching ice melt
   (E) directing a Shakespearean tragedy

17. According to the passage, **expatriates** are people who no longer live in their _____ lands.

    (A) native
    (B) adopted
    (C) favorite
    (D) holy
    (E) underdeveloped

18. In the passage, what characterizes people who travel **incognito**?

    (A) They are members of royalty.
    (B) They are Shakespearean scholars.
    (C) They are in disguise.
    (D) They are exiles.
    (E) They are wealthy.

19. In the passage, when Viola **feigns** being a duke's page, it means that she

    (A) learns
    (B) refuses
    (C) faints
    (D) tries
    (E) pretends

20. Because some characters have an amusing **bravado,** the writer compares them by simile to

    (A) stalking cats disguised as mice
    (B) cats that are afraid of mice
    (C) mice and cats that travel in disguise
    (D) cartoon mice that show false bravery against cats
    (E) actors who portray brave cats and mice

READING NEW WORDS IN CONTEXT

Lesson 3 | **CONTEXT: Literary Figures**

The passage gives you an opportunity to expand your vocabulary. Below are twenty vocabulary words that are used in the passage and in the exercises that follow it.

amorphous	exhort	nonentity	scurrilous
ascetic	facile	parsimonious	seraphic
decorum	guile	proffer	sundry
doggerel	inveigle	protégé	tacit
dogma	nondescript	sanguine	vociferous

Christina Rossetti's Goblins

"Goblin Market" is a haunting narrative poem by Christina Rossetti (1830 – 1894), an English poet identified with the Pre-Raphaelites, members of an artistic movement of the mid-1800s. "Goblin Market," her most famous work, tells a fantastic story that is excitingly presented and easily understood. However, the poem also has **tacit** (1) meanings beyond the expressed story.

The Story of "Goblin Market"

In the poem, two sisters, Lizzie and Laura, pass the Goblin Market each day. The goblins' **sundry** (2) or varied offerings include dozens of fruits—apples, lemons, apricots, and strawberries. With much **guile** (3), or cunning, the goblins **exhort** (4) the young women to buy the fruit. The goblins are not subtle in their urgings. In fact, they are loud and demanding to the point of being **vociferous** (5). Yet as noisy as they are, the goblins are never **scurrilous** (6); they are far too sly to risk offending the girls with foul language.

Lizzie tells Laura, who is plainly curious, not to look at the goblins' wares: "Their offers should not charm us,/Their evil gifts would harm us." At first, neither sister is enticed by the goblins' continual cries of "Come buy, come buy." Finally, though, the tricky goblins

inveigle (7) Laura to buy fruit from them. She says she has no money, but the goblins aren't to be foiled. They are no doubt used to tricking both the poor and those people who have money but are too **parsimonious** (8) to spend any of it. The goblins offer to let Laura pay for the fruit with a golden curl of her hair. Laura accepts, and she **proffers** (9) a lock of her hair, offering it in exchange for the fruit.

Finding out what Laura has done, Lizzie becomes upset. She reminds Laura about a friend of theirs who ate the goblins' fruit and died because she wanted more but could not have it. People who have tasted the goblins' fruit once can thereafter no longer hear the goblins' calls or buy their fruits. Horribly, however, their cravings for the fruit grow ever stronger.

Lizzie's warning is well-founded, for soon, like the goblins' other victims, Laura begins to fade away. She starts to die slowly because she cannot taste the goblins' fruit a second time. Lizzie, who fortunately has a **sanguine** (10) temperament, is, as usual, optimistic and hopeful, even in the face of tragedy. She decides to go to the Goblin Market, confident that she can somehow save Laura's life.

Lizzie finds the goblins. Rossetti does not present these supernatural beings as nondescript (11) creatures but describes them as "[c]at-like and rat-like." The goblins will not sell Lizzie any fruit to take back to Laura unless Lizzie herself will taste the fruit. Lizzie staunchly refuses the temptation. Her refusal makes the goblins angry, and they squeeze their fruits against Lizzie's face. Lizzie holds fast against the goblins' assault, and she avoids eating the fruit. The goblins finally give up, and Lizzie goes home. She lets Laura drink the fruit juices and eat the pulp remaining on her face. In this way, Lizzie saves Laura by letting her have a second taste of goblin fruit. Laura stops fading away and is restored to her former seraphic (12) appearance; she looks like an angel with "gleaming locks," sweet breath, and dancing eyes.

Lasting Appeal

Rossetti's poem, still the most famous of all her works, holds the reader's attention from beginning to end. One reason for the poem's appeal is that the story revolves around strange creatures and their magical abilities. The story thus appeals to the reader's interest in the unusual and fantastic. Of course, the reader knows that goblins, like ghosts and trolls, exist only in the imagination. Yet even though goblins are nonentities (13), they seem real enough in the fantastical world of Rossetti's poem.

    Another reason for the poem's lasting appeal is its lively meter and inventive rhymes:

> Backwards up the mossy glen
> Turned and trooped the goblin men,
> With their shrill repeated cry,
> "Come buy, come buy."

Such lines are examples of very good poetry, not doggerel (14). It appears that Rossetti was a facile (15) writer, that she smoothly and easily fashioned her imaginings into concise, refined verse. "Goblin Market" is a well-organized narrative with a definite plot and structure, not an amorphous (16), rambling tale about mysterious creatures.

"Goblin Market" is more than an entertaining story, however. The poem may be viewed as a moralistic tale that warns people not to give in to evil or dangerous temptations. The poem may also be viewed as a religious story. Some critics have noted that the theme ties in with the biblical account of Eve because Laura eats the "fruit forbidden" that brings death. Some readers see the story as a Christian parable and point out that salvation from death, what Rossetti refers to in the poem as "life out of death," comes through love and suffering—Lizzie's sacrifice for Laura.

The Goblins' Creator

Such interpretations of "Goblin Market" seem consistent with its author's personality traits. Christina Rossetti was a very religious woman who believed in the teachings of the Church of England and strictly adhered to that dogma (17) all her life. She lived as an ascetic (18), denying herself fashionable clothes and other worldly pleasures and comforts. She was a shy, private person, raised in a loving, artistic household where decorum (19), or polite behavior, was stressed. It is perhaps hard to imagine that such a retiring person would have the courage to make her poetry—much of which involved themes of death and unfulfilled love—known to the outside world. In fact, some people credit her brother, the poet and painter Dante Gabriel Rossetti, with being her primary influence and critic, the one who helped her to create a bridge between her private world and the outer world. Still, she was far from being merely her brother's protégé (20). Although he did in many ways act as a mentor to her by promoting her career as a poet, Christina Rossetti had a firm grasp of her own talent and often disregarded her more famous brother's advice. Today, many critics regard her as the superior poet and see her talent as evidence not only of true originality but also of genius.

EXERCISE 1 *Finding Synonyms*

Directions. Reread the preceding passage. Then write on the line provided a synonym for each of the words in boldface. If you cannot think of an exact synonym, you may write a brief definition of the word.

1. tacit _____

2. sundry _____

3. guile _____

4. exhort _____

5. vociferous _____

6. scurrilous _____

7. inveigle _____

8. parsimonious _____

9. proffers _____

10. sanguine _____

11. nondescript _____

12. seraphic _____

13. nonentities _____

14. doggerel _____

15. facile _____

16. amorphous _____

17. dogma _____

18. ascetic _____

19. decorum _____

20. protégé _____

EXERCISE 2   *Reading Strategically* ✍

Directions. Now that you have read the passage and thought about the words in boldface, circle the letter of the correct answer to each of the following items. The numbers of the items are the same as the numbers of the boldface vocabulary words in the passage.

1. What strategy does the writer use to tell us that **tacit** means implied, or understood without being expressed?
    (A) The writer refers to a fascinating, fantastic story.
    (B) The writer uses figurative language as an illustration.
    (C) The writer contrasts the words **tacit** meanings with the words expressed story.
    (D) The writer links **tacit** to a series of synonyms.
    (E) The writer gives a quotation from the poem as an example.

2. In the passage, what does it mean that the goblins' offerings are **sundry**?
    (A) There is only one kind of offering.
    (B) The offerings are not clean.
    (C) There are only a few offerings.
    (D) The offerings are sold on Sunday.
    (E) There is a variety of offerings.

3. In the passage, the word that provides a clue to the meaning of **guile** is
    (A) offerings
    (B) cunning
    (C) curious
    (D) urgings
    (E) untrustworthy

4. In the passage, when the goblins **exhort** people to buy the fruit, they strongly
    (A) expect people to buy it
    (B) warn people not to buy it
    (C) prevent people from buying it
    (D) urge people to buy it
    (E) praise people who buy it

5. If the goblins are always **vociferous** in their urgings, as the writer of the passage suggests, we may expect
    (A) the market always to be noisy with the goblins' loud demands
    (B) people to be unaware of the goblins' presence
    (C) the market to be very quiet and peaceful
    (D) the goblins to be quietly charming and rather humorous
    (E) the goblins to be quiet and undemanding

6. We can infer from the passage that if someone is **scurrilous,** that person
    (A) is trustworthy
    (B) moves around quickly
    (C) speaks softly and politely
    (D) uses foul language
    (E) is like a squirrel

7. In the passage, the words _____ provide a clue to the meaning of **inveigle**.
   (A) money and foiled
   (B) offers and gifts
   (C) curious and charm
   (D) wares and buy
   (E) enticed and tricky

8. In the passage, what does it mean to be **parsimonious**?
   (A) It means to be generous.
   (B) It means to be poor.
   (C) It means to be stingy.
   (D) It means to be wealthy.
   (E) It means to be curious.

9. In the passage, **proffers** means
   (A) tricks
   (B) offers
   (C) steals
   (D) takes away
   (E) refuses

10. When we read in the passage that Lizzie has a **sanguine** temperament, we should realize that she is
   (A) violent and dangerous
   (B) optimistic and confident
   (C) bossy and overbearing
   (D) depressed and melancholy
   (E) quiet and unconcerned

11. According to the passage, why are the goblins not **nondescript** creatures?
   (A) The goblins are never described by Rossetti.
   (B) All of the goblins look alike.
   (C) The goblins are angels in disguise.
   (D) The goblins are described as having distinctive qualities.
   (E) The goblins are imaginary and therefore have no qualities.

12. When Laura is restored to her former **seraphic** appearance, the writer compares her by simile to
   (A) a goblin
   (B) a magician
   (C) an angel
   (D) fruit juice
   (E) a sacrifice

13. In the passage, what does it mean that the goblins are **nonentities**?
   (A) They are imaginary.
   (B) They are strange.
   (C) They are appealing.
   (D) They are popular.
   (E) They are real.

14. We can infer from the passage that **doggerel** is
- (A) bad poetry
- (B) a quotation
- (C) rhyming poetry
- (D) a poem about dogs
- (E) a complex rhyme scheme

15. In the passage, **facile** means
- (A) influential
- (B) fake
- (C) easy
- (D) definite
- (E) religious

16. If a narrative is **amorphous**, as the writer of the passage says "Goblin Market" is not, we may expect it to be
- (A) well organized and concise
- (B) vague and rambling
- (C) interesting and imaginative
- (D) creepy and unsettling
- (E) mysterious and subtle

17. In the passage, Rossetti's adherence to the **dogma** of the Church of England shows that she believed in the _____ of the Church.
- (A) progress
- (B) poetry
- (C) teachings
- (D) restoration
- (E) formation

18. When we read in the passage that Rossetti was an **ascetic**, we should realize that she
- (A) practiced self-denial and self-discipline
- (B) wasted money
- (C) wore fancy clothes and shoes
- (D) was too poor to afford even necessities
- (E) had a biting wit and a bad temper

19. In the passage, **decorum** means
- (A) worldly possessions
- (B) strict discipline
- (C) shy, private person
- (D) artistic household
- (E) polite behavior

20. In the passage, why should we consider Christina Rossetti to be more than merely her brother Dante Gabriel's **protégé**?
- (A) Christina Rossetti never listened to or trusted her brother.
- (B) Dante Gabriel never cared about his sister's work.
- (C) Although in many ways he acted as her mentor, she often disregarded his advice.
- (D) Dante Gabriel was never her mentor in the first place.
- (E) Although Christina Rossetti was a poor poet, her brother Dante Gabriel promoted her work.

READING NEW WORDS IN CONTEXT

Lesson 4 | CONTEXT: Literary Figures

The passage gives you an opportunity to expand your vocabulary. Below are twenty vocabulary words that are used in the passage and in the exercises that follow it.

absolve	erudite	infringe	retroactive
antipathy	extol	nettle	specious
antipodes	gratuitous	ostensible	subjugate
broach	immutable	predispose	truism
charlatan	indigent	prerogative	venerate

Chinua Achebe: A Criticism of Joseph Conrad's Heart of Darkness

Renowned Nigerian author Chinua Achebe (b. 1930) finds little light in *Heart of Darkness*, the famous novella by Polish-born English novelist Joseph Conrad (1857–1924). Although Conrad's story about colonial exploitation of Africans in the Belgian Congo has been generally **venerated** (1) since its 1902 publication (it was, in fact, the inspiration for Francis Ford Coppola's famous film *Apocalypse Now*), Achebe does not regard the novella with respect. In fact, Achebe considers Conrad's viewpoint racist and believes *Heart of Darkness* reflects Conrad's strong dislike of, or **antipathy** (2) toward, African people.

To begin with, Achebe says, in *Heart of Darkness* Conrad uses Africa as a symbol of a primitive world in contrast to the civilized European world. Achebe maintains that in Conrad's mind Africa and Europe are opposites. As **antipodes** (3), the two worlds can never share a common ground. Conrad seems to think it is his exclusive privilege, his **prerogative** (4) as a "civilized" European, to look down on all that is African, Achebe asserts. Achebe believes that Conrad attempts to pass off a falsehood as a **truism** (5) to his readers:

Conrad portrays Africa as a primitive, uncivilized heart of darkness as if that view were obviously the true one. Achebe refutes Conrad's stand by pointing out the respected accomplishments of African artists at the time Conrad wrote his story.

Achebe on Conrad's Racial Bias

Even more disturbing to Achebe than Conrad's use of Africa as a symbol of a primitive world is Conrad's depiction of the African people. Some readers claim that Conrad should be declared blameless since the racially biased views expressed belong to the fictional narrator, not to Conrad himself. But Achebe is not willing to **absolve** (6) Conrad of responsibility for distorted portrayals of Africans. Achebe is irritated by Conrad's descriptions of Africans as a "prehistoric" people who have a "remote kinship" with Europeans. He also is **nettled** (7) by Conrad's depiction of most Africans as being incapable of speech and uttering instead "a violent babble of uncouth sounds." Conrad apparently regards Africans as **immutable** (8) savages unchanged since prehistoric times. Achebe notes that the Africans in *Heart of Darkness* seem to have no function in their lives other than to plague Marlow, the European narrator.

Achebe indicates that he is not swayed in his opinion of *Heart of Darkness* by arguments that Conrad's apparent purpose was to show the terrible atrocities committed against the **indigent** (9) or poor people of the Congo by King Leopold of Belgium. Leopold's goal was to **subjugate** (10) the Congo for its rich resources, to conquer the land and its people. In a trip to the Congo in 1890, Conrad saw firsthand how ruthlessly Leopold was **infringing** (11), or trespassing, on the rights of the Congo's inhabitants. For Achebe, however, this **ostensible** (12) purpose of Conrad's is overshadowed by what he regards as Conrad's hidden motive to dehumanize Africa and Africans. In Conrad's time, Africans were looked down upon, Achebe says, and this atmosphere of prejudice **predisposed** (13) Conrad, or made him susceptible, to a racist attitude toward Africans. Achebe also points out that Conrad had a personal obsession with issues of race and revealed a fixation with skin color that at times was irrational.

Are Achebe's Views Justified?

Achebe admits that Conrad's story does have some literary merit, and he praises Conrad's writing abilities. Yet Achebe says he cannot **extol** (14) the work as a whole because of its blatant racism. Achebe clearly believes his attacks on *Heart of Darkness* are not **gratuitous** (15). Rather, they are justified, he says, because Conrad's racism and stereotyped descriptions of Africa should be exposed and considered as central elements in the story.

Achebe introduced, or **broached** (16), the subject of Conrad's racism in an **erudite** (17), or scholarly, lecture in 1975. This lecture later was published in a scholarly review. As a result, writers and teachers took note of Achebe's comments about Conrad. They took his comments very seriously because they knew Achebe is not a literary **charlatan** (18); he possesses expert knowledge and skills. In fact, many critics rate him as Nigeria's greatest novelist and one of the finest English-language novelists in the world. His novels include *Things Fall Apart* and *Arrow of God*, both of which concern Nigeria's early colonization. Achebe has also been a professor, diplomat, and lecturer.

After reading Conrad's *Heart of Darkness*, you can decide for yourself whether you think Achebe's arguments are **specious** (19) or whether they actually are reasonable and true. Those who agree with Achebe may wish that his views could automatically become the accepted outlook of one hundred years ago, like a **retroactive** (20) law that would go into effect in 1890. Of course, time travel is not possible, but there is still much today that can be done to reduce racial prejudice. Achebe, no doubt, would approve of any light of racial equality shining through to transform Conrad's "heart of darkness."

EXERCISE 1 *Finding Synonyms* ✍

Directions. Reread the preceding passage. Then write on the line provided a synonym for each of the words in boldface. If you cannot think of an exact synonym, you may write a brief definition of the word.

1. venerated _____

2. antipathy _____

3. antipodes _____

4. prerogative _____

5. truism _____

6. absolve _____

7. nettled _____

8. immutable _____

9. indigent _____

10. subjugate _____

11. infringing _____

12. ostensible _____

13. predisposed _____

14. extol _____

15. gratuitous _____

16. broached _____

17. erudite _____

18. charlatan _____

19. specious _____

20. retroactive _____

EXERCISE 2 *Reading Strategically* ✍

Directions. Now that you have read the passage and thought about the words in boldface, circle the letter of the correct answer to each of the following items. The numbers of the items are the same as the numbers of the boldface vocabulary words in the passage.

1. In the passage, how does Achebe's opinion of Conrad's work differ from the opinions of those who have **venerated** Conrad?
   (A) Achebe highly respects Conrad's work.
   (B) Most people have little respect for *Heart of Darkness*.
   (C) Achebe dismisses Conrad's writing as unimportant.
   (D) Achebe thinks Conrad's work is not appreciated enough.
   (E) Achebe does not regard Conrad's work with respect.

2. In the passage, what does it mean that Conrad felt **antipathy** toward Africans?
   (A) He respected them.
   (B) He strongly disliked them.
   (C) He had an understanding of them.
   (D) He was sympathetic to them.
   (E) He lived in Africa among them.

3. In the passage, **antipodes** are

(A) opposites
(B) similarities
(C) activities
(D) assertions
(E) symbols

4. According to the passage, Conrad seems to think it is his **prerogative,** or _____ , to look down on everything African.

(A) portrayal
(B) burden
(C) privilege
(D) task
(E) exclusion

5. What strategy does the writer use to tell us that a **truism** is a statement that is generally regarded as true?

(A) The writer links **truism** with the synonym falsehood.
(B) The writer gives a definition of **truism.**
(C) The writer uses figurative language to illustrate **truism.**
(D) The writer contrasts **truism** with the antonym falsehood.
(E) The writer uses a pronoun reference to explain **truism.**

6. In the passage, why is Achebe unwilling to **absolve** Conrad?

(A) Achebe believes Conrad has done nothing wrong.
(B) Achebe believes Conrad is guilty of racism.
(C) Achebe wants everyone to read and respect Conrad.
(D) Achebe does not feel justified in criticizing Conrad.
(E) Achebe does not feel any anger toward Conrad.

7. In the passage, the word that provides a clue to the meaning of **nettled** is

(A) depiction
(B) violent
(C) regarded
(D) intentions
(E) irritated

8. In the passage, what does it mean to be **immutable**?

(A) It means to be unchangeable.
(B) It means to be hard of hearing.
(C) It means to live forever.
(D) It means to have prehistoric traits.
(E) It means to be bothersome.

9. In the passage, **indigent** means

(A) meek
(B) tall
(C) weak
(D) poor
(E) fast

10. In the passage, the word that provides a clue to the meaning of **subjugate** is

(A) resources
(B) atrocities
(C) conquer
(D) trespassing
(E) rights

11. If Leopold was **infringing** on the rights of the Congo people, we may expect

(A) the Congo's inhabitants to have had their rights supported
(B) the Congo's inhabitants to have encouraged Leopold's efforts
(C) Leopold to have improved the conditions of the Congo's inhabitants
(D) the Congo's inhabitants to have lost many of their rights
(E) Leopold not to have known about the rights of the Congo's inhabitants

12. What strategy does the writer use to tell us that **ostensible** is defined as apparent?

(A) The writer uses **ostensible** with a series of synonyms.
(B) The writer contrasts **ostensible** with the words hidden motive.
(C) The writer uses a quotation as an example of **ostensible**.
(D) The writer relates **ostensible** to the verb dehumanize.
(E) The writer declares that all purposes are **ostensible**.

13. When we read in the passage that the time in which Conrad lived **predisposed** him to racist attitudes, we should realize that

(A) Conrad was in no way influenced by the thinking of the time
(B) Conrad was his own person and formed his own conclusions
(C) the thinking of the time made Conrad susceptible to racism
(D) Conrad had to keep his motives hidden because he was sincere
(E) other people were unable to understand Conrad's attitudes

14. We can infer from the passage that to **extol** something is to

(A) criticize it
(B) publicize it
(C) absorb it
(D) despise it
(E) praise it

15. The writer provides a clue to the meaning of **gratuitous** by

(A) linking it to the word descriptions
(B) using the word blatant to describe racism
(C) contrasting **gratuitous** with the word justified
(D) using the word stereotyped
(E) implying that **gratuitous** means justified

16. In the passage, **broached** means

(A) introduced
(B) learned
(C) subjected
(D) criticized
(E) controlled

17. According to the passage, why did writers and teachers take note of Achebe's **erudite** lecture?

    (A) Achebe is very critical of Conrad.

    (B) Achebe is a very learned and scholarly person.

    (C) Achebe wrote only to offend other Conrad scholars.

    (D) Achebe is a very entertaining writer.

    (E) Achebe is too familiar with Conrad's writing.

18. When we read in the passage that Achebe is not a literary **charlatan,** we should realize that

    (A) a **charlatan** is a skilled and knowledgeable expert

    (B) Achebe has never been a published author

    (C) Achebe has expert knowledge and skills

    (D) Achebe has learned to speak and write in English

    (E) Achebe pretends to be something that he is not

19. We can infer from the passage that arguments that are **specious**

    (A) are actually reasonable and true

    (B) are never publicly written or spoken

    (C) are made by suspicious people

    (D) seem reasonable and true but are not

    (E) can easily be proven to be acceptable

20. Because many people will agree with Achebe's views, they might wish his views could be **retroactive**. To reinforce this point, the writer uses a simile of

    (A) the accepted outlook one hundred years ago

    (B) a law that is made now but goes into effect in the past

    (C) a law that was established in 1890

    (D) a person who dwells on historic facts

    (E) a light that shines into darkness

READING NEW WORDS IN CONTEXT

Lesson 5 | CONTEXT: Literary Figures

The passage gives you an opportunity to expand your vocabulary. Below are twenty vocabulary words that are used in the passage and in the exercises that follow it.

abnegation	eulogy	humdrum	paragon
ascribe	euphony	idiosyncrasy	poignant
copious	extraneous	inconsequential	progeny
elegy	hackneyed	introvert	sonorous
engender	homily	mundane	tenure

The Journals of Dorothy Wordsworth

William Wordsworth (1770–1850) was one of the greatest of England's Romantic poets. Yet many people are unaware that the great poet owed much of his success to another talented member of the Wordsworth family: his sister Dorothy Wordsworth (1771–1855). Dorothy's role as her brother's "dearest Friend," as he described her in the poem "Tintern Abbey," and her contributions to his life and works are clearly seen in the journals Dorothy began keeping in 1797. Through these journals, we know that Dorothy helped produce a harmonious home life for William. We also discover that her journal writings helped **engender** (1) or bring about some of her brother's finest poetry.

Making the Most of a Quiet Life

Dorothy Wordsworth was a shy, quiet person, an **introvert** (2). Beginning at the age of six, she lived with various relatives after her mother died. **Abnegation** (3) was second nature to her; having little money, she became accustomed to self-denial. At an early age she chose to devote her life to her brother William. Her desire to set up a household with William was realized in 1795. Even when William married in 1802, Dorothy remained with him, living in the same house with the couple.

The journals that Dorothy kept about the Wordsworth households may be called **copious** (4) because they are filled with information. She recorded many details about the ordinary or **mundane** (5) activities of their lives in England's Lake District. She wrote, for example, of the simple pleasures of going for walks with her brother, attending to domestic chores, and talking to friends. "We had sunshine and showers, pleasant talk, love and cheerfulness," she wrote of one outing in 1802. She found poetry in all aspects of life. She could write of the **sonorous** (6) sounds of waves tumbling against a lake shore, calling forth their deep and rich tones with her well-chosen words. She could just as poetically write of baking pies and ironing clothes. Dorothy also enjoyed children and often cared for the **progeny** (7) of William and his wife, Mary. Some people might describe Dorothy's life as **humdrum** (8), but it apparently wasn't dull to her.

Dorothy's talents as a writer are evident in her journals. Her writing is admired for its vivid descriptions, rich details, frankness, and energy. Her style is fresh and original, not **hackneyed** (9). For example, you may note the absence of trite expressions in the following excerpt from a January 31, 1809, journal entry:

> "I found a strawberry blossom in a rock. The little slender flower had more courage than the green leaves, for *they* were but half expanded and half grown, but the blossom was spread full out. I uprooted it rashly, and I felt as if I had been committing an outrage, so I planted it again. It will have but a stormy life of it, but let it live if it can."

Her journals show that Dorothy frequently took delight in happenings that might seem **inconsequential** (10) to someone else. To her they were not unimportant; they had great significance. Her writing is insightful but not overly sentimental. She was direct and to the point, and was not one to write a long, moralizing **homily** (11) where a brief description would do. She was not, after all, writing sermons for a lengthy Sunday service; she was recording the realities of everyday life.

In addition to her journals, Dorothy wrote poems, short stories, and letters. One of her works is a **eulogy** (12) to a couple who were killed in a snowstorm in 1808 and who left behind eight children. This tribute is a **poignant** (13) one, especially in its emotionally touching depiction of the eldest child, an eleven-year-old girl, who must become a mother to her younger siblings.

Dorothy's Influence on William Wordsworth

As you can imagine, Dorothy's writings are important sources of biographical information about her more famous brother, William Wordsworth. Through Dorothy's journals, we discover some details relating to William's personal peculiarities—his **idiosyncrasies** (14)—and to his writing habits.

Dorothy's journals were also valuable sources for William himself. When writing poems, he frequently consulted his sister's journals for details and descriptions. Some famous lines and images attributed to William actually should be **ascribed** (15) to Dorothy. For example, in her journal Dorothy wrote, "At once the clouds seemed to cleave asunder, and left her in the centre of a black-blue vault." In his poem "A Night-piece," William wrote, "—the clouds are split / Asunder,—and above his head he sees / The clear Moon, and the glory of the heavens." Both excerpts have an agreeable sound; their **euphony** (16) is, in fact, similar. Neither writer cluttered his or her thoughts with **extraneous** (17) words, but rather carefully chose only relevant, necessary words to evoke certain moods or images.

With Dorothy providing help and support in the background, William developed into one of England's foremost poets. Like a crown jewel among lesser stones, his writing is considered a **paragon** (18), a perfect example, of English Romantic poetry. Among his exemplary poems are lyrical ballads and **elegies** (19). (An **elegy** is a mournful poem, often about someone who is dead.) In 1843, William Wordsworth was made poet laureate of England. His **tenure** (20) in that office lasted until his death. Dorothy Wordsworth, on the other hand, knew no such earthly fame in her lifetime. For many decades, scholars, if they studied her writings at all, did so with an eye only to learning more about William Wordsworth. Today, however, an increasing number of scholars are finding much to admire in Dorothy's journals and letters. Even without the benefit of the kind of education her brother—and other male writers of the time—received, Dorothy managed to develop a perspective and a literary voice all her own.

EXERCISE 1 *Finding Synonyms*

Directions. Reread the preceding passage. Then write on the line provided a synonym for each of the words in boldface. If you cannot think of an exact synonym, you may write a brief definition of the word.

1. engender _____

2. introvert _____

3. abnegation _____

4. copious _____

5. mundane _____

6. sonorous _____

7. progeny _____

8. humdrum _____

9. hackneyed _____

10. inconsequential _____

11. homily _____

12. eulogy _____

13. poignant _____

14. idiosyncrasies _____

15. ascribed _____

16. euphony _____

17. extraneous _____

18. paragon _____

19. elegies _____

20. tenure _____

EXERCISE 2 *Reading Strategically* ✍

Directions. Now that you have read the passage and thought about the words in boldface, circle the letter of the correct answer to each of the following items. The numbers of the items are the same as the numbers of the boldface vocabulary words in the passage.

1. In the passage, the words that provide a clue to the meaning of **engender** are
   (A) clearly seen
   (B) journal writings
   (C) bring about
   (D) finest poetry
   (E) harmonious home life

2. According to the passage, what does **introvert** mean?
   (A) It means a social situation.
   (B) It means a loud voice.
   (C) It means a journalist.
   (D) It means a shy, quiet person.
   (E) It means an orphan.

3. In the passage, **abnegation** means
   (A) appreciation
   (B) accommodation
   (C) selfishness
   (D) activity
   (E) self-denial

4. In the passage, **copious** means
   (A) without mistakes
   (B) domestic
   (C) full of information
   (D) unable to cope
   (E) disorganized

5. The writer provides a clue to the meaning of **mundane** by
   (A) linking **mundane** to two antonyms
   (B) using the prepositional phrase "of their lives"
   (C) using the simile of simple pleasures
   (D) relating **mundane** to the word activities
   (E) linking **mundane** to the synonym ordinary

6. In the passage, **sonorous** means
   (A) high and thin
   (B) deep and thin
   (C) high and loud
   (D) deep and rich
   (E) slow and loud

7. We can infer from the passage that Dorothy was well suited to caring for William and Mary Wordsworth's **progeny** because
(A) she baked pies
(B) she liked children
(C) she never did housework
(D) she was rich
(E) she had children of her own

8. In the passage, the word that provides a clue to the meaning of **humdrum** is
(A) dull
(B) life
(C) written
(D) enjoyed
(E) rich

9. According to the passage, what characterizes a **hackneyed** style?
(A) Vivid descriptions characterize it.
(B) Journals written by the sisters of poets characterize it.
(C) Frankness and energy characterize it.
(D) Stale writing and trite expressions characterize it.
(E) Writing that is obscure and difficult characterizes it.

10. In the passage, what does it mean for happenings to be **inconsequential**?
(A) It means for them to be important.
(B) It means for them to be unimportant.
(C) It means for them to be outdoors.
(D) It means for them to be insightful.
(E) It means for them to occur frequently.

11. Dorothy never wrote a **homily**, but the writer of the passage suggests that many **homilies** are
(A) lively, fresh, descriptive passages
(B) tightly written poems
(C) funny, cheerful, and short articles
(D) long and involved jokes
(E) long and moralizing pieces of writing

12. We can infer from the passage that a **eulogy** is a
(A) cheerful letter to a friend
(B) description of a family friend
(C) question about something
(D) tribute to someone who has died
(E) commentary on the meaning of life

13. When we read in the passage that Dorothy's tribute is a **poignant** one, we should realize that it is
(A) not well written
(B) a very famous poem
(C) the only thing she wrote
(D) emotionally touching
(E) emotionally detached

14. In the passage, **idiosyncrasies** means

(A) personal details

(B) religious practices

(C) personal sleep habits

(D) personal peculiarities

(E) family members and friends

15. In the passage, the word that provides a clue to the meaning of **ascribed** is

(A) valuable

(B) attributed

(C) consulted

(D) sources

(E) descriptions

16. Dorothy's journal writing and William's poetry have a **euphony** because they both have _____ sounds when read aloud.

(A) noisy

(B) sad

(C) agreeable

(D) unnatural

(E) exciting

17. If the Wordsworths did not use **extraneous** words, as the writer of the passage suggests, we may expect

(A) the words they used to be relevant and necessary to the subject

(B) their writing to ramble on about uninteresting things

(C) their writing to be very difficult to understand

(D) their writing to be cluttered with unnecessary descriptions

(E) the words they used to apply to all subjects

18. Because William Wordsworth's writing is regarded as a **paragon** of English Romantic poetry, the writer compares it by simile to

(A) Dorothy Wordsworth's writing

(B) the death of a loved one

(C) a pyramid in the desert

(D) a crown jewel among lesser stones

(E) lyrical ballads written by Coleridge

19. What strategy does the writer use to tell us the meaning of **elegies**?

(A) The writer uses an example of an **elegy**.

(B) The writer defines **elegy**.

(C) The writer uses the synonym ballad for **elegy**.

(D) The writer uses the antonym mournful for **elegy**.

(E) The writer uses a simile about someone who is dead.

20. When we read in the passage that William Wordsworth's **tenure** lasted until his death, we should realize that

(A) **tenure** has to do with writing poetry

(B) **tenure** is the length of time a position is held

(C) a person has to die to obtain **tenure**

(D) **tenure** always lasts multiples of ten years

(E) people who write poetry lose **tenure** when they die

READING NEW WORDS IN CONTEXT

| Lesson 6 | **CONTEXT: History and Society**

The passage gives you an opportunity to expand your vocabulary. Below are twenty vocabulary words that are used in the passage and in the exercises that follow it.

aberration	captivate	deduce	proponent
adjudge	chicanery	diurnal	refute
artifice	configuration	extant	retrospect
augury	corroborate	herculean	salient
candor	dearth	ludicrous	scrupulous

Two British Mysteries

The First Mystery: Stonehenge

You stand within a circle of massive stones and stare at a strange **configuration** (1), wondering why the stones are arranged to form such an outline. Many stones are capped with other stones, forming open doorway-like constructions. Beyond the giant stones you can see the rolling farmlands of the Salisbury Plain in southern England.

You are standing at Stonehenge, one of England's greatest mysteries and tourist attractions. Stonehenge is a **salient** (2) feature on the grassy plain, as noticeable and conspicuous as a house in the middle of an otherwise vacant field. The stones obviously are very ancient, and you are amazed that they have not been destroyed but are **extant** (3) today. When and how did these rugged, giant stones come to be placed here? Who placed them, and why?

In the twelfth century, British chronicler Geoffrey of Monmouth wrote that an ancient king erected Stonehenge as a monument. According to the story, the magician Merlin told the king to travel to Ireland and bring back a group of sacred stones. But it would have taken someone with the superhuman strength of the Greek hero Hercules to accomplish this feat; certainly the king's soldiers were unable

to carry out the **herculean** (4) task of moving the stones. Merlin came up with an alternative: He constructed magic machines that moved the stones across the water from Ireland.

Is this story ridiculous, merely a **ludicrous** (5) fairy tale? Perhaps, but in the 1950s, the researcher Richard J. C. Atkinson believed that he had identified Merlin's so-called magic machines. Reasoning from historical knowledge, Atkinson **deduced** (6) that the stones were transported on rafts along the west coast of Britain and then up rivers on canoes. Thus, Atkinson, in a sense, confirmed or **corroborated** (7) the tale of Merlin's magic machines.

Today, we know that the construction of Stonehenge began about 2800 B.C. No records of its construction were ever made, but there is no lack, or **dearth** (8), of speculations about the purposes for which Stonehenge was built.

Why Was Stonehenge Built?

Recent investigations have revealed that the stones were assembled by early peoples of Western Europe, not by visitors from foreign civilizations. But why was Stonehenge built? What possible purpose did it serve? One researcher, Professor Gerald S. Hawkins, believes he has the answer. In the early 1960s, he made **scrupulous** (9) calculations, as precise as those a computer could produce, to identify the positions of the sun and the moon during the period of Stonehenge's construction in 2800 B.C. From these exact calculations, he concluded that the monument was actually an observatory for studying the nocturnal, or nightly, cycles of the moon and the **diurnal** (10), or daily, cycles of the sun. Scholars have supposed that religious ceremonies tied to the summer and winter solstices were held by early British peoples at Stonehenge. Perhaps Stonehenge even functioned as a daily calendar.

The Second Mystery: Crop Circles

You are standing in a field located a few hours' drive from Stonehenge. It is summer, and you can hear the faint rumbling of farm equipment in the distance. Looking around, you notice that an eerily precise clearing has been made in a field of wheat four feet high. It looks as though someone has mown away part of the wheat field. If you could get a clear bird's-eye view, you would see that a circle with a circumference of almost one hundred feet has been made in the wheat. The wheat all around the circle is standing tall, as is the wheat in the middle of the circle. You glance over at your guide, who is standing on another flattened area that seems to be shaped like a key. "How did these get here?" you ask her. Her honest and direct answer reveals a welcomed **candor** (11). "We don't know," she says frankly, obviously as baffled as you are. "They appeared overnight."

You are in the middle of a crop circle. You have become totally **captivated** (12) by the mystery of your surroundings. Fascinated, you explore further and find other patterns in the wheat: rectangles, crosses, and bars. You notice that the crops were not destroyed when these strange patterns were made.

How Are Crop Circles Created?

From 1990 through 1991, more than six hundred examples of crop circles were found throughout Britain. They are definitely **aberrations** (13), deviations from the normal. But what caused them? Some people believe they were caused by swirling currents of electrically charged air. Other people, **proponents** (14) of the UFO theory, speculate that the crop circles were caused by extraterrestrial beings trying to communicate with us. The UFO theorists see the circles as omens, or **auguries** (15), that aliens eventually will make meaningful contact with humanity.

Time magazine recently discounted these explanations, however, after two men claimed that they had created the patterns at night by attaching wooden boards to their feet and moving about the fields. According to the article in *Time,* the **artifice** (16) of these men—their artful trick—was the explanation that would disprove or **refute** (17) all other theories.

Problems, however, remain with this explanation. How could these men, even if they were able to deceive many by their **chicanery** (18), have created six hundred patterns in a year? And how could they have extended their trickery to twenty-nine other countries, where similar crop-circle patterns have been discovered? Unfortunately, the answer to this mystery is not one that can be **adjudged** (19) in a law court; perhaps it cannot be decided by any law, natural or supernatural.

The creation of the crop circles remains a mystery. Perhaps, however, in 3,500 years our descendants will examine the past. In the same way that we have, in **retrospect** (20), developed plausible theories about the origin of Stonehenge, perhaps they will be able to offer satisfying explanations for the mystery of the crop circles.

EXERCISE 1 *Finding Synonyms*

Directions. Reread the preceding passage. Then write on the line provided a synonym for each of the words in boldface. If you cannot think of an exact synonym, you may write a brief definition of the word.

1. configuration _____

2. salient _____

3. extant _____

4. herculean _____

5. ludicrous _____

6. deduced _____

7. corroborated _____

8. dearth _____

9. scrupulous _____

10. diurnal _____

11. candor _____

12. captivated _____

13. aberrations _____

14. proponents _____

15. auguries _____

16. artifice _____

17. refute _____

18. chicanery _____

19. adjudged _____

20. retrospect _____

EXERCISE 2 Reading Strategically ✍

Directions. Now that you have read the passage and thought about the words in boldface, circle the letter of the correct answer to each of the following items.

1. In the passage, the word that provides a clue to the meaning of **configuration** is
    (A) massive
    (B) strange
    (C) stones
    (D) outline
    (E) wonder

2. To illustrate what a **salient** feature Stonehenge is, the writer compares it by simile to
    (A) a house in the middle of an otherwise vacant field
    (B) the rolling farmlands of the Salisbury Plain
    (C) magic machines moving stones across the water
    (D) rugged, giant stones in Ireland
    (E) a circle of massive stones capped with smaller stones

3. According to the passage, why is it amazing that Stonehenge is **extant** today?
    (A) It is amazing because Stonehenge no longer exists.
    (B) It is amazing because of the location of Stonehenge.
    (C) It is amazing because of the age of Stonehenge.
    (D) It is amazing because we know everything about it.
    (E) It is amazing because the rocks are not from the earth.

4. According to the passage, a **herculean** job requires someone who is very _____.
    (A) sacred
    (B) honest
    (C) ancient
    (D) young
    (E) strong

5. What strategy does the writer use to tell us that **ludicrous** is defined as laughable or absurd?
    (A) The writer links **ludicrous** to the synonym ridiculous.
    (B) The writer contrasts **ludicrous** with the words fairy tale.
    (C) The writer defines **ludicrous** as happy.
    (D) The writer describes a **ludicrous** machine.
    (E) The writer compares **ludicrous** to the word magical.

6. What strategy does the writer use to tell us that **deduced** is defined as concluded by means of logic?
    (A) The writer describes the method used to transport the stones.
    (B) The writer links **deduced** to the phrase "Reasoning from historical knowledge."
    (C) The writer uses an antonym for **deduced**.
    (D) The writer uses a simile to describe Merlin's method of transporting the stones.
    (E) The writer uses **deduced** to explain different theories.

7. In the passage, **corroborated** means
  (A) refuted
  (B) praised
  (C) sensed
  (D) confirmed
  (E) disproved

8. We can infer from the passage that if there is no **dearth** of speculations, there are
  (A) only incorrect speculations
  (B) no speculations
  (C) many speculations
  (D) a few speculations
  (E) fewer than a hundred speculations

9. According to the passage, what does it mean to be **scrupulous**?
  (A) It means to be careless.
  (B) It means to be electronic.
  (C) It means to be exact.
  (D) It means to produce.
  (E) It means to estimate.

10. If the sun has **diurnal** cycles, as the writer of the passage says, we may expect them to be related to
  (A) the night
  (B) the tides
  (C) moonlight
  (D) the day
  (E) spring

11. According to the passage, what does it mean for people to speak with **candor**?
  (A) It means they speak secretly.
  (B) It means they can't be understood.
  (C) It means they don't tell the truth.
  (D) It means they speak quietly.
  (E) It means they speak frankly.

12. In the passage, the word that provides a clue to the meaning of **captivated** is
  (A) totally
  (B) fascinated
  (C) surroundings
  (D) destroyed
  (E) patterns

13. In the passage, **aberrations** are
  (A) revelations of mysteries
  (B) deviations from the normal
  (C) usual circumstances
  (D) currents of electrically charged air
  (E) seasonal rotations of crops

14. According to the passage, the people who are **proponents** of the UFO theory _____ that the crop circles are caused by extraterrestrial beings.

   (A) believe
   (B) deny
   (C) question
   (D) fear
   (E) disproved

15. In the passage, **auguries** means

   (A) circles
   (B) extraterrestrial beings
   (C) omens, or signs
   (D) alien contact
   (E) natural events

16. If the two men are successful in their **artifice**, the writer of the passage suggests that they will have

   (A) honestly created art
   (B) explained ancient signs
   (C) harvested crops
   (D) artfully tricked people
   (E) questioned authorities

17. In the passage, the word that provides a clue to the meaning of **refute** is

   (A) answers
   (B) artful
   (C) convince
   (D) mystery
   (E) disprove

18. When we read in the passage that the men used **chicanery**, we should realize that

   (A) they honestly tried to solve the mystery
   (B) they deliberately intended to deceive people
   (C) they hoped to perfect their methods
   (D) they became rich and famous for their work
   (E) they used electronic devices to make the crop circles

19. We can infer from the passage that if the mystery could be **adjudged** in a law court, it could be

   (A) decided
   (B) tried
   (C) denied
   (D) confused
   (E) extended

20. The writer provides a clue to the meaning of **retrospect** by

   (A) describing the creation of the crop circles
   (B) using an antonym for **retrospect**
   (C) saying that our descendants will examine the past
   (D) linking **retrospect** to the origin of the circles
   (E) using the word solve

READING NEW WORDS IN CONTEXT

Lesson 7 | CONTEXT: History and Society

The passage gives you an opportunity to expand your vocabulary. Below are twenty vocabulary words that are used in the passage and in the exercises that follow it.

affront	effusion	guffaw	patrimony
buffoon	exhilaration	indulgent	precocious
capitulate	foible	magnanimous	propitious
civility	germane	munificent	punctilious
connoisseur	gregarious	obsequious	querulous

Samuel Johnson: A Great Man of Letters

Samuel Johnson (1709–1784) was an expert in the English language as well as a **connoisseur** (1) of eighteenth-century English literature and culture. He is famous for a variety of writings, including *A Dictionary of the English Language*, which remained the definitive English dictionary for more than a century and a half.

A Witty Eccentric

Johnson was so popular in English society that many people wrote down their impressions of him. These accounts tell us that Johnson was not only a scholarly writer but also a lively conversationalist. When he conversed with equally witty friends, the **effusion** (2) of clever, amusing remarks was like water gushing from a fountain. The **exhilaration** (3) his listeners felt was no greater than the excitement Johnson himself experienced during such rapid-fire exchanges of wit. Johnson was **gregarious** (4) by nature; he always enjoyed the company of others. Although he was certainly no **buffoon** (5) who spent all his time clowning around, he was certain to **guffaw** (6) appreciatively at a clever joke. In fact, one of Johnson's friends wrote of him that "no man loved laughing better."

Of course, Johnson wasn't perfect; he had his **foibles** (7). For example, he could be abrupt or rude, and he sometimes grew impatient with the people who came to him for advice. Since Johnson didn't like being fussed over and flattered, one can imagine that he had little tolerance for visitors who seemed **obsequious** (8). In addition, he no doubt offended some people with his casual attitude toward conventions of behavior. Johnson was no more **punctilious** (9) about details of etiquette than he was exact and careful about his personal appearance. Most people, though, overlooked his shortcomings, for they valued his kindness and generosity and admired his honesty, courage, and spirit.

A Self-Made Man

Although Johnson was unusually mature and intelligent as a young man, he apparently was not **precocious** (10) as a small child. He was extremely frail, and his first few years were dominated by illness. One incident from his childhood may be **germane** (11) or pertinent to the development of Johnson's character. In Johnson's time, many people believed that the touch of a royal person could cure certain ailments. Seeking a cure for her son,

Johnson's mother took him to London, where he and two hundred other sick children were touched by Queen Anne. The queen showed great **civility** (12) or courtesy to the children, and she gave the young Johnson a religious medal to wear on a ribbon around his neck. Perhaps this early experience helped shape Johnson's generous, noble spirit, his **magnanimous** (13) nature.

Johnson didn't become rich and famous as soon as he set a pen to paper. Much of his life was a struggle for survival. His father, an unsuccessful bookstore owner, died poor and therefore left Johnson no **patrimony** (14). Yet Johnson wasn't **querulous** (15) or complaining about the lack of an inheritance. For many years he supported himself and his wife by writing articles for periodicals. Then, in the 1750s, he began publishing a highly successful series of essays on moral and religious themes. These and other essays eventually made Johnson famous throughout England. King George III recognized Johnson's literary achievements by awarding him a pension of three hundred pounds a year. This **propitious** (16) or favorable event ensured that Johnson would never have to worry about money again. **Munificent** (17) by nature, Johnson showed his extreme generosity by supporting several less-fortunate people and allowing them to live in his house. Some people may have thought that Johnson was too **indulgent** (18) with his guests. Yet it seems out of character for someone as direct and self-assured as Johnson to be overly kind or lenient with others. Johnson no doubt simply treated them with the same kind of respect and kindness that he would have expected others to show him.

Johnson's Dictionary

Johnson may have been relaxed about social conventions, but he was never casual about scholarship. He spent nine years painstakingly compiling his definitive *Dictionary of the English Language*, which included more than forty thousand words and many definitions. Reading some of the entries, one might conclude that Johnson took any misuse of the language as an **affront** (19), an intentional insult, to his person. For example, he expressed his disapproval for then-colloquial words such as fun and slim. Exacting a scholar as he was, Johnson couldn't resist the opportunity to add some humor to his dictionary. For example, he illustrated the meaning of the word dull by writing the sentence "To make dictionaries is dull work."

Johnson's dictionary remained the authoritative dictionary of the English language until 1928, when supporters of Johnson's book **capitulated** (20) or yielded to the establishment of a new authority, now called the *Oxford English Dictionary*. Neither Johnson nor his works have faded into obscurity, however; he is still acknowledged as one of England's greatest literary figures and one of its most engaging characters.

EXERCISE 1 *Finding Synonyms*

Directions. Reread the preceding passage. Then write on the line provided a synonym for each of the words in boldface. If you cannot think of an exact synonym, you may write a brief definition of the word.

1. connoisseur _____

2. effusion _____

3. exhilaration _____

4. gregarious _____

5. buffoon _____

6. guffaw _____

7. foibles _____

8. obsequious _____

9. punctilious _____

10. precocious _____

11. germane _____

12. civility _____

13. magnanimous _____

14. patrimony _____

15. querulous _____

16. propitious _____

17. munificent _____

18. indulgent _____

19. affront _____

20. capitulated _____

EXERCISE 2   *Reading Strategically* ✍

Directions. Now that you have read the passage and thought about the words in boldface, circle the letter of the correct answer to each of the following items. The numbers of the items are the same as the numbers of the boldface vocabulary words in the passage.

1. In the passage, the word that provides a clue to the meaning of **connoisseur** is
   (A) famous
   (B) expert
   (C) language
   (D) literature
   (E) culture

2. In the passage, the **effusion** of Johnson's clever remarks is compared by simile to
   (A) an explosion of fireworks
   (B) a radio broadcast
   (C) water gushing from a fountain
   (D) the sound of gunfire
   (E) water bursting from a broken dam

3. The writer provides a clue to the meaning of **exhilaration** by

    (A) linking **exhilaration** to the word excitement

    (B) linking **exhilaration** to the word greater

    (C) implying that it is a conversation

    (D) describing Johnson's remarks as clever and amusing

    (E) contrasting **exhilaration** with an antonym

4. We can infer from the passage that **gregarious** means

    (A) private

    (B) enjoyable

    (C) valuable

    (D) sociable

    (E) exciting

5. We can infer from the passage that a **buffoon** is a

    (A) clown

    (B) prank

    (C) laugh

    (D) scholar

    (E) friend

6. When we read in the passage that Johnson was known to **guffaw**, we should realize that he

    (A) probably laughed loudly

    (B) sometimes wrote about his friends

    (C) was very sarcastic to others

    (D) was well known for his temper

    (E) had no sense of humor

7. According to the passage, what does it mean to have **foibles**?

    (A) It means to have a bad temper.

    (B) It means to be perfect.

    (C) It means to have many friends.

    (D) It means to have integrity.

    (E) It means to have shortcomings.

8. In the passage, why would Johnson be irritated by **obsequious** visitors?

    (A) Johnson was too poor to have valets or other servants.

    (B) Johnson was known to prefer servants who were inefficient.

    (C) Johnson didn't like to have people fussing over him and flattering him.

    (D) Johnson's friends were jealous of Johnson having a servant.

    (E) Johnson treated servants very harshly and drove them away.

9. If Johnson wasn't **punctilious**, as the writer of the passage states, we may expect that he

    (A) carefully followed etiquette and was careful about his appearance

    (B) hated visitors and let them know it

    (C) was never on time for anything

    (D) was not exact and careful about etiquette or his personal appearance

    (E) was very demanding of everyone except himself

10. According to the passage, what does it mean to be **precocious**?

    (A) It means to be healthy.
    (B) It means to be unusually mature.
    (C) It means to be frail.
    (D) It means to be very young.
    (E) It means to be slow-witted.

11. What strategy does the writer use to tell us that **germane** is defined as pertinent?

    (A) The writer uses the word or to link **germane** to the word pertinent.
    (B) The writer gives examples that illustrate the meaning or **germane**.
    (C) The writer defines **germane** in an earlier paragraph.
    (D) The writer uses **germane** in an extended metaphor.
    (E) The writer contrasts **germane** with words of opposite meaning.

12. According to the passage, what does it mean not to treat someone with **civility**?

    (A) It means to treat them courteously.
    (B) It means to be honest with them.
    (C) It means to ignore them.
    (D) It means to treat them with kindness.
    (E) It means to be impolite to them.

13. If Samuel Johnson had a **magnanimous** nature, as the writer of the passage suggests, we may expect him to be

    (A) selfish and demanding
    (B) argumentative and sarcastic
    (C) a famous author
    (D) frail and sickly
    (E) kind and generous

14. According to the passage, what does it mean to receive a **patrimony**?

    (A) It means to support oneself.
    (B) It means to leave great wealth.
    (C) It means to inherit something from one's father.
    (D) It means to dislike one's father.
    (E) It means to receive money in a divorce settlement.

15. We can infer from the passage that a **querulous** person

    (A) complains
    (B) questions
    (C) struggles
    (D) stumbles
    (E) supports

16. In the passage, **propitious** means

    (A) doubtful
    (B) worrisome
    (C) favorable
    (D) proper
    (E) unnatural

17. In the passage, the words that provide a clue to the meaning of **munificent** are
   (A) less fortunate
   (B) extreme generosity
   (C) direct and self-assured
   (D) favorable event
   (E) out of character

18. According to the passage, Johnson may have seemed **indulgent** or _____ with his guests.
   (A) overly kind
   (B) self-assured
   (C) too strict
   (D) less fortunate
   (E) very cruel

19. In the passage, an **affront** is
   (A) a compliment
   (B) a scholarly work
   (C) an intentional insult
   (D) a colloquial expression
   (E) an argument

20. When we read in the passage that users of Johnson's dictionary **capitulated** to the establishment of a new source, we should realize that they
   (A) searched for a better dictionary
   (B) realized that they hated Johnson's dictionary
   (C) faded into obscurity
   (D) insisted that Johnson's book was best
   (E) yielded to a more definitive source

READING NEW WORDS IN CONTEXT

Lesson 8 | CONTEXT: History and Society

The passage gives you an opportunity to expand your vocabulary. Below are twenty vocabulary words that are used in the passage and in the exercises that follow it.

abeyance	discrepancy	inscrutable	perfidious
chastise	emanate	intercede	pervade
demagogue	harbinger	inundate	prevaricate
deplore	homogeneous	irrevocable	primordial
detriment	illicit	obnoxious	sumptuous

Tyranny in the Congo

As captain of a river steamer that journeyed to the Belgian Congo in 1890, adventurer and novelist Joseph Conrad (1857–1924) received an unsettling view of conditions there. The region was in turmoil, and conditions didn't improve until more than a decade later.

Conrad found the country **primordial** (1). He felt that sailing on the River Congo was like "traveling back to the earliest beginnings of the world." He later described the mysterious land and its equally **inscrutable** (2) atmosphere in his novella *Heart of Darkness*. Some readers object to Conrad's descriptions of the Congo and its people because they find these accounts offensive; but Conrad was not intentionally **obnoxious** (3) in his descriptions. He depicted the Congo as he perceived it.

The journey to the Congo was not a pleasant one for Conrad. His ship was a simple "tin-pot" steamer; it was not **sumptuous** (4) at all. Many of his crew members were sick, and Conrad himself later became ill and had to return home to England.

However, it was not the primitiveness of the land or of his sailing conditions that upset Conrad but rather what foreigners were doing to the land and the people. Conrad **deplored** (5) the looting of Africa's natural

riches by Europeans. His strong disapproval is evident in the harsh words he uses to describe the situation. He calls the exploitation of Africa "the vilest scramble for loot that ever disfigured the history of human conscience."

Leopold's Reign of Tyranny

The **detriment** (6) or damage to Africa from European businesses and governments had begun about a decade before Conrad sailed. By 1900, most of Africa was **inundated** (7) by foreign imperialists. These outsiders overwhelmed the land like locusts. The country was eventually divided into European colonies. Because so many different races and cultures coexisted there after colonization, the Congo would never again be a **homogeneous** (8) area with a uniform population.

One greedy, power-hungry man—King Leopold II of Belgium—was the main force behind the early exploitation of the Congo. He founded the International Association for the Exploration and Civilization of Africa in 1876. His stated purposes were noble: to bring civilization to Africa and to stop the slave trade. But his true motive was far from noble. Leopold was a **demagogue** (9), a leader who stirred up people by appealing to their emotions. He persuaded other European powers to go along with him and to recognize him as ruler and owner of the Congo Free State. This action was only a **harbinger** (10), a forerunner, of trickery to come.

Leopold was actually interested in Africa's riches—ivory from elephant tusks and rubber from rubber trees. The new industrial Europe needed all the rubber it could get. Leopold didn't have to worry about how he went about obtaining what he wanted. Were his actions **illicit** (11)? No, they weren't forbidden by law because Leopold made the laws—and made them in his best interest. For example, in 1885, he decreed that all the Congo's "vacant" land was his own property; he then set about making the land vacant.

Leopold's power **pervaded** (12) the Congo. To help spread his power throughout the area, Leopold appointed explorer Henry Stanley as his chief agent in the Congo. Stanley set up garrisons and signed treaties with chiefs of African tribes. Leopold was particularly interested in improving transportation—steamship routes and railways—through Africa so that goods and troops could be moved faster. Leopold soon controlled the commercialization of rubber plantations.

Strict and cruel means of taxation **emanated** (13) or issued from Leopold's court. Government or company officials were required to collect taxes from the people of the Congo. Leopold established his own network of slavery in the Congo. Taxes had to be paid in labor or in flesh. Any African worker who did not bring in the established quota of ivory or rubber could lose a hand. Atrocities were commonplace. You can imagine what forms of punishment **perfidious** (14) acts would

bring if merely failing to meet a quota resulted in maiming. Leopold most certainly would not have tolerated treachery.

Did He Get Away with It?

Eventually, the world became aware that there was a huge **discrepancy** (15) between Leopold's account of activities in the Congo and the actual conditions there. Roger Casement, appointed British Consul for the Congo Free State in 1898, investigated Leopold's methods and in 1904 published a report about Leopold's crimes. In his report, Casement did not **prevaricate** (16) but told the truth about Leopold's activities. Casement's report, documenting activities between 1901 and 1903, revealed cruelties that were highly objectionable to civilized people everywhere.

Leopold's cruelties so shocked the world that people demanded reforms in the Congo government. A Congo Reform Association was formed in England. Leopold himself was widely **chastised** (17). The severity of the criticisms made it obvious that more than a temporary suspension or **abeyance** (18) of Leopold's rule was needed. Of course, the cruelties inflicted during Leopold's rule of more than two decades in the Congo were **irrevocable** (19). However, Leopold's laws and methods, at least, could be reversed. A Belgian commission was formed to investigate the crimes described in Casement's report, and the commission agreed with Casement's findings. Apparently no one **interceded** (20) on Leopold's behalf, although Leopold did plead for himself. In 1906, the Belgian government voted to annex the Congo Free State. The Belgian government restored free trade to the area and brought an end to Leopold's tyrannical reign over the Congo.

EXERCISE 1 *Finding Synonyms*

Directions. Reread the preceding passage. Then write on the line provided a synonym for each of the words in boldface. If you cannot think of an exact synonym, you may write a brief definition of the word.

1. primordial _____

2. inscrutable _____

3. obnoxious _____

4. sumptuous _____

5. deplored _____

6. detriment _____

7. inundated _____

8. homogeneous _____

9. demagogue _____

10. harbinger _____

11. illicit _____

12. pervaded _____

13. emanated _____

14. perfidious _____

15. discrepancy _____

16. prevaricate _____

17. chastised _____

18. abeyance _____

19. irrevocable _____

20. interceded _____

EXERCISE 2 *Reading Strategically* ✍

Directions. Now that you have read the passage and thought about the words in boldface, circle the letter of the correct answer to each of the following items. The numbers of the items are the same as the numbers of the boldface vocabulary words in the passage.

1. What strategy does the writer use to tell us that **primordial** is defined as primitive?
   (A) The writer uses the word turmoil.
   (B) The writer describes Conrad's ship.
   (C) The writer contrasts the word **primordial** with a series of antonyms.
   (D) The writer quotes Conrad's reference to "the earliest beginnings of the world."
   (E) The writer uses synonyms in a series with **primordial**.

2. If the land and its atmosphere are equally **inscrutable**, as the writer of the passage suggests, we may expect them to be
   (A) pleasant
   (B) rugged
   (C) mysterious
   (D) dangerous
   (E) easily described

3. When we read in the passage that Conrad wasn't intentionally **obnoxious**, we should realize that
   (A) he didn't expect his views to be accepted
   (B) he didn't mean to be offensive
   (C) he didn't want to describe the Congo
   (D) he didn't mean to be mysterious
   (E) he didn't realize that people would read his descriptions

4. In the passage, what does it mean to be **sumptuous**?
   (A) It means to be simple.
   (B) It means to be luxurious.
   (C) It means to be poor.
   (D) It means to be mysterious.
   (E) It means to be unpleasant.

5. In the passage, the words that give a clue to the meaning of **deplored** are
   (A) the primitiveness
   (B) sailing conditions
   (C) disfigured the history
   (D) natural riches
   (E) strong disapproval

6. In the passage, **detriment** means
   (A) wealth
   (B) damage
   (C) decade
   (D) imperialism
   (E) benefit

7. Because imperialists **inundated** Africa, the writer compares the imperialists by simile to
   (A) governments
   (B) businesses
   (C) races
   (D) locusts
   (E) colonies

8. In the passage, what does it mean for a country to be **homogeneous**?
   (A) It means a country contains similar races and cultures.
   (B) It means a country contains different races and cultures.
   (C) It means a country is uncivilized.
   (D) It means a country is filled with imperialists.
   (E) It means a country is divided into different regions.

9. What strategy does the writer use to tell us what **demagogue** means?
   (A) The writer links **demagogue** to the synonym stirred.
   (B) The writer uses a series of adjectives.
   (C) The writer provides a definition of **demagogue**.
   (D) The writer compares **demagogue** by simile to locusts.
   (E) The writer links **demagogue** to the antonym leader.

10. In the passage, **harbinger** means
    (A) follower
    (B) trickery
    (C) favorite
    (D) forerunner
    (E) ruler

11. We can infer from the passage that if something is **illicit** it is
    (A) illegal
    (B) vacant
    (C) industrial
    (D) legal
    (E) obtainable

12. The writer provides a clue to the meaning of **pervaded** by
    (A) telling about Henry Stanley
    (B) relating **pervaded** to the phrase "spread his power"
    (C) explaining the use of treaties in the Congo
    (D) providing a definition of **pervaded**
    (E) relating **pervaded** to the word transportation

13. In the passage, what does it mean that tax measures **emanated** from Leopold's court?
    (A) It means that the government asked for voluntary tax donations.
    (B) It means that the Congolese had to bring their taxes directly to the court.
    (C) It means that the tax measures were kept secretly within the court.
    (D) It means that Leopold's court let the Congolese vote on the taxes.
    (E) It means that the tax measures issued from Leopold's court.

14. In the passage, **perfidious** acts probably would bring about _____ punishment.
   (A) gentle
   (B) legal
   (C) severe
   (D) acceptable
   (E) fair

15. If there was a big **discrepancy** between what Leopold said he was doing and what he was actually doing, we may expect
   (A) that what he said he did and what he really did were the same
   (B) that he had trouble carrying out his plans
   (C) that he was telling the truth about actual conditions
   (D) that there was a great difference between what he said and what he did
   (E) that people around the world had access to the facts

16. We can infer from the passage that to **prevaricate** is to
   (A) lie
   (B) delay
   (C) spy
   (D) say
   (E) hesitate

17. In the passage, the words that provide a clue to the meaning of **chastised** are
   (A) reforms, government
   (B) temporary suspension
   (C) shocked, demanded
   (D) cruelties inflicted
   (E) severity, criticisms

18. According to the passage, what effect would an **abeyance** of Leopold's rule have had on the Congo?
   (A) It would have changed everything permanently.
   (B) It would not have lasted long enough to do any good.
   (C) It would have rid the Congo of Leopold's laws.
   (D) It would have created more transportation routes.
   (E) It would have stopped the flow of information.

19. When we read in the passage that the cruelties inflicted during Leopold's rule were **irrevocable**, we should realize that
   (A) they could be reversed
   (B) they could not be forgiven
   (C) they could not be reversed
   (D) they could not be repeated
   (E) they could be forgiven

20. According to the passage, **interceded** means
   (A) punished
   (B) agreed
   (C) pleaded
   (D) listened
   (E) traded

READING NEW WORDS IN CONTEXT

Lesson 9 | CONTEXT: History and Society

The passage gives you an opportunity to expand your vocabulary. Below are twenty vocabulary words that are used in the passage and in the exercises that follow it.

anarchy	elocution	maim	residual
cadaverous	ethnology	menial	restitution
cajole	extricate	nadir	strident
commodious	impair	pestilence	subversion
consign	incorrigible	rampant	virulent

The English Slave Trade

Call him Jared. He was born in 1740 in a small village in West Africa. Eighteen years later, he, along with hundreds of other Africans, was captured by English slave traders. Jared had no chance to **extricate** (1) himself from the situation, just as a prisoner, chained hand and foot, has no chance to escape from his captors. Slave traders did not release their captives; slaves were worth far too much.

Jared had become a statistic in England's infamous era of slave trade. From 1690 to 1807, England imported an estimated 2,807,100 slaves. During the 1700s, England was the top carrier of slaves from Africa. Profit-hungry slave traders no doubt considered this period the zenith or highest point in England's commercial history. Yet people concerned with human rights must have held the opposite to be true: The era of slave trading was the **nadir** (2) of the country's history.

Many English shipping merchants and businesspeople spoke in favor of the slave trade, which uprooted the lives of such Africans as Jared. Some merchants were particularly adept at **elocution** (3), the art of public speaking; they argued persuasively that the slaves were needed to help England achieve commercial success in its colonial possessions. The British crown created slave-trading companies to gather slaves from its colonies in West Africa and to transport them to its colonies in the West Indies and North America. In addition, there were many independent slave traders.

Surviving the Journey
Jared and his companions were herded aboard a slave ship by a rough Englishman with a **strident** (4) voice. "Move on, move on!" the man yelled harshly. Jared was thrown into a room below deck that could hardly be considered **commodious** (5) for the number of people it held. In fact, the room had so little space that its one hundred occupants literally could not move. Africans of both sexes and of all ages were kept in the room and put into irons so they wouldn't escape.

The voyage was miserable. Rats scampered over Jared's legs. He thought his right leg would be permanently **maimed** (6) from the irons. He feared that his right arm might be similarly crippled from being crushed between two wooden posts. He had wedged himself between the posts to try to get some breathing room. The slave hold had little air, and its floors were cleaned rarely, if ever. The man next to Jared looked **cadaverous** (7) because he was so ill and gaunt; his deathlike face was sad and haunted. **Pestilences** (8), contagious and often fatal diseases that spread rapidly, were **rampant** (9) in the slave hold. The captives had no way to prevent the spread of **virulent** (10) or deadly diseases. Many of the slaves who didn't die aboard ship had their health **impaired** (11) for the rest of their lives by the illnesses they suffered aboard ship. Jared, fortunately, had only a minor illness that didn't injure him permanently.

On Jared's ship, the captain did not enforce any laws or try to maintain order among his men. As a result, **anarchy** (12) prevailed; the ship was in a state of disorder, with no leadership. Some of the stronger slaves wanted to escape from their irons and overthrow the crew, but there was no way to manage such **subversion** (13).

The ship landed in the English West Indies, and agents on the islands arranged for the sale of the slaves. Strong slaves were especially needed to work the sugar plantations on islands such as Jamaica. Able slaves also were needed for the tobacco fields in England's North American colonies. Some weak, elderly, or very young slaves would be sold for **menial** (14), low-level work such as cleaning house and waiting on people.

Sold to the Highest Bidder

Jared was placed on a platform and examined by many buyers. He was sold to a large white-haired man and **consigned** (15) to one of the sugar plantations. Immediately, Jared was loaded onto a wagon and taken to his unpleasant assignment. About twenty other young men were put on the wagon, along with several older men who looked ill. The agent apparently had **cajoled** (16) or coaxed Jared's buyer into paying a reduced price for the older men. Perhaps after the buyer paid for the slaves he really wanted, he used his **residual** (17) funds to buy the less-desirable slaves. It would probably not have taken much in the way of leftover funds to purchase older people with health problems.

Jared lived the rest of his life, about thirty years, working on the plantation. He was one of thousands of slaves who helped feed England's sweet tooth. (Sugar was England's most valuable colonial product.) In his first years on the plantation, Jared tried to rebel, but he reformed his ways after a few beatings because he realized that his survival depended on his accepting his situation. Some of his friends, however, refused to give in. They were considered **incorrigible** (18) because they made a habit of causing trouble for the cruel overseers. No matter how they were punished, these slaves persisted in their bid for freedom.

The British and American governments abolished the slave trade in 1808, but the damage had already been done. There could be no **restitution** (19) for two centuries of disrupted and lost lives. How could governments ever compensate a people for such damage? How could anyone restore to the slaves all that they had lost?

Today, professors interested in the branch of anthropology known as **ethnology** (20) frequently go back to slave records to find information about the origins, cultures, and characteristics of Africans in the West Indies and in North America. Yet these records have little to say about the suffering of individual human beings, like Jared, whose lives were stolen from them by slave traders.

EXERCISE 1   *Finding Synonyms*

Directions. Reread the preceding passage. Then write on the line provided a synonym for each of the words in boldface. If you cannot think of an exact synonym, you may write a brief definition of the word.

1. extricate _____

2. nadir _____

3. elocution _____

4. strident _____

5. commodious _____

6. maimed _____

7. cadaverous _____

8. pestilences _____

9. rampant _____

10. virulent _____

11. impaired _____

12. anarchy _____

13. subversion _____

14. menial _____

15. consigned _____

16. cajoled _____

17. residual _____

18. incorrigible _____

19. restitution _____

20. ethnology _____

EXERCISE 2 Reading Strategically ✍️

Directions. Now that you have read the passage and thought about the words in boldface, circle the letter of the correct answer to each of the following items. The numbers of the items are the same as the numbers of the boldface vocabulary words in the passage.

1. Because Jared couldn't **extricate** himself from the clutches of slave traders, the writer compares Jared to

   (A) a statistic in England's history

   (B) a fish caught in a net

   (C) a prisoner chained by his captors

   (D) a boy about to become an adult

   (E) a village in West Africa

2. In the passage, why might the era of slave trade be considered the **nadir** of England's commercial history?

   (A) It was the time of England's greatest commercial success.

   (B) It was the time when England was the top carrier of cargo.

   (C) It was the time when England made very little money.

   (D) It was England's lowest possible point for human rights.

   (E) It was the time of great social upheaval and change.

3. In the passage, why would merchants adept at **elocution** have great influence?

   (A) They would write letters to newspapers supporting slavery.

   (B) They would make persuasive speeches in support of slavery.

   (C) They would make a great amount of money from selling slaves.

   (D) They would be able to make changes in the laws.

   (E) They would own most of the slave-trading companies.

4. In the passage, what does it mean to speak with a **strident** voice?

   (A) It means to speak softly.

   (B) It means to speak kindly.

   (C) It means to speak harshly.

   (D) It means to speak persuasively.

   (E) It means to speak continuously.

5. We can infer from the passage that a **commodious** room is

   (A) very small

   (B) very crowded

   (C) smaller than needed

   (D) commonly used

   (E) very spacious

6. How does the writer provide a clue to the meaning of **maimed**?

   (A) The writer gives an explanation of the meaning of **maimed**.

   (B) The writer uses the word permanently to link **maimed** to the future.

   (C) The writer uses synonyms in a series to define **maimed**.

   (D) The writer links **maimed** to the word crippled by using the word similarly.

   (E) The writer implies that **maimed** has to do with a voyage.

7. In the passage, what does it mean for people to look **cadaverous**?
  (A) It means that they look gaunt and corpselike.
  (B) It means that they look like caverns.
  (C) It means that they look strong and healthy.
  (D) It means that they look carefree and happy.
  (E) It means that they look kind and friendly.

8. What strategy does the writer use to tell us what **pestilences** means?
  (A) The writer uses a series of antonyms.
  (B) The writer uses pronoun references.
  (C) The writer uses examples.
  (D) The writer uses figurative language.
  (E) The writer defines **pestilences**.

9. When we read in the passage that deaths were **rampant**, we should realize that
  (A) there were very few deaths
  (B) the death count was growing unchecked
  (C) deaths were usually avoided
  (D) deaths were instantaneous
  (E) deaths were due to unnatural causes

10. In the passage, **virulent** means
  (A) deadly
  (B) clean
  (C) captive
  (D) protected
  (E) healthy

11. In the passage, the word that provides a clue to the meaning of **impaired** is
  (A) health
  (B) minor
  (C) aboard
  (D) injure
  (E) deadly

12. In the passage, what does it mean that **anarchy** prevailed on the ship?
  (A) It means that the captain laid down strict laws.
  (B) It means that the crew was rebelling.
  (C) It means that the ship was in disorder.
  (D) It means that most of the crew members were ill.
  (E) It means that the captain had stopped a rebellion.

13. In the passage, **subversion** by the slaves would have resulted in the _____ of the crew.
  (A) drowning
  (B) friendship
  (C) overthrow
  (D) understanding
  (E) orderliness

14. We can infer from the passage that **menial** work is
   (A) hard, physical field labor
   (B) done only by men
   (C) work that requires education
   (D) strictly mental exercise
   (E) done by or fit for servants

15. In the passage, the words that provide a clue to the meaning of **consigned** are
   (A) unpleasant assignment
   (B) loaded onto
   (C) sugar plantations
   (D) examined by many
   (E) large man

16. In the passage, **cajoled** means
   (A) reduced
   (B) worried
   (C) punished
   (D) coaxed
   (E) questioned

17. If a buyer uses **residual** funds, as the writer of the passage suggests, we may expect the buyer to
   (A) borrow money
   (B) use leftover funds
   (C) expect to make money
   (D) purchase real estate
   (E) be financially limited

18. When we read in the passage that some of Jared's friends were considered **incorrigible**, we should realize that they
   (A) changed the way they behaved
   (B) continued to rebel and cause trouble
   (C) learned to get along with the overseers
   (D) acted the way Jared told them to act
   (E) were so weak from past illnesses that they could not work

19. According to the passage, **restitution** cannot be made because nothing can _____ for two centuries of damaged lives.
   (A) suffer
   (B) rebel
   (C) compensate
   (D) continue
   (E) legislate

20. In the passage, **ethnology** is
   (A) a branch of economics that deals with foreign cultures
   (B) the study of petroleum products
   (C) the study of logic and ethics
   (D) the study of the history of slavery
   (E) the study of the origins and characteristics of a culture

READING NEW WORDS IN CONTEXT

Lesson 10 | CONTEXT: History and Society

The passage gives you an opportunity to expand your vocabulary. Below are twenty vocabulary words that are used in the passage and in the exercises that follow it.

auspices	dissent	mollify	sedentary
austerity	foment	obese	solicitous
calumny	hiatus	recant	temerity
clandestine	impassive	retaliate	vestige
contingency	litigation	saline	vindicate

The British and Mahatma Gandhi

One person came to mind immediately when I was asked to write about my greatest hero: Mohandas K. Gandhi (1869–1948). A leader in India's fight for independence from Great Britain, Gandhi always tried to **circumvent** (1) violent demonstrations. He wanted to avoid violence and bring about change through courageous, nonviolent action. He called his philosophy of nonviolence *satyagraha*, a Hindu word meaning "a grasping for truth."

Fighting for Indian Rights
Gandhi's civil rights work actually began in South Africa. Gandhi was trained as a lawyer in London and in 1893 went to South Africa to practice law. On a train in South Africa, Gandhi experienced racial discrimination. Because he was an Indian, Gandhi was ordered to leave his first-class compartment and go instead to the baggage car. In an act of **temerity** (2), Gandhi protested. However, his rashness only got him thrown off the train. This incident began his interest in fighting against discrimination. He handled the **litigations** (3), or lawsuits, of many Indians in South Africa and worked to obtain equal rights for them. During this time, Gandhi began forming his philosophy of nonviolent action.

He returned to India in 1915 but stayed out of the public eye for a year. After this **hiatus** (4), or interruption, in his public work, Gandhi became involved in various disputes on behalf of Indian workers. In 1920, Gandhi began a national campaign called the noncooperation movement to convince the people of India to resist British rule in nonviolent ways. For example, he urged people to boycott British goods and jobs. He thus began a unique political revolution that led in 1947 to Britain's decision to grant India independence. To thousands of people in India, Britain's exodus, or departure, **vindicated** (5) their faith in Gandhi and also justified the title they gave him—Mahatma, or "Great Soul."

Gandhi: A Moral Force in India
True, Gandhi's methods sometimes **fomented** (6) unrest despite his peaceful intentions. For stirring up trouble, he and his followers were often imprisoned. Still, Gandhi never **recanted** (7) or retracted his beliefs. He maintained that moral force, when used to defend truth, triumphs over physical force. Gandhi's efforts were under the **auspices** (8)—that is, with the approval and support—of the Indian National Congress, of which he was president for one year.

In 1929, after the Congress called for independence from Britain, Gandhi led a resistance campaign against the unpopular Salt Acts. These acts made it illegal for citizens to buy salt from any source other than the government, which held a monopoly on salt. Gandhi led fifty thousand people on a two-hundred-mile march to the sea to make salt from sea water, which is naturally **saline** (9). In this way, the people could procure salt without paying a tax. Police attacked the marchers, but the marchers did not **retaliate** (10). Instead of returning the injuries, the marchers kept going until they were struck down. The police probably thought they had prepared for every **contingency** (11), but they hadn't prepared for the possible occurrence of passive resistance. The march attracted worldwide attention.

Although he might have seemed **impassive** (12), Gandhi was an emotional man with strong beliefs. He staged several long hunger strikes to protest various wrongs. In 1932–1933, for example, Gandhi fasted four times to protest discrimination against poor Indians known as "untouchables." During these fasts, his followers were greatly concerned about his welfare. If you have seen pictures of Gandhi, you know he certainly wasn't **obese** (13) or even slightly overweight. He was mostly **sedentary** (14) during the fasts because he didn't have the strength to move much.

Gandhi's Legacy

Gandhi lived a life of severe simplicity and harsh self-discipline. His **austerity** (15) is seen in a lack of concern for or interest in worldly pleasures and possessions. He dressed simply in hand-woven cloth made from hand-spun thread. Gandhi himself spun thread for cloth every day. Spinning was a very important activity for Gandhi because he considered it a symbol of India's self-sufficiency.

In the last years of his life, Gandhi worked to bring Hindus and Muslims together. He was always **solicitous** (16) of other people's opinions and beliefs, but he was also attentive to his own conviction that India should remain united. He **dissented** (17) with those who wanted to divide India into two nations. Although he disagreed, he supported a plan to create two nations, India and Pakistan, in order to insure independence. Gandhi was involved in both open and **clandestine** (18) meetings with Muslim leaders in an attempt to unite Hindus and Muslims. Right up until his death, Gandhi tried to **mollify** (19) or soothe the different factions within his beloved country.

Gandhi and his beliefs have continued to be a source of inspiration for people around the world—including the American civil rights leader Martin Luther King, Jr. In his fight against racial discrimination in the United States, King was greatly influenced by Gandhi's philosophy of nonviolent action. Thus, more than a trace, a **vestige** (20), of Gandhi's philosophy can be found in King's compelling speeches. Based on King's example, I'm convinced that the world would be a better place if more leaders took Gandhi's words and actions to heart.

EXERCISE 1 *Finding Synonyms* 👉

Directions. Reread the preceding passage. Then write on the line provided a synonym for each of the words in boldface. If you cannot think of an exact synonym, you may write a brief definition of the word.

1. circumvent _____

2. temerity _____

3. litigations _____

4. hiatus _____

5. vindicated _____

6. fomented _____

7. recanted _____

8. auspices _____

9. saline _____

10. retaliate _____

11. contingency _____

12. impassive _____

13. obese _____

14. sedentary _____

15. austerity _____

16. solicitous _____

17. dissented _____

18. clandestine _____

19. mollify _____

20. vestige _____

EXERCISE 2 *Reading Strategically* ☞

Directions. Now that you have read the passage and thought about the words in boldface, circle the letter of the correct answer to each of the following items. The numbers of the items are the same as the numbers of the boldface vocabulary words in the passage.

1. In the passage, the word that provides a clue to the meaning of **circumvent** is
   (A) violent
   (B) method
   (C) fight
   (D) change
   (E) avoid

2. In the passage, what was the result of Gandhi's act of **temerity** on the train?
   (A) Gandhi refused to ride the train.
   (B) Gandhi was thrown off the train.
   (C) Gandhi wished he had spoken up.
   (D) Gandhi refused to protest his treatment.
   (E) Gandhi learned to accept discrimination.

3. In the passage, **litigations** are

(A) rights
(B) protests
(C) lawsuits
(D) equalities
(E) incidents

4. What strategy does the writer use to let us know that **hiatus** is defined as a break in continuity?

(A) The writer uses figurative language.
(B) The writer restates **hiatus** with the word interruption.
(C) The writer gives a series of synonyms for **hiatus**.
(D) The writer uses an antonym.
(E) The writer uses a metaphor.

5. In the passage, the word that provides a clue to the meaning of **vindicated** is

(A) exodus
(B) urged
(C) boycotted
(D) justified
(E) involved

6. In the passage, what happened when Gandhi's methods **fomented** unrest?

(A) Gandhi became tired of nonviolence and urged his followers to attack.
(B) The authorities began to like the idea of nonviolence and started using it themselves.
(C) Gandhi influenced the Indians to raise an army to defeat the British.
(D) Gandhi's influence was so great that no one ever used any other method.
(E) Trouble resulted and Gandhi and his followers were imprisoned.

7. In the passage, what does it mean that Gandhi never **recanted** his beliefs?

(A) He continuously maintained his beliefs.
(B) He frequently changed his opinions and goals.
(C) Other people began believing what he believed.
(D) He gave up his beliefs when they failed.
(E) He refused to struggle to succeed.

8. According to the passage, Gandhi's efforts were under the **auspices** of the Indian National Congress. In other words, the Congress _____ what Gandhi was doing.

(A) often questioned
(B) complained about
(C) approved of
(D) voted on
(E) did not like

9. We can infer from the passage that **saline** means

(A) watery
(B) taxed
(C) independent
(D) salty
(E) natural

10. In the passage, why did the marchers not **retaliate** when they were attacked?

    (A) They did not understand why they were being attacked.

    (B) They would not go against their belief in nonviolence.

    (C) Gandhi told them to return violence with more violence.

    (D) They were waiting until more people came to help fight.

    (E) They wanted to anger the authorities and provoke a fight.

11. In the passage, what does it mean to prepare for every **contingency**?

    (A) It means to be able to handle everything except nonviolence.

    (B) It means to have a plan for everything that might happen.

    (C) It means to ignore the possibilities you don't understand.

    (D) It means to be able to take care of only nonviolent events.

    (E) It means to be aware that there are people who disagree.

12. We can infer from the passage that **impassive** means

    (A) wrong

    (B) unemotional

    (C) strong

    (D) hungry

    (E) weak

13. What strategy does the writer use to tell us that **obese** is defined as extremely overweight?

    (A) The writer defines **obese** as slightly overweight.

    (B) The writer uses **obese** with a series of synonyms.

    (C) The writer contrasts **obese** with the words slightly overweight.

    (D) The writer describes a person who is extremely overweight.

    (E) The writer provides examples of **obese** people who fast.

14. In the passage, what does it mean to be **sedentary**?

    (A) It means to be very active.

    (B) It means to be strong.

    (C) It means to be hungry.

    (D) It means to be inactive.

    (E) It means to be concerned.

15. How does the writer provide a clue to the meaning of **austerity**?

    (A) The writer describes Gandhi's life as one of "severe simplicity and harsh self-discipline."

    (B) The writer gives examples of worldly pleasures.

    (C) The writer uses the synonyms worldly pleasures and possessions.

    (D) The writer describes Gandhi's interest in teaching people how to spin.

    (E) The writer assumes the reader knows that **austerity** comes from a lack of concern.

16. When we read in the passage that Gandhi was **solicitous** of other people's opinions and beliefs, we should realize that he

    (A) did not care about them

    (B) was attentive to them

    (C) was worried about them

    (D) misunderstood them

    (E) was secretive about his thoughts

17. In the passage, **dissented** means

    (A) discussed
    (B) contracted
    (C) disagreed
    (D) battled
    (E) sided

18. We can infer from the passage that **clandestine** meetings are

    (A) open
    (B) secret
    (C) illegal
    (D) legal
    (E) violent

19. In the passage, **mollify** means

    (A) anger
    (B) destroy
    (C) update
    (D) soothe
    (E) understand

20. In the passage, the word that provides a clue to the meaning of **vestige** is

    (A) trace
    (B) philosophy
    (C) beliefs
    (D) speeches
    (E) actions

READING NEW WORDS IN CONTEXT

Lesson 11 | CONTEXT: Science and Technology

The passage gives you an opportunity to expand your vocabulary. Below are twenty vocabulary words that are used in the passage and in the exercises that follow it.

chauvinism	empirical	officious	sagacity
cosmopolitan	epitome	quiescent	scathing
devoid	facetious	regimen	tenuous
differentiate	inexorable	renounce	testimonial
disparity	moot	repository	treatise

A Lesson from the Scientific Revolution

Gulliver's Travels, by Jonathan Swift (1667–1745), is today regarded as a literary classic. From the time it was first published in 1726, it was a great success. *Gulliver's Travels* was read, as the poet John Gay (1685–1732) wrote, "from the cabinet council to the nursery."

Swift's book is most often remembered for its description of the **officious** (1) Lilliputians, an overbearing race of people small in height but large in ego. Readers also often recall the giant inhabitants of Brobdingnag. Gulliver's third voyage, however, is often less memorable to readers, but it is very telling in its depiction of the scientific climate of Swift's era. In this voyage, Gulliver travels to the Grand Academy of Lagado, where all time and energy is devoted to useless scientific experiments. Gulliver discovers here a great **disparity** (2) between common sense and scientific practice. At the Academy of Projectors, for example, Gulliver finds men attempting such absurd experiments as trying to extract sunshine from cucumbers.

What readers often do not realize is that Gulliver's third voyage is a **scathing** (3) or bitterly harsh satire of the Royal Society in London. This group was the very **epitome** (4) of science in Great Britain at the time, the essence of the scientific community of the eighteenth century.

A Background to the Scientific Revolution

It would be impossible to isolate a single cause for the scientific revolution. Any single explanation would be simplistic and would do no more than inspire debates. Instead of pursuing such a **moot** (5) point, then, it is better to realize that the new worldview of the eighteenth century was a natural outgrowth of the work of philosophers and scientists during the Middle Ages.

Members of the Royal Society engaged in a new method of scientific inquiry that differed greatly from medieval scholarship, which emphasized philosophical or religious interpretations of the natural world. Indeed, the new science, argumentative in nature, would not produce scientists as **quiescent** (6) as those of the Middle Ages. Instead, it would produce thinkers who were bold, aggressive, and questioning.

Three basic characteristics of the new science produced this new breed of "show me" experimental investigators. First, the new science was **empirical** (7), relying on direct experience and observation rather than on hand-me-down ideas and assumptions. Scientists of the eighteenth century gave careful attention to what we now call the scientific method: stating an experimental aim, forming a hypothesis, conducting an experiment, gathering results, and drawing conclusions. The scientists' **regimen** (8) or routine of careful observation and meticulous attention to detail was at the heart of the scientific revolution.

Second, the new science relied on technological innovations. The telescope, for example, allowed people to **differentiate** (9) objects in the night sky that could not be detected by the unaided eye. Scientists thus were able to distinguish better than ever before the differences between celestial bodies such as stars and planets.

Third, the new science was **cosmopolitan** (10), or international, rather than simply national. During the seventeenth century, universities throughout Europe had established centers for the study of science. Also, European governments established learned societies to foster scientific inquiry. The government of England, for example, formed the Royal Society that Swift satirized in *Gulliver's Travels*. This society and others like it printed journals to circulate information on scientific discoveries. *Philosophical Transactions*, begun in 1664, was the **repository** (11) of the ideas of the Royal Society: If the Royal Society thought it, this journal would print it. Such journals became forums for sometimes heated debates and allowed scientists both to voice their agreement with and on occasion to **renounce** (12) one another's work.

The Contributions of Sir Isaac Newton

In England, one name in particular continues to be associated with the scientific revolution: the mathematician Isaac Newton (1642–1727). Newton is best known for his work *Mathematical Principles of Natural Philosophy* (1687). Newton believed that the universe was a single uniform machine that operated according to **inexorable** (13) laws, laws that could not be altered or discontinued. Educated at Trinity College, Cambridge, Newton made his first contact with the Royal Society when he presented his theory of light and colors in 1672. In 1703, Newton was elected president

of the Royal Society and was reelected annually until his death. A statue was erected in his honor at Trinity College. On it are inscribed these lines by the poet William Wordsworth as a **testimonial** (14) to Newton's brilliance:

> The marble index of a mind for ever
> Voyaging through strange seas of Thought
> alone.

Women of the Scientific Revolution

During the Middle Ages, women who sought a life of learning were severely hampered because of the **chauvinism** (15) of the men who dominated society. These men, for the most part, believed that only men could fully benefit from formal education. In fact, during the scientific revolution, Benedict Spinoza (1632–1677) argued that an educated woman was similar to an antique gun "which one shows to the curious, but which has no use at all, any more than a carousel horse." Spinoza's comment was obviously based on **tenuous** (16) or flimsy evidence, for women in science were in fact making important contributions.

Anna Maria Sibylla Merian (1647–1717), a contemporary of Newton's, established a reputation as an entomologist, or one who studies insects. Her studies resulted in her first **treatise** (17), *Wonderful Metamorphosis and Special Nourishment of Caterpillars*, an important book in her day. At the end of the seventeenth century, she made an expedition to the colony of Surinam to study insect and plant life. Her **sagacity** (18) as a scientist is revealed in the work for which she is best known, *Metamorphosis of the Insects of Surinam*, a penetrating and insightful work.

The Influence of the Scientific Revolution

Why, you might ask, did Swift satirize scientists such as Isaac Newton in *Gulliver's Travels*? Wasn't science improving the quality of life? Why then is Swift so **facetious** (19) in his description of the Academy of Projectors? Why does he make such obvious fun of scientists? While he recognized that science could be beneficial, Swift also recognized that science could be **devoid** (20) of practical concerns and completely lacking in ethics. Therefore, in its worst manifestations science was removed from the everyday lives of most people and was possibly even dangerous to society. As in Swift's time, many people today, having seen nuclear destruction and other examples of unchecked technology, find science terrifying in its implications.

What was Swift's message? How should we view science today? We should remember that, in the final analysis, science is a search for knowledge. That is the lesson we should learn from studying the scientific revolution. It is up to us to direct the use of science and to make sure that it does not dominate our world but instead is used to work for the common good.

EXERCISE 1 *Finding Synonyms*

Directions. Reread the preceding passage. Then write on the line provided a synonym for each of the words in boldface. If you cannot think of an exact synonym, you may write a brief definition of the word.

1. officious _____

2. disparity _____

3. scathing _____

4. epitome _____

5. moot _____

6. quiescent _____

7. empirical _____

8. regimen _____

9. differentiate _____

10. cosmopolitan _____

11. repository _____

12. renounce _____

13. inexorable _____

14. testimonial _____

15. chauvinism _____

16. tenuous _____

17. treatise _____

18. sagacity _____

19. facetious _____

20. devoid _____

EXERCISE 2 *Reading Strategically* ✍

Directions. Now that you have read the passage and thought about the words in boldface, circle the letter of the correct answer to each of the following items. The numbers of the items are the same as the numbers of the boldface vocabulary words in the passage.

1. How does the writer provide a clue to the meaning of **officious**?
   (A) The writer tells us that the Lilliputians are overbearing and small in height but large in ego.
   (B) The writer tells us that *Gulliver's Travels* was read "from the cabinet council to the nursery."
   (C) The writer tells us that *Gulliver's Travels* was a great success when it was published in 1726.
   (D) The writer tells us that Gulliver visited the Grand Academy of Lagado.
   (E) The writer implies that Gulliver is, in fact, a spokesperson for Swift himself.

2. The **disparity** between common sense and scientific practice may also be viewed as the _____ between the two.
   (A) commonality
   (B) equality
   (C) difference
   (D) correlation
   (E) equivalency

3. How does the writer let us know that a **scathing** satire may be defined as an attack with cruel language?
   (A) The writer tells us that men in the Academy of Projectors attempted to extract sunshine from cucumbers.
   (B) The writer tells us that the Royal Society in London typified eighteenth-century science.
   (C) The writer implies that *Gulliver's Travels* is a satire.
   (D) The writer links the words bitterly harsh to **scathing**.
   (E) The writer uses alliteration to link **scathing** to the word society.

4. In the passage, a synonym for **epitome** is
   (A) report
   (B) description
   (C) essence
   (D) satire
   (E) key

5. In the passage, why is it a **moot** point to isolate a single cause of the scientific revolution?
   (A) There is no single cause of the scientific revolution.
   (B) No one likes to discuss the scientific revolution.
   (C) The single cause was so ridiculous that it is not worth discussing.
   (D) Since people already know what the single cause was, there is no point in discussing it.
   (E) As far as anyone can tell, there were no causes at all of the scientific revolution.

6. In the passage, a **quiescent** scientist is one who might be described as
   (A) curious and probing
   (B) eccentric and suspicious
   (C) argumentative and aggressive
   (D) quiet and accepting
   (E) gullible and naive

7. According to the passage, an **empirical** science
  (A) is based on philosophical speculation
  (B) depends on government funding
  (C) disregards direct experience and observation
  (D) relies on direct experience and observation
  (E) does not follow the scientific method

8. How does the writer provide a clue to the meaning of **regimen**?
  (A) The writer tells us that the scientific method relies on direct experience.
  (B) The writer tells us that the scientists were careful.
  (C) The writer tells us that the scientific method allowed scientists to explore the earth.
  (D) The writer tells us that scientists during the scientific revolution adhered to a special routine.
  (E) The writer tells us that the new science relied on technology.

9. In the passage, what does it mean to **differentiate** objects in the universe?
  (A) It means to view by telescope.
  (B) It means to use empirical methods.
  (C) It means to perceive different objects.
  (D) It means to rely on technology.
  (E) It means to share technological innovations.

10. When we are told that the new science was **cosmopolitan,** we should realize that
  (A) it was taught in universities
  (B) it extended beyond national boundaries
  (C) it was interested in the structure of the universe
  (D) it was the object of satire
  (E) it was empirical

11. A **repository** may be defined as a box, chest, or room where things are kept. How could *Philosophical Transactions* be a **repository** for the ideas of the Royal Society?
  (A) The Royal Society was, in reality, a library.
  (B) The Royal Society was, in reality, a journal.
  (C) The writer suggests that books are places where ideas can be kept safely.
  (D) The writer suggests that ideas are like boxes, closets, or rooms.
  (E) The writer realizes readers know that scientific journals are printed.

12. Why would scientists who read journals such as the *Philosophical Transactions* **renounce** each other's work?
  (A) The scientists would **renounce** work they did not agree with.
  (B) The scientists would agree with the work they **renounced**.
  (C) The scientists would either agree with each other or dispute each other's ideas.
  (D) The scientists used direct observation and relied on technology to **renounce** each other's work.
  (E) The scientists were influenced by the printing press.

13. The writer provides a clue to the meaning of **inexorable** by
  (A) linking **inexorable** to the phrase "could not be altered or discontinued"
  (B) linking **inexorable** to Newton's *Mathematical Principles of Natural Philosophy*
  (C) linking **inexorable** to the words operated according to
  (D) using **inexorable** as an adverb
  (E) using **inexorable** as a synonym for empirical

14. Wordsworth's lines on Newton are a **testimonial** to the scientist's brilliance because
   (A) they are written by a poet
   (B) they are a tribute to Newton's ideas
   (C) they are a satire of modern science
   (D) they remind us that Newton was English
   (E) they are a bitter criticism

15. How does the writer let us know that **chauvinism** may be defined as an unreasoning devotion to one's own country or group?
   (A) The writer tells us that men believed only other men could benefit from education.
   (B) The writer tells us that educated women were considered ridiculous.
   (C) The writer tells us that women made inroads into the scientific community.
   (D) The writer clearly defines **chauvinism** in the next three sentences.
   (E) The writer contrasts the Middle Ages with the eighteenth century.

16. In the passage, a synonym for **tenuous** is
   (A) clear
   (B) strong
   (C) despicable
   (D) flimsy
   (E) warranted

17. According to the passage, Anna Maria Sibylla Merian's *Wonderful Metamorphosis and Special Nourishment of Caterpillars* is a **treatise** because
   (A) it is a formal, systematic discussion of a subject
   (B) it is a large, hard-to-read volume
   (C) it is the work of an entomologist
   (D) it is about insects
   (E) it is an unpublished manuscript

18. When we are told that Anna Maria Sibylla Merian demonstrated her **sagacity** as a scientist, we should realize that she
   (A) continued to write books throughout her life
   (B) used the scientific method
   (C) had sound judgment and a keen mind
   (D) had refined powers of observation
   (E) was very stubborn

19. Because Swift's description of the Academy of Projectors is **facetious**, the description is
   (A) vindictive
   (B) satirical
   (C) harsh
   (D) accurate
   (E) inaccurate

20. According to the passage, if science is **devoid** of practical concerns, it is
   (A) completely without practical concerns
   (B) absorbed in practical concerns to the exclusion of everything else
   (C) exempt from practical concerns because they are not relevant
   (D) the subject of harsh satire
   (E) part of the modern world

READING NEW WORDS IN CONTEXT

Lesson 12 CONTEXT: Science and Technology

The passage gives you an opportunity to expand your vocabulary. Below are twenty vocabulary words that are used in the passage and in the exercises that follow it.

acrimonious	coerce	expound	misnomer
atrophy	consternation	firmament	mottled
benevolence	desist	gauntlet	precursor
bode	enigma	loquacious	terra firma
burnish	esoteric	mete	voluminous

The Plow and the Stirrup: Technology in the Dark Ages

The Time: A.D. 899

The Place: The Anglo-Saxon Kingdom of Mercia

The lord looked out across his vast estate. It was sunset. Down long strips of fields, a farmer was forcing his oxen to pull a mold-board plow. He **coerced** (1) the reluctant beasts with a long whip.

"What an invention this plow is!" the lord remarked to his guest, a knight visiting from the neighboring shire of Lichfield. "See how it splits the soil with the front blade? Notice how the iron plowshare then cuts deeply down? See how the moldboard throws the soil to the side? Before, with the scratch plow, my farmers were barely able to break the surface of the solid earth. But this new mold-board plow cuts deeply into the **terra firma** (2). We shall have a rich harvest this year."

The guest smiled at the remarks of his **loquacious** (3) host. Although the knight himself was not usually given to conversation—he was certainly not as talkative as his host—he wanted his host to continue the conversation, for he loved hearing about inventions. Glancing down at his stirrups, the knight discovered a new source of conversation.

"Indeed," the knight said, "inventions are wondrous! Why, my grandfather told me that

he had to be a foot soldier for most of his life. Why? Simply because it was impossible for him and many others to stay on the backs of their horses. With these stirrups, I can now stay safely mounted on my horse during an attack. Let no farmer ever fear for the safety of his family as they plow the fields. Steady on my horse, armed and armored, I will **mete** (4) out severe injury to any foe!" The thought of giving out punishment to his enemies made the Lichfield knight raise the **gauntlet** (5) on his hand in defiance. The metal-plated glove glistened in the sunlight. His manner and speech were **acrimonious** (6)—bitter and sharp. He always became angry when he thought about threats to his land and people, for he had seen the deaths of many loved ones over the years. Lost in his angry imaginings, he reached instinctively for his sword.

For a moment, the host was filled with **consternation** (7) at his guest's behavior, but he soon controlled his shock and resulting confusion when he realized that the knight was merely momentarily overcome with emotion.

"**Desist** (8) from this rage. Stay your sword, my friend," said the host. "No threat is here."

The knight, rather embarrassed at his outburst, calmed down. "Yes," the host went on,

"I agree that these inventions are wondrous! With the plow and the stirrup, there is no telling how much our people can accomplish. The **benevolence** (9) of God our Maker is great. Although he remains hidden in the **firmament** (10) above, his acts of kindness and charity fall freely from the clouds that conceal his presence. Truly, God has blessed us with marvelous things."

The two nobles turned their horses and headed back to the dining hall. Both of the horses were **mottled** (11) with spots of black, gray, and white that shone like speckled marble against the evening landscape. The farmer, in the meantime, unhitched the eight oxen. Slowly, he led the oxen away into the rosy dusk. Before the next day's toil, he would **burnish** (12) the metal on the harnesses until it gleamed.

The Time: The Present

The Place: Where You Are

The scene just described could actually have taken place in the English kingdom of Mercia in the ninth century. The moldboard plow used by the farmer had been introduced in England by the ninth century. The stirrup had been introduced just one hundred years earlier. These two noblemen were just as fascinated with these technological innovations as you might be intrigued by laser discs or the possibilities of virtual-reality equipment.

Traditionally, historians have considered the period from A.D. 500 to 1000 to be the Dark Ages. During this period, Latin, once the standard language of scholarship, became a riddle, an **enigma** (13), as so few people were taught to speak and write it. As a result, classical texts became **esoteric** (14) documents that only a few learned scholars could understand. During this time, the Church would traditionally allow schooling for only a privileged few; most people remained uneducated and illiterate. Circumstances did not **bode** (15) well for England. In fact, the situation foretold grim problems for the future of all of Western civilization.

Did civilization just **atrophy** (16) during the Dark Ages? Did it waste away as completely as the name of the period implies? No. Scholars have written many volumes indicating that the Dark Ages may not have been so dark after all. There is, in fact, **voluminous** (17) evidence that the Early Middle Ages may be seen as a **precursor** (18) to our own age. This ancient period is sometimes viewed as a forerunner to our modern age because it too was marked by exciting innovations and advances.

The historian L. S. Stavrianos **expounds** (19) this position in detail in his book *The Promise of the Coming Dark Age*. He explains that the Early Middle Ages was a time when Western European civilization was being born. To ignore the evidence of that birth in such innovations as the stirrup and the moldboard plow is to ignore this dynamic period of civilization. Have historians, then, incorrectly named this period? With Stavrianos's argument in mind, we may feel that the description of the Early Middle Ages as the Dark Ages is, indeed, a **misnomer** (20).

EXERCISE 1   *Finding Synonyms*

Directions. Reread the preceding passage. Then write on the line provided a synonym for each of the words in boldface. If you cannot think of an exact synonym, you may write a brief definition of the word.

1. coerced _____

2. terra firma _____

3. loquacious _____

4. mete _____

5. gauntlet _____

6. acrimonious _____

7. consternation _____

8. desist _____

9. benevolence _____

10. firmament _____

11. mottled _____

12. burnish _____

13. enigma _____

14. esoteric _____

15. bode _____

16. atrophy _____

17. voluminous _____

18. precursor _____

19. expounds _____

20. misnomer _____

EXERCISE 2 Reading Strategically

Directions. Now that you have read the passage and thought about the words in boldface, circle the letter of the correct answer to each of the following items. The numbers of the items are the same as the numbers of the boldface vocabulary words in the passage.

1. In the passage, what does it mean that the farmer **coerced** the oxen?
    (A) It means that he stopped them.
    (B) It means that he forced them.
    (C) It means that he bribed them.
    (D) It means that he turned them.
    (E) It means that he rode on them.

2. In the passage, the words that provide a clue to the meaning of **terra firma** are
(A) scratch plow
(B) cuts deeply
(C) break the surface
(D) solid earth
(E) barely able

3. In the passage, the knight talks enthusiastically about stirrups, becoming as **loquacious**, or _____, as his host.
(A) talkative
(B) fearful
(C) defiant
(D) old
(E) remarkable

4. In the passage, the knight vows to **mete** out or _____ injury to his enemies.
(A) surrender
(B) give out
(C) decipher
(D) standardize
(E) forget about

5. According to the passage, a **gauntlet** is a
(A) sword
(B) drinking cup
(C) type of stirrup
(D) raised fist
(E) metal-plated glove

6. What strategy does the writer use to tell us that **acrimonious** is defined as bitter or sharp in language or manner?
(A) The writer describes the knight with a simile.
(B) The writer links **acrimonious** with the words kind and gentle.
(C) The writer restates **acrimonious** with the words bitter and sharp.
(D) The writer provides an antonym for **acrimonious**.
(E) The writer compares riding a horse with plowing a field.

7. When we read in the passage that the host was filled with **consternation**, we should realize that
(A) he fully expected his guest's response
(B) he was ready to fight his guest if necessary
(C) he agreed with his guest's remark
(D) he was shocked and confused by his guest's outburst
(E) he wanted to tell his guest to leave

8. According to the passage, why did the host say to his guest, "**Desist** from this rage"?
(A) The host hoped to make his guest even angrier.
(B) The guest obviously was only pretending to be angry.
(C) The host wanted his guest to stop being angry.
(D) The host wanted to have a sword fight with his guest.
(E) The host was pointing out a threatening situation.

9. What strategy does the writer use to tell us that **benevolence** is defined as an act resulting from a desire to do good?

(A) The writer contrasts **benevolence** with kindness and sympathy.
(B) The writer links **benevolence** to acts of kindness and charity.
(C) The writer uses **benevolence** as a synonym for something hidden.
(D) The writer describes **benevolence** as a wondrous invention.
(E) The writer links **benevolence** to plows and stirrups.

10. We can infer from the passage that the **firmament** is

(A) the earth
(B) time
(C) an accomplishment
(D) charity
(E) the sky

11. To describe how the **mottled** horses look, the writer compares them by simile to

(A) dining halls
(B) spotted oxen
(C) speckled marble
(D) black, gray, and white
(E) shiny metal

12. According to the passage, what does it mean to **burnish** metal?

(A) It means to polish it.
(B) It means to scratch it.
(C) It means to reshape it.
(D) It means to paint it.
(E) It means to sharpen it.

13. In the passage, the word that provides a clue to the meaning of **enigma** is

(A) language
(B) standard
(C) period
(D) riddle
(E) classical

14. We can infer from the passage that something is **esoteric** if

(A) it is widely taught and understood
(B) it is part of common, everyday knowledge
(C) it is from a traditional society
(D) it is misunderstood by very few people
(E) it is understood by only a few people

15. In the passage, **bode** means

(A) foretell
(B) listen
(C) remember
(D) abide
(E) speak

16. According to the passage, what leads us to believe that civilization did not **atrophy** during the Dark Ages?

(A) Virtually nothing changed during the Dark Ages.
(B) Civilization wasted away completely during this time.
(C) There were exciting innovations during this time.
(D) There were many problems throughout the period.
(E) It was a grim time.

17. According to the passage, there is **voluminous** evidence, enough to fill many _____, that the period known as the Dark Ages was not so dark.

(A) buildings
(B) civilizations
(C) ships
(D) volumes
(E) periods

18. In the passage, the word that provides a clue to the meaning of **precursor** is

(A) evidence
(B) forerunner
(C) innovations
(D) ancient
(E) problems

19. In the passage, **expounds** means

(A) positions
(B) explains
(C) questions
(D) ignores
(E) denies

20. The writer provides a clue to the meaning of **misnomer** by

(A) relating **misnomer** to the Early Middle Ages
(B) describing the Dark Ages as truly dark
(C) comparing **misnomer** to a dynamic period of civilization
(D) linking **misnomer** to the words incorrectly named
(E) relating **misnomer** to historians

READING NEW WORDS IN CONTEXT

Lesson 13 │ CONTEXT: Science and Technology

The passage gives you an opportunity to expand your vocabulary. Below are twenty vocabulary words that are used in the passage and in the exercises that follow it.

assiduous	corollary	extenuate	inordinate
avarice	denizen	fissure	mercurial
aver	duress	impeccable	pecuniary
cessation	equanimity	incarcerate	quell
conciliate	espouse	iniquity	tenable

Going Places: England's Railroads

Imagine a machine that could instantly take you anywhere in the world. One minute, you're standing in your swimsuit in sunny California. Two minutes later, you're freezing in Alaska. How do you feel about the power of this machine? At first you are thrilled. Then you begin to have doubts. Everything changes so quickly and unpredictably. You aren't at all sure if you can be as **mercurial** (1) as the technological world you live in.

The Coming of the Railroad
If you can imagine the impact of the machine described above, then you can get some idea of the impact of the railroad on Victorian England. The coming of the railroad changed almost every aspect of British life. Before the railroad, life was simple and familiar for the **denizens** (2) of England. Afterward, life was complex and strange for these same inhabitants.

The history of the steam locomotive began with the invention of the steam engine. By the early nineteenth century, a British mining engineer, Richard Trevithick, had built a small locomotive powered by a steam engine. Its job was to pull mining cars in Wales. By 1820, George Stephenson, a self-educated engineer, perfected steam-powered locomotives. He

had worked **assiduously** (3), and his perseverance was rewarded. He was given the task of building the Stockton and Darlington, the world's first public railroad. In 1829, Stephenson and his son designed the *Rocket,* which historians declare was the first practical locomotive. They also **aver** (4) that the *Rocket* was a symbol of a force that changed life in England forever.

Everything in Britain now seemed closer together. For travel, the railroad was the **tenable** (5) choice. It was reasonable for travelers to choose the railroad because it quickly covered distances once thought vast. To meet the growing demand for rapid travel, laborers laid over five thousand miles of railway line in Britain between 1830 and 1848. Train tracks, bridges, tunnels, viaducts, and train sheds checkered a countryside that had remained essentially unchanged since the Middle Ages.

The Railroad Changes the Face of Britain
Britain's countryside had always been divided by geographical barriers such as mountains and rivers. Each section of the country had developed its own dialect, cultural heritage, and even its own economy. The cracks

in England's social structure were obvious. Indeed, England's social **fissures** (6) went as deep as the underground coal mines in Wales. Suddenly, however, all of England's people became neighbors because of the railroads. Regrettably, however, the **equanimity** (7) of the quiet country life was left behind with the introduction of the railroad. Such calmness and balance disappeared with the horse-drawn coaches and the simple cottage industries. The railroad had come and it would not be stopped; there would be no **cessation** (8) of progress.

The railroads forced the Victorians to consider time and space in totally new, unfamiliar ways. For example, the railroads altered people's perceptions of time. Before the railways came, a person could travel only twelve to fifteen miles per hour by horse-drawn coach. Such speeds were tripled by railroad express trains. Moreover, travel by rail demanded **impeccable** (9) timekeeping. For example, people waiting for trains departing from London had to read exactly the same time on their watches as the train's engineers. Railroads and travelers alike depended on standardized clocks to time arrivals and departures. Travelers had to learn to be prompt. People who missed a scheduled departure could defend themselves by claiming **extenuating** (10) circumstances, but pleading wouldn't help; train schedules could not accommodate human excuses.

The Social Price of Progress

The railroad industry was greedy and intent on financial gain at almost any cost. Because of its **avarice** (11), the industry demanded immediate production of materials such as railroad ties, bridge materials, and other iron products. England's merchants saw great possibilities for **pecuniary** (12) gain with the railroads. Money would come to those who could use the new technology to their advantage. Those who **espoused** (13) industry and progress began to realize profits; those who did not support the new technology were left far behind.

As demand and production grew, laborers began to move into England's most crowded spaces: the cities. The growth of the cities, therefore, was a definite **corollary** (14) to the growth of the railroad industry. The years from 1821 to 1831 saw a gain of 50 percent in the population of all major industrial cities in Britain. Never before had there been such rapid population growth. The cities were totally unprepared for such an **inordinate** (15), excessive influx of workers and their families.

Thus began the horrors of urban slums. **Iniquities** (16) against the poor were abundant, because many employers, businesspeople, and property owners treated the poor in wicked and unrighteous ways. Ironically, because technology rendered their old economics obsolete, many country people were forced to leave their comfortable homes to make a living in the cities. In a very real sense, these workers became urban prisoners, **incarcerated** (17) by the greed of an industry that had become their jailers. The workers' spirits were **quelled** (18) by exhausting work, poor pay, and horrible living conditions. In addition, the workers were suppressed by the **duress** (19) that was frequently used by those in power. There was no real protection against the use of force or threats to compel the weaker to serve the stronger. England's men, women, and children served the needs of industry, but their only reward, it seemed, was to have industry confine them even further. Industry did little to **conciliate** (20) the workers and make their lives easier. There were no friendly acts to foster goodwill among the working class.

The railroad affected every aspect of life in Victorian England. It altered not only the geographical landscape but also the social landscape. It changed the way people thought about time. It brought people to the cities and affected living and working conditions. Who would have predicted that a simple steam engine would have such a wide-ranging effect?

EXERCISE 1 — *Finding Synonyms* ✍

Directions. Reread the preceding passage. Then write on the line provided a synonym for each of the words in boldface. If you cannot think of an exact synonym, you may write a brief definition of the word.

1. mercurial _____

2. denizens _____

3. assiduously _____

4. aver _____

5. tenable _____

6. fissures _____

7. equanimity _____

8. cessation _____

9. impeccable _____

10. extenuating _____

11. avarice _____

12. pecuniary _____

13. espoused _____

14. corollary _____

15. inordinate _____

16. iniquities _____

17. incarcerated _____

18. quelled _____

19. duress _____

20. conciliate _____

EXERCISE 2 *Reading Strategically* ☞

Directions. Now that you have read the passage and thought about the words in boldface, circle the letter of the correct answer to each of the following items. The numbers of the items are the same as the numbers of the boldface words in the passage.

1. If the world continues to change in a **mercurial** way, as the writer of the passage suggests, we may expect
    (A) slow and predictable changes
    (B) change that results in benefits for everyone
    (C) a lack of progress and change
    (D) no growth in transportation
    (E) quick and unpredictable changes

2. In the passage, **denizens** are
    (A) transportations
    (B) newspapers
    (C) inhabitants
    (D) railroads
    (E) categories

3. How does the writer provide a clue to the meaning of **assiduously**?
    (A) The writer links **assiduously** to the word perseverance.
    (B) The writer relates **assiduously** to being self-educated.
    (C) The writer links **assiduously** to the first railroad.
    (D) The writer contrasts **assiduously** with an antonym.
    (E) The writer repeats **assiduously** in the next paragraph.

4. According to the passage, what does **aver** mean?
    (A) It means to deny.
    (B) It means to swerve.
    (C) It means to avoid.
    (D) It means to declare.
    (E) It means to question.

5. What strategy does the writer use to tell us that **tenable** is defined as reasonable?
    (A) The writer uses figurative language to define **tenable**.
    (B) The writer says it was reasonable for travelers to choose the railroad.
    (C) The writer gives an example of travel by railroad.
    (D) The writer uses **tenable** to describe the growing demand for railway travel.
    (E) The writer lists a series of railroad properties.

6. Because the **fissures** that separated the social classes in England were deep, the writer compares them by simile to
    (A) Britain's geographical barriers
    (B) the days of horse-drawn coaches
    (C) the simple cottage industries
    (D) train tracks that checkered Britain's countryside
    (E) underground coal mines in Wales

7. According to the passage, why was the **equanimity** of country life left behind?
(A) The people who lived in the country preferred the excitement of the city.
(B) Calmness and balance disappeared with horse-drawn carriages and simple cottage industries.
(C) Horse-drawn coaches began racing about and competing with the railroads.
(D) Neighbors began to argue over the depth of Welsh coal mines.
(E) Simple cottage industries were boring.

8. According to the passage, if progress continues without **cessation,** we may expect
(A) temporary progress
(B) continuous progress
(C) occasional progress
(D) declining progress
(E) an end to progress

9. When we read in the passage that travel by rail demanded **impeccable** timekeeping, we should realize that
(A) trains always ran late
(B) it never mattered what time it was
(C) perfect time had to be kept
(D) watches kept imperfect time
(E) trains ran on random schedules

10. We can infer from the passage that **extenuating** circumstances are ones for which there are
(A) solutions
(B) excuses
(C) limits
(D) schedules
(E) punishments

11. What strategy does the writer use to tell us that **avarice** is defined as an excessive desire for money?
(A) The writer describes the railroad industry as greedy.
(B) The writer gives an example of materials used in building railroads.
(C) The writer contrasts **avarice** with financial losses.
(D) The writer says the government is more generous than the railroad industry.
(E) The writer implies that **avarice** is synonymous with progress.

12. When we read in the passage that merchants saw great possibilities for **pecuniary** gain, we should realize that
(A) they believed that the railroads would fail
(B) they were afraid of losing their money through the use of railroads
(C) they saw that they could make money through the use of railroads
(D) they wanted to maintain their simple country lifestyle
(E) they thought everyone was dishonest

13. According to the passage, those who **espoused** industry and progress _____ it.
(A) stopped
(B) changed
(C) established
(D) criticized
(E) supported

14. According to the passage, why is the growth of the cities a **corollary** to the growth of the railroad industry?

(A) The growth of the cities declined as the growth of the railroad industry increased.
(B) The growth of the cities increased as the growth of the railroad industry declined.
(C) The railroads grew because the cities increased greatly in industry and population.
(D) The growth of the cities resulted directly from the growth of the railroad industry.
(E) A great amount of money could be made in the railroad industry and in cities that grew along the railways.

15. In the passage, the word that provides a clue to the meaning of **inordinate** is

(A) growth
(B) intense
(C) excessive
(D) influx
(E) unprepared

16. According to the passage, what are **iniquities**?

(A) **Iniquities** are buildings in an urban slum.
(B) **Iniquities** are wicked and unrighteous acts.
(C) **Iniquities** are jobs offered to the poor.
(D) **Iniquities** are kindnesses done for poor people.
(E) **Iniquities** are buildings of unequal size.

17. Because workers in crowded cities were, in a sense, **incarcerated** by the greed of industry, the writer uses a metaphor to compare workers to

(A) firefighters
(B) peasants
(C) prisoners
(D) economists
(E) landowners

18. In the passage, the word that provides a clue to the meaning of **quelled** is

(A) suppressed
(B) similarly
(C) compelled
(D) exhausting
(E) conditions

19. In the passage, **duress** is

(A) a common way of setting up a system
(B) a depressing way of combating technology
(C) hiring workers at high wages
(D) a term used by railroad engineers
(E) the use of force or threats

20. We can infer from the passage that because industry did little to **conciliate** the workers, industry

(A) was concerned about the workers
(B) cared very little about the workers
(C) was interested in improving conditions
(D) did everything it could to help
(E) preferred to hire good workers

Name _____ Date _____ Class _____

READING NEW WORDS IN CONTEXT

Lesson 14 | CONTEXT: Science and Technology

The passage gives you an opportunity to expand your vocabulary. Below are twenty vocabulary words that are used in the passage and in the exercises that follow it.

abstruse	commiserate	gambol	pallor
apostasy	evanescent	ingenuous	promontory
bauble	festoon	iridescent	remuneration
bullion	fresco	maudlin	usury
caricature	frugal	opulence	venal

England and the Industrial Revolution

Art can tell us a great deal about the values of a culture. Giotto di Bondone (c. 1267–1337) was one of Italy's greatest painters. In **frescoes** (1) such as *Flight into Egypt*, the images of the Virgin Mary and the Christ Child, painted on fresh plaster, reflect the period in which Giotto lived. In this painting, we see the first flowering of the humanitarian qualities that were part of the Italian Renaissance. Similarly, *Rain, Steam, and Speed: The Great Western Railway*, a dramatic painting by J.M.W. Turner (1775–1851), reflects the spirit of England at the beginning of the Industrial Revolution.

Considered by many to be Britain's greatest artist, Turner captured the coming industrialization of England in oil on canvas. In *Rain, Steam, and Speed*, a locomotive seems almost **evanescent** (2), a fleeting image speeding through the vapor of rain and wind across a viaduct. The scene seems to be observed from the perspective of a person standing on a **promontory** (3), a high point of land extending into a body of water. Like the unseen observer, we look down from on high at a landscape completely altered by the pale, swirling rainbow colors of the **iridescent** (4) rain. The misty rain has obscured the natural, deep colors of the landscape and makes it

seem as washed-out and unnaturally pale as the **pallor** (5) of a sick person's flesh. The misty, hazy backdrop heightens the driving energy of the dark locomotive, making its speed even more apparent. If we compare Turner's painting to Giotto's much earlier religious fresco, we can see at a glance the stark contrast between the complex, sophisticated world of the Industrial Revolution and the simple, **ingenuous** (6) world of the Italian Renaissance.

Britain was the first country in the world to experience the Industrial Revolution. As a historical period, the Industrial Revolution began in the 1780s and continued to overwhelm the British economic and social structures into the twentieth century. For many people, the Industrial Revolution was a time of **apostasy** (7), for they abandoned age-old beliefs and principles as a result of their changing views of the world. During the Industrial Revolution, some people lived in **opulence** (8), while many others lived in poverty. The rich could afford to waste money on trinkets, or **baubles** (9); the poor could barely afford food. The homes of the wealthy were elaborately **festooned** (10); the homes of the poor remained virtually undecorated.

The Importance of Iron

No material played a more critical role in Britain's economic transformation than iron. This metal became one of Britain's most important natural resources because it was a source material for cast iron, wrought iron, and steel. To avoid **abstruse** (11) definitions of these terms, we can simply say that iron built the nineteenth century. Masses of the metal poured from Britain's foundries. The resulting iron bars could be regarded as the gold bars, or **bullion** (12), of the Industrial Revolution.

Britain made so much iron that British production surpassed that of the rest of the world in 1870. Ironworking began at the blast furnace. There, molten iron poured out of a blast furnace along a system of channels. At the end of the process, pig iron—iron in its crudest form—was taken to a foundry, remelted, and poured into molds that shaped the iron into needed products. This was a backbreaking process in which unskilled laborers called puddlers worked for far too little **remuneration** (13), or pay. The puddlers had the hardest job in the blast furnace, working in thirty-minute shifts to stir the molten iron. As the metal hardened, it became more and more difficult to stir; the puddlers had to work harder and harder.

The days of the puddlers were numbered, however, for new technologies were developed that allowed greater mechanization and less manual labor. Today, early blast furnace work seems like a **caricature** (14) of modern iron-production processes. The exertions of the puddlers seem satirically exaggerated when compared to the more modern Bessemer process, which employs chemists instead of puddlers.

It should be noted that England's production of iron paled next to America's once America's natural resources were unlocked.

England's production of iron was almost insignificant when compared to the tremendous output of the factories of American businessman Andrew Carnegie. Carnegie was known for his **frugality** (15); he watched every penny. His devotion to economy made him among the world's richest men. Carnegie was never accused of being **maudlin** (16) or excessively sentimental. In fact, his tough and practical approach often made him appear coldhearted, for he would scrap an entire manufacturing plant for profit.

A Difficult Time for the Working Class

During England's Industrial Revolution, merchants, landowners, and city authorities were not generally concerned with social responsibility and thus had little sympathy or compassion for workers. Consequently, they indulged in very little **commiseration** (17) with workers concerning the crowded and often unsanitary living conditions in the cities. Low-paid laborers were sometimes easy victims of corruption. For example, many were harmed by the practice of **usury** (18), in which some merchants and bankers charged excessively high interest rates on loans.

Of course, there were honest as well as **venal** (19) merchants and employers. Over time, employers and union officials in England collaborated to set wages and to maintain industrial relations. It would be incorrect and misleading to paint a whimsical picture of the relations between management and labor, however. The two factions were not like children **gamboling** (20) on a playground; there was little lighthearted frolicking and a great deal of interpersonal conflict. Nevertheless, conditions in England improved as employers increased safety measures for workers, provided insurance programs, and shortened the workday.

EXERCISE 1 *Finding Synonyms*

Directions. Reread the preceding passage. Then write on the line provided a synonym for each of the words in boldface. If you cannot think of an exact synonym, you may write a brief definition of the word.

1. frescoes _____

2. evanescent _____

3. promontory _____

4. iridescent _____

5. pallor _____

6. ingenuous _____

7. apostasy _____

8. opulence _____

9. baubles _____

10. festooned _____

11. abstruse _____

12. bullion _____

13. remuneration _____

14. caricature _____

15. frugality _____

16. maudlin _____

17. commiseration _____

18. usury _____

19. venal _____

20. gamboling _____

EXERCISE 2 *Reading Strategically* ✍

Directions. Now that you have read the passage and thought about the words in boldface, circle the letter of the correct answer to each of the following items. The numbers of the items are the same as the numbers of the boldface vocabulary words in the passage.

1. In the passage, **frescoes** are
   (A) refreshing soft drinks
   (B) oil paintings done on stretched canvas
   (C) paintings done on fresh plaster
   (D) sculptures copied by Giotto di Bondone
   (E) paintings of industrialized society

2. Which word in the passage provides a clue to the meaning of **evanescent**?
   (A) painting
   (B) perspective
   (C) viaduct
   (D) fleeting
   (E) industrialization

3. According to the passage, why does it seem as though the painting is observed from the perspective of a person standing on a **promontory**?
   (A) We seem to be looking down at the scene.
   (B) The painting shows us standing on a **promontory**.
   (C) The locomotive is shown on a **promontory**.
   (D) We are forced to look up to see the painting.
   (E) We cannot see anything because of the rain.

4. In the passage, **iridescent** means
   (A) rain mixed with snow
   (B) heavy rain that causes floods
   (C) something dark that has faded
   (D) the darkness of nature
   (E) swirling rainbow colors

5. According to the passage, why is the landscape compared to the **pallor** of a sick person's flesh?
   (A) The misty rain makes the landscape seem pale and washed-out.
   (B) The colors of the landscape are darker than normal.
   (C) It is night and no color is visible on the landscape.
   (D) The sun is bright enough to fade the colors of the landscape.
   (E) The landscape is intensely colored like a person with a fever.

6. What strategy does the writer use to tell us that **ingenuous** is defined as simple or innocent?
   (A) The writer provides a definition of **ingenuous**.
   (B) The writer contrasts **ingenuous** with the words complex and sophisticated.
   (C) The writer uses a series of synonyms for **ingenuous**.
   (D) The writer uses the metaphor of the Industrial Revolution.
   (E) The writer implies that **ingenuous** is a word of Italian origin.

7. If the Industrial Revolution was a time of **apostasy,** as the writer of the passage suggests, we may expect other times of technological advance to
   (A) cause people to appreciate Italian art
   (B) bring about higher prices on new products
   (C) result in people abandoning long-held beliefs and principles
   (D) change the way people travel and communicate
   (E) force people to compete for new occupations

8. According to the passage, during the Industrial Revolution some people lived in **opulence** and therefore were _____ enough to spend money on elaborate decorations.
   (A) poor
   (B) educated
   (C) wealthy
   (D) resentful
   (E) overworked

9. In the passage, **baubles** are
   (A) changing views
   (B) trinkets
   (C) homes
   (D) festivals
   (E) age-old beliefs

10. In the passage, how does the reference to **festooned** homes point out the difference in the economic levels of the people?
   (A) It shows that everyone during the Industrial Revolution had enough money to have parties and parades and decorations.
   (B) It shows that the Industrial Revolution produced new products that were used for decorations.
   (C) It shows that the wealthy people were concerned about the poor and gave festivals for them.
   (D) It shows that since all people had good jobs as a result of the Industrial Revolution, there were no longer economic differences.
   (E) It shows that some people had money to spend on unnecessary decorative things, while many people struggled merely to exist.

11. When we read in the passage that there are **abstruse** definitions, we should realize that
   (A) they are easily understood
   (B) they are detailed and hard to understand
   (C) they will not be avoided
   (D) the writer doesn't know them
   (E) they require little knowledge

12. Because the iron bars were a source of great wealth, they are compared by simile to **bullion,** which is
   (A) pig iron
   (B) molten iron
   (C) precious gems
   (D) gold bars
   (E) thin soup

13. In the passage, the word _____ provides a clue to the meaning of **remuneration.**
   (A) end
   (B) pay
   (C) job
   (D) iron
   (E) poor

14. The writer provides a clue to the meaning of **caricature** by
- (A) describing the Bessemer process
- (B) comparing the puddlers to a painting
- (C) linking **caricature** to the words satirically exaggerated
- (D) using an antonym for **caricature**
- (E) implying that **caricature** means mechanization

15. According to the passage, Carnegie's **frugality** meant that he was _____ with money.
- (A) generous
- (B) seldom
- (C) cursed
- (D) never
- (E) careful

16. In the passage, the words _____ provide a clue to the meaning of **maudlin**.
- (A) social responsibility
- (B) excessively sentimental
- (C) city authorities
- (D) generally concerned
- (E) entire manufacturing plant

17. In the passage, **commiseration** is
- (A) a commission
- (B) living conditions
- (C) insincere concern
- (D) sympathy and compassion
- (E) an easy victim

18. We can infer from the passage that because of the practice of **usury,**
- (A) merchants and bankers never charged interest
- (B) some poor people had to pay too much interest
- (C) poor people were protected from paying too much interest
- (D) low-paid laborers sometimes turned to crime
- (E) poor people were lucky to be able to borrow money

19. What strategy does the writer use to tell us that **venal** is defined as dishonest?
- (A) The writer describes a **venal** employer.
- (B) The writer uses a synonym for **venal**.
- (C) The writer contrasts **venal** with the word honest.
- (D) The writer uses a metaphor for **venal**.
- (E) The writer includes **venal** in a series of synonyms.

20. When we read in the passage that laborers and employers were not like children **gamboling** on a playground, we should realize that
- (A) laborers and employers were not getting along playfully and lightheartedly
- (B) laborers and employers fought like children on a playground
- (C) employers gambled with laborers' benefits
- (D) labor and management never collaborated and never reached any agreement
- (E) laborers and employers were too old to be considered children

READING NEW WORDS IN CONTEXT

Lesson 15 CONTEXT: Science and Technology

The passage gives you an opportunity to expand your vocabulary. Below are twenty vocabulary words that are used in the passage and in the exercises that follow it.

abscond	circumvent	extort	malinger
adjure	elicit	fiasco	prognosis
aspersion	emaciate	ignominy	remonstrate
biennial	equivocal	longevity	reprisal
capricious	ethereal	malign	taciturn

Environmental Pollution in England

When it entered the Industrial Revolution, England also entered the age of pollution. In the nineteenth century, more and more people crowded into England's cities. Britain's industry was in full throttle, and no one had to **extort** (1) manufacturers in order to get them to increase production. It was the promise of profits, not the threat of harm, that motivated manufacturers.

Pollution problems arose on all fronts. Water supplies were contaminated, waste disposal was not regulated, and the air itself became polluted. Pollution actually began to negatively affect the people's **longevity** (2), or length of life. In London, citizens regularly fell prey to various diseases. An investigator in 1838 reported that of the six people occupying a single small room, two were ill and **emaciated** (3), wasting away with fever.

The story was the same throughout Britain. Although many employers accused their employees of **malingering** (4), the truth of the situation was that many workers were indeed sick. They had become ill from inhaling, drinking, or eating toxic substances. It takes little effort for us to **elicit** (5) the truth about the effects of industrial pollution. Research brings forth information verifying that each technological advantage—railways, home coal furnaces, and industrial chimneys— produced its own environmental problems. Under the pretense of increasing prosperity, industry had, like a thief in the night, **absconded** (6) with the clean environment.

At the height of the Industrial Revolution, however, the forecast for Britain's ailing environment was guardedly optimistic. This improved **prognosis** (7) came about because the nation had at last begun to deal with the reality of its environmental problems. The Town Improvement Act of 1847, for example, required railroad engines to consume their own smoke. Further legislation in the mid-1920s attempted to regulate industrial pollution. Still, environmental pollution remained severe in spite of these measures.

Damage to the Air and the Land

In 1952, air pollution reached a crisis point in London. Even usually **taciturn** (8) or uncommunicative people began remarking on the unhealthy haze that hung over London. The haze resulted from a combination of industrial pollutants, London's natural fog, and the burning of home fuels—wood, coal, and peat. In an effort to **circumvent** (9) continued problems, the British government introduced a preventive measure, the Clean Air Act, in

1956. This act forbade the emission of smoke and soot in areas designated as smokeless zones.

Not only the air, but the land itself, sustained great damage from industry. Sensitive to their surroundings, England's poets often celebrated the **ethereal** (10) as well as the earthly beauties of the countryside before the Industrial Revolution. For example, in 1807 William Wordsworth (1770–1850) wrote of wandering "lonely as a cloud / That floats on high o'er vales and hills." But a little more than a century and a half later, Wordsworth's lovely vales and hills had changed. No longer were they crowded with yellow daffodils or the **biennial** (11) thistles that once could be counted on to bloom every second year. Instead, the countryside was littered with mass-produced farm equipment and showed evidence of the damage that could be inflicted by harmful chemical methods of soil nourishment. In a 1974 poem titled "Going, Going," poet Philip Larkin (1922–1985) **remonstrated** (12) against the lack of environmental planning. He protested industrial growth and warned that one day all of the countryside would be covered with concrete.

A Response to the Problem

In response to the industrialization of the countryside, a massive conservationist movement arose in England. This movement refused to be **equivocal** (13) about environmental protection. Because of the movement's decided stand, there was rapid growth in the Council for the Preservation of Rural England (and Wales). There was nothing **capricious** (14) about Britain's decision to save the environment. Once the British decided to take a firm stand on environmental concerns, they did not erratically stray from their course. Rather, they continued to unswervingly pursue measures that would cut down on pollution and conserve natural resources. In 1982, for instance, Britain passed the

Wildlife and Countryside Act. This law states that it is best to have local management set its own environmental provisions rather than to command or **adjure** (15) the national government to make environmental laws.

Today in England, the environment is not treated carelessly, as it was during so many decades of the Industrial Revolution. If pollution has not disappeared completely, it has at least faded measurably. There is even a political party—the Green Party—founded on environmental concerns.

The Future of Britain's Environment

Many in Britain believe that the environment suffered under the conservative Prime Minister Margaret Thatcher (b. 1925). A common complaint is that Thatcher's allegiance to industry compromised her devotion to the environment. Some people label this charge a political **aspersion** (16), or slander. However, the loss of confidence in Mrs. Thatcher by her own party, which forced her resignation in 1989, may be viewed in some ways as a **reprisal** (17) concerning her environmental record. In other words, members of Britain's growing "green" movement injured Mrs. Thatcher politically because they believed she had injured the environment.

What does the future hold for Britain's environment? It is clear that current and future governments must address environmental concerns or run the risk of creating a **fiasco** (18), a complete failure. If John Major, Great Britain's prime minister, does not address environmental concerns, he may repeat the political fate of his predecessor. The situation is hopeful because politicians want to avoid public disgrace and save their reputations; they do not want to suffer **ignominy** (19). If they are to avoid being **maligned** (20) or slandered by an aggressive British press for taking a passive position on the environment, British leaders must make sure that environmental issues remain high on the nation's agenda.

EXERCISE 1 *Finding Synonyms* ✍

Directions. Reread the preceding passage. Then write on the line provided a synonym for each of the words in boldface. If you cannot think of an exact synonym, you may write a brief definition of the word.

1. extort _____

2. longevity _____

3. emaciated _____

4. malingering _____

5. elicit _____

6. absconded _____

7. prognosis _____

8. taciturn _____

9. circumvent _____

10. ethereal _____

11. biennial _____

12. remonstrated _____

13. equivocal _____

14. capricious _____

15. adjure _____

16. aspersion _____

17. reprisal _____

18. fiasco _____

19. ignominy _____

20. maligned _____

EXERCISE 2 *Reading Strategically* ✍️

Directions. Now that you have read the passage and thought about the words in boldface, circle the letter of the correct answer to each of the following items. The numbers of the items are the same as the numbers of the boldface vocabulary words in the passage.

1. In the passage, **extort** means
  - (A) threaten
  - (B) prevent
  - (C) coax
  - (D) shout at
  - (E) argue with

2. If pollution negatively affects people's **longevity,** as the writer of the passage suggests, we may expect people
  - (A) to live longer
  - (B) to get taller each year
  - (C) to lose their patience
  - (D) to learn to live with pollution
  - (E) not to live as long

3. How does the writer provide a clue to the meaning of **emaciated**?
  - (A) The writer describes different kinds of pollution.
  - (B) The writer blames London for being polluted.
  - (C) The writer says six people lived in a small room.
  - (D) The writer links **emaciated** to the words wasting away.
  - (E) The writer provides an antonym for **emaciated**.

4. When we read in the passage that employees were not **malingering,** we should realize that they
  - (A) were pretending to be sick
  - (B) were not patient enough to stay with their jobs
  - (C) really were sick
  - (D) were hoping to become sick
  - (E) were unable to live in a single room

5. In the passage, what does it mean to **elicit** the truth?
  - (A) It means to bring forth the truth.
  - (B) It means to cover up the truth.
  - (C) It means to avoid the truth.
  - (D) It means to change the truth.
  - (E) It means to repeat the truth.

6. Because industry **absconded** with the clean environment, it is compared by simile to
  - (A) increasing prosperity
  - (B) a thief in the night
  - (C) industrial chimneys for manufacturing
  - (D) a coal furnace in the home
  - (E) an optimistic forecast

7. In the passage, the word _____ provides a clue to the meaning of **prognosis**.

   (A) problems
   (B) forecast
   (C) example
   (D) environment
   (E) legislation

8. In the passage, **taciturn** means

   (A) communicative
   (B) polluted
   (C) unpolluted
   (D) remarkable
   (E) uncommunicative

9. What strategy does the writer use to tell us that **circumvent** is defined as avoid or prevent?

   (A) The writer explains what the government did to **circumvent** environmental problems.
   (B) The writer uses a synonym for **circumvent**.
   (C) The writer contrasts **circumvent** with the antonym continued.
   (D) The writer uses a simile to describe what the government did to **circumvent** environmental problems.
   (E) The writer uses a series of words that have similar meanings to **circumvent**.

10. In the passage, poets celebrated **ethereal** or _____ as well as earthly beauties of the countryside.

   (A) natural
   (B) unlikeable
   (C) heavenly
   (D) agricultural
   (E) foreign

11. We can infer from the passage that a **biennial** plant blooms

   (A) every four years
   (B) only in late summer
   (C) in two-year cycles
   (D) in the countryside
   (E) in vales

12. In the passage, the word _____ provides a clue to the meaning of **remonstrated**.

   (A) reminded
   (B) production
   (C) countryside
   (D) inorganic
   (E) protested

13. If people continue to refuse to be **equivocal** on their stand, as the writer of the passage suggests, we may expect

   (A) their undecided natures to give in easily to pressure
   (B) their lack of interest in the environment to be obvious
   (C) their refusal to express an opinion to hurt their cause
   (D) their determination to continue to have an effect
   (E) them never to stick to a single decision or idea

14. In the passage, why is there nothing **capricious** about Britain's decision to save the environment?

(A) All of the environmental problems in Britain have been completely solved.

(B) Since deciding to save their environment, the British have not erratically strayed from their course.

(C) The Industrial Revolution was over a long time ago.

(D) Since deciding to save their environment, the British have erratically and unpredictably wavered in their decision.

(E) No one in Britain is concerned enough to bother with the environment.

15. In the passage, **adjure** means

(A) hurt

(B) treat

(C) command

(D) restore

(E) require

16. In the passage, what does it mean to make an **aspersion**?

(A) It means to make a damaging, slandering remark.

(B) It means to tell the truth about someone.

(C) It means to doubt someone's actions.

(D) It means to make a political statement that has a positive impact.

(E) It means to make a choice.

17. In the passage, a **reprisal** is shown to be _____ done in response to an injury received.

(A) a second chance

(B) an appeal

(C) an injury

(D) a healing

(E) an unnecessary job

18. In the passage, why does no government want to ignore environmental concerns and create a **fiasco**?

(A) Governments can easily solve environmental problems.

(B) Governments are strong enough to ignore such concerns.

(C) No government wants local agencies to set environmental standards.

(D) No government wants to be responsible for creating a complete failure.

(E) It is possible to run a successful government.

19. When we read in the passage that politicians do not want such **ignominy**, we should realize that they

(A) enjoy even negative publicity

(B) do not want public disgrace

(C) are mostly interested in laws

(D) don't like many publications

(E) would rather ignore the issues

20. In the passage, the word _____ provides a clue to the meaning of **maligned**.

(A) aggressive

(B) hopeful

(C) passive

(D) remained

(E) slandered

NOTES

NOTES